TOP
STOCKS

TWENTY-SIXTH EDITION

2020

D1056152

MARTIN ROTH'S

BEST-SELLING ANNUAL

TOP STOCKS

TWENTY-SIXTH EDITION

2020

A SHAREBUYER'S GUIDE TO

LEADING AUSTRALIAN COMPANIES

WILEY

The author and publisher would like to thank Alan Hull (author of *Active Investing*, Revised Edition, *Trade My Way* and *Invest My Way*; www.alanhull.com) for generating the share-price charts.

This twenty-sixth edition first published in 2020 by Wrightbooks

an imprint of John Wiley & Sons Australia, Ltd

42 McDougall Street, Milton Qld 4064

Office also in Melbourne

Typeset in Adobe Garamond Pro Regular 10/12 pt

First edition published as *Top Stocks* by Wrightbooks in 1995

New edition published annually

Cover design: Wiley
Cover image: Financial Chart © Yurchanka Siarhei / Shutterstock

Charts created using TradeStation © TradeStation Technologies, Inc. 2001–2019. All rights reserved. No investment or trading advice, recommendation or opinions are being given or intended.

10 9 8 7 6 5 4 3 2 1

Disclaimer

Contents

Preface   vii
Introduction   xvii

PART I: the companies

PART II: the tables

Preface

Economic uncertainty, political instability, trade wars, currency volatility and more seem to be exerting a growing influence on global financial markets. Yet, in the midst of this environment, numerous fine companies continue to emerge in Australia, with great potential for investors.

In *Top Stocks 2020* there are 25 new companies, including 18 that have never appeared in any previous edition of the book. This is the second-highest number of new companies in the 26-year history of the book.

They are often smaller to medium-sized corporations. Some will be unfamiliar to investors. But all meet the stringent *Top Stocks* criteria, including solid profits and moderate debt levels.

Guiding investors towards value stocks has been one of the paramount aims of the book from the very first edition. Indeed, one of the rationales for the book has always been to highlight the truth that Australia boasts many excellent companies that enjoy high profits — and growing profits — regardless of the direction of the markets. Despite the title, *Top Stocks* is actually a book about companies.

Right from the start it has been an attempt to help investors find the best public companies in Australia, using strict criteria. These criteria are explained fully later. But, in essence, all companies in the book must have been publicly listed for at least five years and must have been making a profit and paying a dividend for each of those five years. They must also meet tough benchmarks of profitability and debt levels. It is completely objective. My own personal views count for nothing. In addition, share prices have never been relevant.

Of course, such stocks could not withstand the tidal wave of a substantial market sell-off. They too would be affected. But they should be affected less. And if they are good companies they will continue to thrive and to pay dividends. And they will bounce back faster than many others.

Of the 105 companies in *Top Stocks 2020* — 10 more than in last year's edition — fully 74 reported a higher after-tax profit in the latest financial year (June 2019 for most of them), including 44 with double-digit profit growth and a further three that achieved triple-digit growth. In addition, 73 recorded higher earnings per share and 68 paid a higher dividend.

And though, as I wrote above, share prices are not relevant for selection to *Top Stocks*, more than half the companies in the book have provided investor returns — share price appreciation plus dividends — of an average of at least 10 per cent per year over a five-year period.

Australian companies with overseas activities

Each year I try to identify trends among the companies of *Top Stocks*. The weakening dollar has for several years become a feature of local financial markets. It has benefited exporters and companies with extensive overseas business. Conversely, it can hurt importers.

For investors interested in this theme, here are companies in *Top Stocks 2020* that generate a substantial amount of their revenues abroad. Do note, however, that this does not automatically mean that they are beneficiaries of a weaker dollar. Some have a hedging program — or some other arrangement — in place that limits the potential gains from a weak dollar.

- ALS provides laboratory analysis services around the world, with nearly 70 per cent of revenues from abroad.
- Altium is a high-tech company with most of its activities overseas.
- Ansell is a global leader in safety and healthcare products, with more than 90 per cent of sales overseas.
- ARB exports its automotive accessories to more than 100 countries, with overseas business nearly 30 per cent of total sales.
- BHP Group is a huge diversified resources company, with activities and sales around the world.
- Blackmores is selling a lot of its healthcare products to Asia.
- Brambles, a leader in the supply of pallets for global trade, derives most of its income abroad.
- Breville Group sells its home appliances in more than 65 countries, with foreign revenues about 80 per cent of the total.
- Clover Corporation makes nutrients for food products, with about half of its sales overseas.
- Cochlear derives about 90 per cent of the sales for its ear implants from overseas customers.
- Codan sells its metal detectors and high-frequency radios to more than 150 countries, representing 85 per cent of company turnover.
- Corporate Travel Management derives more than 70 per cent of its revenues from overseas activities.
- Flight Centre gets around half of its income from its overseas branches.

- Fortescue Metals Group sells most of its iron ore abroad.
- Hansen Technologies continues to expand its billing service activities, with overseas business now more than 80 per cent of total income.
- Infomedia has most sales of its electronic car parts catalogues outside Australia.
- Integrated Research's specialised performance monitoring software is mainly sold abroad.
- IPH gets about 35 per cent of its intellectual property services income from its Asian operations.
- IRESS derives more than half its revenues for its financial software from overseas customers.
- Macquarie Group has banking operations in 25 countries, and international business accounts for around two-thirds of total income.
- Mineral Resources is a big iron ore exporter, with much of its income from abroad.
- Northern Star Resources is a major gold producer, with the international gold price determining its sales prices.
- Orora derives half its revenues for its paper and packaging products from its North American operations.
- Pro Medicus sells medical imaging software, with more than 80 per cent of revenues from abroad.
- Regis Resources sells its gold on international markets.
- Rio Tinto is a major global supplier of minerals.
- Sandfire Resources sells its copper on the international market.
- Schaffer Corporation sells its leather goods to auto makers around the world.
- Servcorp, the serviced office space provider, has more than two-thirds of its business offshore.
- Sonic Healthcare's fast-growing overseas pathology businesses now account for around 60 per cent of total revenues.
- Treasury Wine Estates markets its wines around the world, with overseas sales more than 55 per cent of company revenues.
- Webjet is now a leader in the international hotel bed intermediary market, with a substantial amount of its revenues coming from overseas.
- Wellcom Group's corporate design services are enjoying increasing demand outside Australia, with overseas business more than a third of total revenues.

Gold

The gold price has been rising during 2019, putting a spotlight on gold stocks. Here are some from this edition of *Top Stocks*.

- Codan is a world leader in the production of gold detectors for small-scale miners.
- GR Engineering Services, an engineering consulting and contracting company, has a specialty in the construction of processing plants for the gold industry.

- Northern Star Resources is one of Australia's largest gold producers. It sold 840 580 ounces of gold in the June 2019 year, with a forecast of 800 000 ounces to 900 000 ounces for June 2020.
- Orica is a supplier of commercial explosives and sodium cyanide, with the gold sector representing around 20 per cent of sales.
- Pacific Energy is a prominent supplier of off-grid electricity generating equipment for the mining industry. About two-thirds of its business is with the gold sector.
- Regis Resources, a smaller gold production company, sold 369 721 ounces of gold in the June 2019 year.
- Sandfire Resources is predominantly a copper miner, but in the June 2019 year it also produced 44 455 ounces of gold.

High-tech companies

It was back in *Top Stocks 2011* that I first alerted readers to the phenomenon of a growing number of high-tech companies making it into the book. Ten years earlier only one technology company — Computershare — had been in *Top Stocks*. But since 2011 a dozen or so have regularly made it.

The Information Technology sector represents only around 4 per cent of market capitalisation in Australia (in the US it is more than 20 per cent), yet some of these companies have been outstanding performers.

They are generally small companies and it can sometimes be difficult for outsiders to understand just how they make their money. In addition, some are on high price/earnings ratios with low dividend yields. Thus, many investors avoid them.

But technology has infiltrated virtually every facet of our lives, and the best of these companies are set to grow. It is worth taking the time to learn more about them.

Information technology companies

	Year-on-year after-tax profit growth (%)	Dividend yield (%)
Altium	48.9	0.9
Citadel Group	−24.1	2.8
Codan	9.8	1.9
Data#3	28.7	4.2
DWS	5.5	7.3
Hansen Technologies	−18.7	1.8
Infomedia	25.0	1.7
Integrated Research	13.9	2.4

IRESS	7.3	3.8
Objective	22.6	1.3
Technology One	14.6	1.2

Money management companies

Another trend — first noted a year ago — is the rise of listed fund management companies. One of these, Perpetual, has been in the book for many years. But others, like APN Property Group and Australian Ethical Investment, are new.

The companies are beneficiaries of the huge — and steadily growing — pool of superannuation money in Australia. Nevertheless, it must be recognised that their fortunes are linked to the financial markets. Their profits will take a hit if the markets fall badly. But they should also recover quickly once investors become active again.

Money management companies

	Year-on-year after-tax profit growth (%)	Dividend yield (%)
APN Property Group	7.1	5.0
Australian Ethical Investment	30.9	2.3
Fiducian Group	12.5	4.6
Magellan Financial Group	35.5	3.0
Pendal Group	29.5	7.8
Perpetual	−16.6	6.9
Platinum Asset Management	−16.7	7.1

High dividend yields

With interest rates remaining low, many investors have been seeking stocks offering high dividend yields. These are still a worthy target, as they can offer a degree of protection if the market is falling. Table N lists all companies in the book according to their dividend yields.

Six years ago, in *Top Stocks 2014*, with investors looking for smaller companies with high dividend yields, I published a list of smaller companies from the book — a market capitalisation of below $450 million — with a dividend yield of at least 5 per cent.

There were 22 such companies in *Top Stocks 2014*. Since then I have repeated the process each year. There were 10 companies in *Top Stocks 2019*. This year there are just seven.

Dividend yield: small companies

	Dividend yield (%)
Bell Financial Group	7.6
Vita Group	7.5
DWS	7.3
GR Engineering Services	6.5
Virtus Health	5.9
Mortgage Choice	5.3
APN Property Group	5.0

Acquisitions

It is a feature of the *Top Stocks* books that they contain many smaller companies. So almost every year one or more of them gets acquired by a larger corporation.

In this latest edition, Capilano Honey, which appeared in *Top Stocks 2019*, is omitted because it was acquired by a private equity firm in 2018.

But something new has occurred with *Top Stocks 2020*. No fewer than three of the companies that qualify for inclusion have announced that they are likely to be taken over. One or more of these friendly acquisitions may even have taken place by the time this book is printed and reaches the bookstores, leading to the delisting of the stock.

It was tempting not to include the companies in the book at all. But I have decided to leave them in. There is a remote possibility that the takeovers will not go ahead. It is unlikely — these are non-hostile takeover bids — but possible that they are voted down by shareholders.

I also remember one year, in the early days of *Top Stocks*, that I removed one company from the book when it appeared it would be acquired by a rival. But the takeover never went ahead.

Here are the three stocks. Please be aware that one or more of them may no longer exist as an independent company by the time you are reading this book.

- Pacific Energy
- Ruralco Holdings
- Wellcom Group

Who is *Top Stocks* written for?

Top Stocks is written for all those investors wishing to exercise a degree of control over their portfolios. It is for those just starting out, as well as for those with plenty of experience but who still feel the need for some guidance through the thickets of nearly 2300 listed stocks.

It is not a how-to book. It does not give step-by-step instructions to 'winning' in the stock market. Rather, it is an independent and objective evaluation of leading companies, based on rigid criteria, with the intention of yielding a large selection of stocks that can become the starting point for investors wishing to do their own research.

A large amount of information is presented on each company, and another key feature of the book is that the data is presented in a common format, to allow readers to make easy comparisons between companies.

It is necessarily a conservative book. All stocks must have been listed for five years even to be considered for inclusion. It is especially suited for those seeking out value stocks for longer-term investment.

Yet, perhaps ironically, the book is also being used by short-term traders seeking a goodly selection of financially sound and reliable companies whose shares they can trade.

In addition, there are many regular readers who buy the book each year, and to them in particular I express my thanks.

What are the entry criteria?

The criteria for inclusion in *Top Stocks* are strict:

- All companies must be included in the All Ordinaries Index, which comprises Australia's 500 largest stocks (out of nearly 2300). The reason for excluding smaller companies is that there is often little investor information available on many of them and some are so thinly traded as to be almost illiquid. In fact, the 500 All Ordinaries companies comprise, by market capitalisation, more than 95 per cent of the entire market.
- It is necessary that all companies be publicly listed since at least the end of 2014, and have a five-year record of profits and dividend payouts, each year.
- All companies are required to post a return-on-equity ratio of at least 10 per cent in their latest financial year.
- No company should have a debt-to-equity ratio of more than 70 per cent.
- It must be stressed that share price performance is NOT one of the criteria for inclusion in this book. The purpose is to select companies with good profits and a strong balance sheet. These may not offer the spectacular share-price returns of a high-tech start-up or a promising lithium miner, but they should also present far less risk.
- There are several notable exclusions. Listed managed investments are out, as these mainly buy other shares or investments. Examples are Australian Foundation Investment Company and all the real estate investment trusts.
- A further exclusion are the foreign-registered stocks listed on the ASX. There is sometimes a lack of information available about such companies. In addition, their stock prices tend to move on events and trends in their home countries, making it difficult at times for local investors to follow them.

It is surely a tribute to the strength and resilience of Australian corporations that, once again, despite the volatility of recent years, so many companies have qualified for the book.

Changes to this edition

A total of 15 companies from *Top Stocks 2019* have been omitted from this new edition.

One company, Capilano Honey, was acquired during the year.

With interest rates remaining low some corporations expanded their borrowings, and three companies from *Top Stocks 2019* saw their debt-to-equity ratio rise above the 70 per cent limit for this book:

- Collection House
- Reece
- Seek

The remaining 11 excluded companies had return-on-equity ratios that fell below the required 10 per cent:

- Bank of Queensland
- CVC
- Event Hospitality and Entertainment
- Evolution Mining
- G8 Education
- IOOF Holdings
- Lendlease Group
- MyState
- Sigma Healthcare
- Tassal Group
- Villa World

There are 25 new companies in this book (although seven of them have appeared in earlier editions of the book but were not in *Top Stocks 2019*).

The new companies in this book are:

- Alumina*
- APN Property Group*
- Australian Ethical Investment*
- Australian Pharmaceutical Industries
- Bapcor*
- Beacon Lighting Group*
- Bell Financial Group*
- Bluescope Steel
- Brambles
- CIMIC Group
- The Citadel Group*

- Clover Corporation*
- Fortescue Metals Group
- IPH*
- Lifestyle Communities*
- McPherson's
- Medibank Private*
- Orora*
- Pacific Smiles Group*
- Regis Resources*
- Schaffer Corporation
- Service Stream*
- SG Fleet Group*
- Smartgroup Corporation*
- Supply Network*

* Companies that have not appeared in any previous edition of *Top Stocks*.

Companies in every edition of *Top Stocks*

This is the 26th edition of *Top Stocks*. Just three companies have appeared in each one of those editions:

- ANZ Banking
- Commonwealth Bank of Australia
- Westpac Banking

Once again it is my hope that *Top Stocks* will serve you well.

Martin Roth
Melbourne
September 2019

Introduction

The 105 companies in this book have been placed as much as possible into a common format, for ease of comparison. Please study the following explanations in order to get as much as possible from the large amount of data.

The tables have been made as concise as possible, though they repay careful study, as they contain large amounts of information.

Note that the tables for the banks have been arranged a little differently from the others. Details of these are provided later in this Introduction.

Head

At the head of each entry is the company name, with its three-letter ASX code and the website address.

Share-price chart

Under the company name is a share-price chart, to September 2019, provided by Alan Hull (www.alanhull.com), author of *Invest My Way*, *Trade My Way* and *Active Investing*.

Small table

Under the share-price chart is a small table with the following data.

Share price

This is the closing price on 2 September 2019. Also included are the 12-month high and low prices, as of the same date.

Market capitalisation

This is the size of the company, as determined by the stock market. It is the share price (again, as of 2 September 2019) multiplied by the number of shares in issue. All companies in this book must be in the All Ordinaries Index, which comprises Australia's 500 largest stocks, as measured by market capitalisation.

Price-to-NTA-per-share ratio

The NTA-per-share figure expresses the worth of a company's net tangible assets—that is, its assets minus its liabilities and intangible assets—for each share of the company. The price-to-NTA-per-share ratio relates this figure to the share price.

A ratio of one means that the company is valued exactly according to the value of its assets. A ratio below one suggests that the shares are a bargain, though usually there is a good reason for this. Profits are more important than assets.

Some companies in this book have a negative NTA-per-share figure—as a result of having intangible assets valued at more than their remaining net assets—and a price-to-NTA-per-share ratio cannot be calculated.

See Table M, in the second part of this book, for a little more detail on this ratio.

Five-year share price return

This is the total return you could have received from the stock in the five years to September 2019. It is based on the share price appreciation (or depreciation) plus dividends, and is expressed as a compounded annual rate of return.

Dividend reinvestment plan

A dividend reinvestment plan (DRP) allows shareholders to receive additional shares in their company in place of the dividend. Usually—though not always—these shares are provided at a small discount to the prevailing price, which can make them quite attractive. And of course no broking fees apply.

Many large companies offer such plans. However, they come and go. When a company needs finance it may introduce a DRP. When its financing requirements become less pressing it may withdraw it. Some companies that have a DRP in place may decide to deactivate it for a time.

The information in this book is based on up-to-date information from the companies. But if you are investing in a particular company in expectations of a DRP, be sure to check that it is still on offer. The company's own website will often provide this information.

Price/earnings ratio

The price/earnings ratio (PER) is one of the most popular measures of whether a share is cheap or expensive. It is calculated by dividing the share price—in this case the closing price for 2 September 2019—by the earnings per share figure. Obviously the share price is continually changing, so the PER figures in this book are for guidance only. Many newspapers publish each morning the latest PER for every stock.

Dividend yield

This is the latest full-year dividend expressed as a percentage of the share price. Like the price/earnings ratio, it changes as the share price moves. It is a useful figure, especially for investors who are buying shares for income, as it allows you to compare this income with alternative investments, such as a bank term deposit or a rental property.

Sector comparisons

It is sometimes useful to compare a company's price/earnings ratio and its dividend yield with those of its sector.

Figures used in this book are those of the S&P/ASX sectors from September 2019.

Company commentary

Each commentary begins with a brief introduction to the company and its activities. Then follow the highlights of its latest business results. For the majority of the companies these are their June 2019 results, which were issued during July and August 2019. Finally, there is a section on the outlook for the company.

Main table

Here is what you can find in the main table.

Revenues

These are the company's revenues from its business activities, generally the sale of products or services. However, it does not usually include additional income from such sources as investments, bank interest or the sale of assets. If the information is available, the revenues figure has been broken down into the major product areas.

As much as possible, the figures are for continuing businesses. When a company sells a part of its operations the financial results for the sold activities are now separated from the core results. This can mean that the previous year's results are restated — also excluding the sold business — to make year-on-year comparisons more valid.

Earnings before interest and taxation

Earnings before interest and taxation (EBIT) is the firm's profit from its operations before the payment of interest and tax. This figure is often used by analysts examining a company. The reason is that some companies have borrowed extensively to finance their activities, while others have opted for alternative means. By expressing profits before interest payments it is possible to compare the performance of these companies more precisely. The net interest figure — interest payments minus interest receipts — has been used for this calculation.

You will also find many companies using a measure called EBITDA, which is earnings before interest, taxation, depreciation and amortisation.

EBIT margin

This is the company's EBIT expressed as a percentage of its revenues. It is a gauge of a company's efficiency. A high EBIT margin suggests that a company is achieving success in keeping its costs low.

Gross margin

The gross margin is the company's gross profit as a percentage of its sales. The gross profit is the amount left over after deducting from a company's sales figure its cost of sales: that is, its manufacturing costs or, for a retailer, the cost of purchasing the goods it sells. The cost of goods sold figure does not usually include marketing or administration costs.

As there are different ways of calculating the cost of goods sold figure, this ratio is better used for year-to-year comparisons of a single company's efficiency, rather than in comparing one company with another.

Many companies do not present a cost of goods sold figure, so a gross margin ratio is not given for every stock in this book.

The revenues for some companies include a mix of sales and services. Where a breakdown is possible, the gross profit figure will relate to sales only.

Profit before tax/profit after tax

The profit before tax figure is simply the EBIT figure minus net interest payments. The profit after tax figure is, of course, the company's profit after the payment of tax, and also after the deduction of minority interests. Minority interests are that part of a company's profit that is claimed by outside interests, usually the other shareholders in a subsidiary that is not fully owned by the company. Many companies do not have any minority interests, and for those that do it is generally a tiny figure.

As much as possible, I have adjusted the profit figures to exclude non-recurring profits and losses, which are often referred to as significant items. It is for this reason that the profit figures in *Top Stocks* sometimes differ from those in the financial media or on financial websites, where profit figures normally include significant items.

Significant items are those that have an abnormal impact on profits, even though they happen in the normal course of the company's operations. Examples are the profit from the sale of a business, or expenses of a business restructuring, the write-down of property, an inventory write-down, a bad-debt loss or a write-off for research and development expenditure.

Significant items are controversial. It is often a matter of subjective judgement as to what is included and what excluded. After analysing the accounts of hundreds of companies, while writing the various editions of this book, it is clear that different companies use varying interpretations of what is significant.

Further, when they do report a significant item there is no consistency as to whether they use pre-tax figures or after-tax figures. Some report both, making it easy to adjust the profit figures in the tables in this book. But difficulties arise when only one figure is given for significant items.

In normal circumstances most companies do not report significant items. But investors should be aware of this issue. It sometimes causes consternation for readers of *Top Stocks* to find that a particular profit figure in this book is substantially different from that given by some other source. My publisher occasionally receives emails from readers enquiring why a profit figure in this book is so different from that reported elsewhere. In virtually all cases the reason is that I have stripped out a significant item.

It is also worth noting my observation that a growing number of companies present what they call an underlying profit (called a cash profit for the banks), in addition to their reported (statutory) profit. This underlying profit will exclude not only significant items but also discontinued businesses and sometimes other related items. Where all the relevant figures are available, I have used these underlying figures for the tables in this book.

It should also be noted that when a company sells or terminates a significant business it will now usually report the profit or loss of that business as a separate item. It will also usually backdate its previous year's accounts to exclude that business, so that worthwhile comparisons can be made of continuing businesses.

The tables in this book usually refer to continuing businesses only.

Earnings per share
Earnings per share is the after-tax profit divided by the number of shares. Because the profit figure is for a 12-month period the number of shares used is a weighted average of those on issue during the year. This number is provided by the company in its annual report and its results announcements.

Cashflow per share
The cashflow per share ratio tells—in theory—how much actual cash the company has generated from its operations.

In fact, the ratio in this book is not exactly a true measure of cashflow. It is simply the company's depreciation and amortisation figures for the year added to the after-tax profit, and then divided by a weighted average of the number of shares. Depreciation and amortisation are expenses that do not actually utilise cash, so can be added back to after-tax profit to give a kind of indication of the company's cashflow.

By contrast, a true cashflow—including such items as newly raised capital and money received from the sale of assets—would require quite complex calculations based on the company's statement of cashflows.

However, many investors use the ratio as I present it, because it is easy to calculate, and it is certainly a useful guide to how much funding the company has available from its operations.

Dividend
The dividend figure is the total for the year, interim and final. It does not include special dividends. The level of franking is also provided.

Net tangible assets per share
The NTA per share figure tells the theoretical value of the company—per share—if all assets were sold and then all liabilities paid. It is very much a theoretical figure, as there is no guarantee that corporate assets are really worth the price put on them in the balance sheet. Intangible assets such as goodwill, newspaper mastheads and patent rights are excluded because of the difficulty in putting a sales price on them, and also because they may in fact not have much value if separated from the company.

As already noted, some companies in this book have a negative NTA, due to the fact that their intangible assets are so great, and no figure can be listed for them.

Where a company's most recent financial results are the half-year figures, these are used to calculate this ratio.

Interest cover

The interest cover ratio indicates how many times a company could make its interest payments from its pre-tax profit. A rough rule of thumb says a ratio of at least three times is desirable. Below that and fast-rising interest rates could imperil profits. The ratio is derived by dividing the EBIT figure by net interest payments. Some companies have interest receipts that are higher than their interest payments, which turns the interest cover into a negative figure, and so it is not listed.

Return on equity

Return on equity is the after-tax profit expressed as a percentage of the shareholders' equity. In theory, it is the amount that the company's managers have made for you — the shareholder — on your money. The shareholders' equity figure used is an average for the year.

Debt-to-equity ratio

This ratio is one of the best-known measures of a company's debt levels. It is total borrowings minus the company's cash holdings, expressed as a percentage of the shareholders' equity. Some companies have no debt at all, or their cash position is greater than their level of debt, which results in a negative ratio, so no figure is listed for them.

Where a company's most recent financial results are the half-year figures, these are used to calculate this ratio.

Current ratio

The current ratio is simply the company's current assets divided by its current liabilities. Current assets are cash or assets that can, in theory, be converted quickly into cash. Current liabilities are normally those payable within a year. Thus, the current ratio measures the ability of a company to repay in a hurry its short-term debt, should the need arise. The surplus of current assets over current liabilities is referred to as the company's working capital.

Where a company's most recent financial results are the half-year figures, these are used to calculate this ratio.

Banks

The tables for the banks are somewhat different from those for most other companies. EBIT and debt-to-equity ratios have little relevance for them, as they have such high interest payments (to their customers). Other differences are examined below.

Operating income

Operating income is used instead of sales revenues. Operating income is the bank's net interest income—that is, its total interest income minus its interest expense—plus other income, such as bank fees, fund management fees and income from businesses such as corporate finance and insurance.

Net interest income

Banks borrow money—that is, they accept deposits from savers—and they lend it to businesses, homebuyers and other borrowers. They charge the borrowers more than they pay those who deposit money with them, and the difference is known as net interest income.

Operating expenses

These are all the costs of running the bank. Banks have high operating expenses, and one of the keys to profit growth is cutting these expenses. Add the provision for doubtful debts to operating expenses, then deduct the total from operating income, and you get the pre-tax profit.

Non-interest income to total income

Banks have traditionally made most of their income from savers and from lending out money. But they are also working to diversify into new fields, and this ratio is an indication of their success.

Cost-to-income ratio

As noted, the banks have high costs—numerous branches, expensive computer systems, many staff, and so on—and they are all striving to reduce these. The cost-to-income ratio expresses their expenses as a percentage of their operating income, and is one of the ratios most often used as a gauge of efficiency. The lower the ratio drops the better.

Return on assets

Banks have enormous assets, in sharp contrast to, say, a high-tech start-up whose main physical assets may be little more than a set of computers and other technological equipment. So the return on assets—the after-tax profit expressed as a percentage of the year's average total assets—is another measure of efficiency.

PART I
THE COMPANIES

1300SMILES Limited

ASX code: ONT   www.1300smiles.com.au

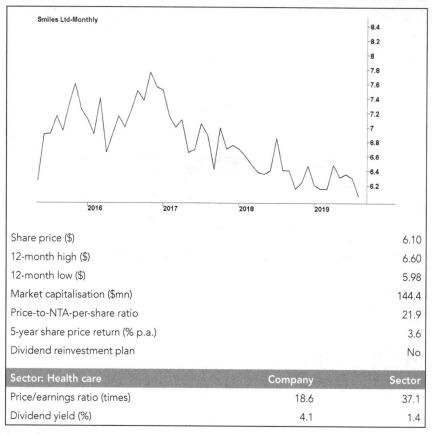

Share price ($)	6.10
12-month high ($)	6.60
12-month low ($)	5.98
Market capitalisation ($mn)	144.4
Price-to-NTA-per-share ratio	21.9
5-year share price return (% p.a.)	3.6
Dividend reinvestment plan	No

Sector: Health care	Company	Sector
Price/earnings ratio (times)	18.6	37.1
Dividend yield (%)	4.1	1.4

Townsville-based 1300SMILES, founded in 2000, runs a chain of more than 35 dental practices in 10 major population centres of Queensland, and has also expanded to South Australia and New South Wales. Its main role is the provision of dental surgeries and practice management services to self-employed dentists, allowing them to focus on dental services. It also manages its own small dental business. The founder and managing director, Dr Daryl Holmes, owns around 60 per cent of the company equity.

Latest business results (June 2019, full year)

Revenues and profits rose modestly as the company continued to expand. The company also reports what it calls over-the-counter revenues, which represent the amount actually received by its dentistry businesses before the deduction of patient fees by self-employed dentists. On this basis — which the company believes gives a fairer measure of the scale of its operations than its reported statutory sales figure — total company revenues rose to $58.9 million in June 2019, from $55.8 million in the previous year. During the year the company acquired new practices in Noosa, Springfield Lakes, Maroochydore and Strathpine, all in Queensland.

Outlook

The dental business in Australia is fragmented, with around 70 per cent of dentists working in their own private practices or in small partnerships. However, as stricter regulatory and compliance requirements drive up costs, a gradual consolidation is taking place, which has led to the rise of what has become known as the Dental Service Organisations sector, and 1300SMILES is one of the leaders in this trend. The company buys dental practices, then retains the dentists, who pay a fee to 1300SMILES for services received, including marketing, administration, billing and collection, facilities certification and licensing. The company also provides support staff, equipment and facilities and sources all consumable goods. It continues to seek out new practices to buy, though it has strict benchmarks concerning the price it will pay. Company management have suggested that a big new wave of consolidation is due to take place, and they believe that 1300SMILES, with its relatively low levels of debt and its strong reputation, will be able to take advantage of this. In particular, the company believes that it may even be able to buy out some of its rival consolidators. In addition, it expects to continue establishing new practices in existing and new regions. It will also build up existing practices through benchmarking, training and mentoring, as well as by expanding those facilities that are at full capacity.

Year to 30 June	2018	2019
Revenues ($mn)	39.1	40.3
EBIT ($mn)	10.4	10.7
EBIT margin (%)	26.6	26.4
Profit before tax ($mn)	10.7	10.8
Profit after tax ($mn)	7.6	7.8
Earnings per share (c)	32.24	32.82
Cash flow per share (c)	41.98	42.40
Dividend (c)	24	25
Percentage franked	100	100
Net tangible assets per share ($)	0.42	0.28
Interest cover (times)	~	~
Return on equity (%)	20.6	19.9
Debt-to-equity ratio (%)	~	21.4
Current ratio	0.9	1.0

Accent Group Limited

ASX code: AX1   www.accentgr.com.au

Share price ($)	1.63
12-month high ($)	1.71
12-month low ($)	1.05
Market capitalisation ($mn)	877.7
Price-to-NTA-per-share ratio	17.4
5-year share price return (% p.a.)	49.0
Dividend reinvestment plan	No

Sector: Consumer discretionary	Company	Sector
Price/earnings ratio (times)	16.3	13.7
Dividend yield (%)	5.1	3.9

Sydney company Accent Group is a nationwide footwear wholesaler and retailer that has grown rapidly through a series of mergers and acquisitions. Its brands now include The Athlete's Foot — established in 1976 — Hype DC, Platypus, Podium Sports, Skechers, Merrell, CAT, Vans, Dr. Martens, Saucony, Timberland, Sperry Top-Sider, Palladium and Stance. The company's wholesale division distributes footwear and apparel. Accent also operates in New Zealand.

Latest business results (June 2019, full year)

Accent overcame a weak retail environment to post a strong result, with double-digit gains in sales and profit. With profit growing at a faster pace than sales, the company was successful in boosting margins. The good result came despite the weakening dollar, which forced up costs for its imported products. Retail sales at company-owned stores rose 16 per cent to $656 million. This included a 2.3 per cent increase in like-for-like sales and a 93 per cent surge in digital sales. Skechers, Platypus, Vans, Dr. Martens, Timberland and Merrell all traded especially well. Wholesale revenues of $116 million were 7 per cent higher than in the previous year, with strong performances from Vans, Dr. Martens, Merrell, CAT and Stance more than offsetting continued weakness from Skechers. Total company sales for the year, including for franchise stores, rose 9 per cent to $935 million. During the year Accent opened 54 new stores and closed 21, resulting in a total of 479 stores and online sites.

Outlook

Accent maintains its ambitious growth strategy and expects profits to continue rising. It plans to open more than 40 new stores during the June 2020 year, with a further 30 to 40 in the ensuing two to three years. In the current weak retail environment it finds that it is able to arrange beneficial deals with landlords that make new stores cashflow-positive from the first month. It is enjoying success with its new The Trybe children and youth brand, launched in October 2018, with the initial stores performing well ahead of expectations. Also performing well ahead of expectations is its new range of socks and shoe accessories, launched in November 2018 under the Hype, Platypus and The Athlete's Foot brands. In September 2018 it acquired Subtype, a boutique retailer of limited-edition premium sneakers, and it expects to expand this business. In 2020 it plans the launch of a new store brand, PIVOT, selling budget-priced footwear. It has also opened some large new CBD Platypus stores in response to the expansion in Australia of British sportswear retailer JD Sports.

Year to 30 June*	2018	2019
Revenues ($mn)	702.4	796.3
EBIT ($mn)	64.7	80.6
EBIT margin (%)	9.2	10.1
Profit before tax ($mn)	60.9	77.0
Profit after tax ($mn)	44.0	53.9
Earnings per share (c)	8.23	10.02
Cash flow per share (c)	12.75	15.28
Dividend (c)	6.75	8.25
Percentage franked	100	100
Net tangible assets per share ($)	0.08	0.09
Interest cover (times)	17.1	22.6
Return on equity (%)	11.6	13.6
Debt-to-equity ratio (%)	8.9	12.3
Current ratio	1.3	1.2

* 1 July 2018

Adelaide Brighton Limited

ASX code: ABC   www.adbri.com.au

Share price ($)	3.02
12-month high ($)	6.53
12-month low ($)	2.98
Market capitalisation ($mn)	2014.8
Price-to-NTA-per-share ratio	2.3
5-year share price return (% p.a.)	2.0
Dividend reinvestment plan	No

Sector: Materials	Company	Sector
Price/earnings ratio (times)	10.3	13.2
Dividend yield (%)	6.6	4.4

Adelaide-based Adelaide Brighton, established in 1882, is one of Australia's leaders in the production and supply of construction materials, notably cement and lime. In addition, its Hy-Tec business and its Mawson Group joint venture are suppliers of pre-mixed concrete, and it has a business as a supplier of aggregates, through Mawson Group and Hurd Haulage. The Adbri Masonry operation is a leading producer of concrete masonry products. Adelaide Brighton's major customers include the residential, non-residential and engineering construction sectors, as well as the infrastructure, alumina, steel and mining industries.

Latest business results (June 2019, half year)

Sales were down and profits fell sharply as the company was hit by weaker residential and civil construction markets. Cement sales fell by 8.6 per cent from the June 2018 half, with higher costs and pricing pressure from imports hurting margins. Concrete volumes were down by 7.8 per cent, and with price increases insufficient to offset the impact of rising raw material and production costs. Concrete product revenues were also down, despite some improvement in Victorian, South Australian and Tasmanian markets. Lime sales were generally stable for the year. On a statutory basis the company actually reported a loss, mainly due to a non-cash after-tax impairment charge of $69.9 million.

Outlook

Adelaide Brighton is a key supplier to the construction and resources industries, and its fortunes are heavily dependent on trends in these sectors. It expects the residential construction market to remain weak until 2021. However, it believes the mining sector will generate an increase in demand for construction materials, and with expansion in iron ore, gold and nickel mining operations boosting sales of cement and lime in Western Australia and the Northern Territory. It also expects infrastructure spending to remain high, with demand from some large new projects expected to arrive during 2020. The company is working to cut expenses, with a target of annual cost savings of $10 million from 2020. It is also boosting its Western Australian lime business, where demand remains firm. It is increasing its concrete and aggregates capacity, through organic growth and acquisition, with a particular view to supplying the south-east Queensland growth corridor. In 2013 Adelaide Brighton initiated the process of selling surplus land and it believes that over 10 years it could realise some $100 million in sales. With the current weakness in its businesses, it plans to bring forward some land sales. The company expects an after-tax profit — excluding property business — of $120 million to $130 million for 2019.

Year to 31 December	2017	2018
Revenues ($mn)	1559.6	1630.6
EBIT ($mn)	289.9	273.5
EBIT margin (%)	18.6	16.8
Gross margin (%)	35.2	35.5
Profit before tax ($mn)	277.8	259.1
Profit after tax ($mn)	198.4	191.0
Earnings per share (c)	30.52	29.36
Cash flow per share (c)	43.21	42.80
Dividend (c)	20.5	20
Percentage franked	100	100
Interest cover (times)	24.0	19.0
Return on equity (%)	16.1	15.4
Half year to 30 June	2018	2019
Revenues ($mn)	806.3	755.7
Profit before tax ($mn)	116.8	76.0
Profit after tax ($mn)	85.2	55.3
Earnings per share (c)	13.10	8.50
Dividend (c)	9	0
Percentage franked	100	~
Net tangible assets per share ($)	1.43	1.30
Debt-to-equity ratio (%)	33.7	45.9
Current ratio	1.3	2.6

AGL Energy Limited

ASX code: AGL

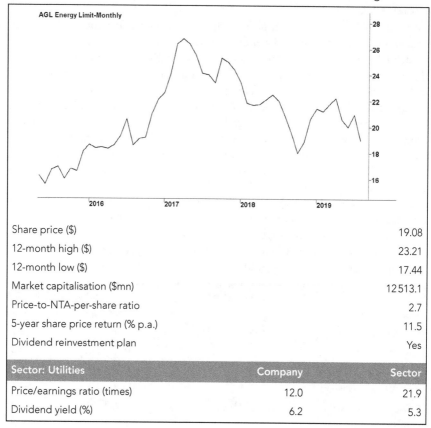

Share price ($)	19.08
12-month high ($)	23.21
12-month low ($)	17.44
Market capitalisation ($mn)	12513.1
Price-to-NTA-per-share ratio	2.7
5-year share price return (% p.a.)	11.5
Dividend reinvestment plan	Yes

Sector: Utilities	Company	Sector
Price/earnings ratio (times)	12.0	21.9
Dividend yield (%)	6.2	5.3

Sydney-based power generator and supplier AGL Energy is one of Australia's oldest companies, founded in 1837 as Australian Gas Light. It owns and operates four major coal- and gas-fired power stations—the Bayswater and Liddell black coal power plants in New South Wales (total 4640 MW), the Loy Yang brown coal mine and power plant in Victoria (2210 MW), and the Torrens gas power plant in South Australia (1280 MW). Its growing portfolio of renewable assets includes wind power generation in South Australia, Queensland, New South Wales and Victoria, hydro-electric power generation in Victoria and New South Wales, and solar power in New South Wales. Through its wholesale and retail businesses AGL supplies electricity and gas to some 3.7 million business and residential customers in New South Wales, Victoria, South Australia, Queensland and Western Australia.

Latest business results (June 2019, full year)

Sales rose and the underlying after-tax profit was up, but at a much more modest pace than in recent years. The key factor behind the rise was margin growth in the company's wholesale business, thanks to higher wholesale electricity prices and lower compliance costs for renewable energy certificates. This was partially offset by a decline in gas volume sales to large businesses and a 10 per cent jump in depreciation and amortisation charges. On a statutory basis profits fell sharply, largely due to changes in the value of electricity derivative contracts. Though the company's wholesale business was responsible for just 42 per cent of company revenues, it generated more than 90 per cent of earnings.

Outlook

AGL has been a short-term beneficiary of rising energy prices in Australia, but it now expects a sharp fall in profits. Its early forecast is that the June 2020 underlying after-tax profit will drop to between $780 million and $860 million. This reflects a range of factors, including the high cost of repairing some extensive damage to one of the units at its Loy Yang plant, rising fuel input costs, lower wholesale power prices, retail price regulatory pressures and higher depreciation charges. Meanwhile, it continues with plans to invest more than $2 billion in a series of projects that will bring on stream some 1215 MW of new generation capacity. It is also expanding its activities in the Western Australian energy market—which it entered in 2017—with the $93 million acquisition of Perth Energy Holdings, the state's third-largest electricity retailer. AGL has also expressed a desire to expand into the provision of data services for households.

Year to 30 June	2018	2019
Revenues ($mn)	12 816.0	13 246.0
Customer markets (%)	60	57
Wholesale markets (%)	39	42
EBIT ($mn)	1 664.0	1 660.0
EBIT margin (%)	13.0	12.5
Gross margin (%)	28.5	27.6
Profit before tax ($mn)	1 444.0	1 467.0
Profit after tax ($mn)	1 018.0	1 040.0
Earnings per share (c)	155.22	158.58
Cash flow per share (c)	241.83	253.88
Dividend (c)	117	119
Percentage franked	80	80
Net tangible assets per share ($)	7.67	7.16
Interest cover (times)	7.6	8.6
Return on equity (%)	12.8	12.4
Debt-to-equity ratio (%)	30.1	32.4
Current ratio	1.6	1.3

ALS Limited

ASX code: ALQ

www.alsglobal.com

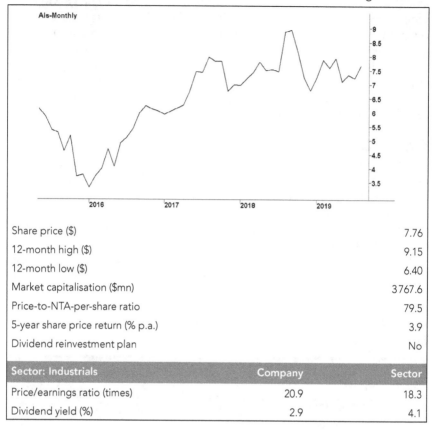

Share price ($)	7.76
12-month high ($)	9.15
12-month low ($)	6.40
Market capitalisation ($mn)	3 767.6
Price-to-NTA-per-share ratio	79.5
5-year share price return (% p.a.)	3.9
Dividend reinvestment plan	No

Sector: Industrials	Company	Sector
Price/earnings ratio (times)	20.9	18.3
Dividend yield (%)	2.9	4.1

Brisbane-based ALS was established in 1863 and has become one of the world's largest providers of laboratory analysis services. It serves numerous industry sectors, and groups these into three divisions—Life Sciences (including environmental, food, pharmaceutical, consumer products and electronics), Commodities (minerals and coal) and Industrial (energy, resources, transportation, infrastructure, asset care and tribology—used oil). It processes more than 40 million samples annually at over 350 locations in 65 countries.

Latest business results (March 2019, full year)

ALS posted another excellent result, with all three divisions achieving growth in sales, although the Industrial division saw its profits fall. The Commodities division enjoyed another strong year, with increased demand from both established mining clients and new exploration companies for mineral-related geochemistry testing. Nevertheless, the company reported a slowdown in the second half, due to uncertain global trading conditions. The Life Sciences division also enjoyed an excellent year, thanks to both organic growth and new acquisitions. There were solid gains for each of the division's revenue streams, environmental and food/pharmaceuticals, with strong profit growth for the former. Both the Commodities and the Life Sciences divisions also benefited from productivity improvements that lowered costs and boosted margins. The Industrial division profited from a substantial increase in orders from Australia and the US. However, lower margins for asset care business hurt profits. During the year the company invested $100 million in acquisitions and growth projects.

Outlook

ALS has developed a five-year strategic plan, with a focus on building and expanding its existing businesses, and with a particular emphasis on its high-margin testing activities. It is also seeking to divest itself of underperforming, lower-margin operations. Early in 2019 it sold two Chinese businesses related to environmental testing and life science consumer testing. Its Commodities division is benefiting from an increase in regulatory requirements in the coal industry, as well as growing demand for high-quality coal in international markets, and has seen some significant growth in orders, especially in Australia. Nevertheless, ALS is working to diversify away from its high exposure to the resources sector, and is seeking further acquisitions in the environmental, pharmaceutical and food sectors in Europe and North America. It may also enter new areas of business. The company's target is that by 2022 it will be achieving annual revenues of $2.2 billion, with EBITDA of at least $500 million—compared with $353 million in the March 2019 year—and with non-resource businesses contributing more than half the profit.

Year to 31 March	2018	2019
Revenues ($mn)	1446.9	1664.8
Life sciences (%)	51	50
Commodities (%)	36	37
Industrial (%)	13	13
EBIT ($mn)	221.3	281.1
EBIT margin (%)	15.3	16.9
Profit before tax ($mn)	195.5	249.1
Profit after tax ($mn)	142.2	181.0
Earnings per share (c)	28.38	37.15
Cash flow per share (c)	42.47	52.50
Dividend (c)	17	22.5
Percentage franked	51	28
Net tangible assets per share ($)	0.26	0.10
Interest cover (times)	8.6	8.8
Return on equity (%)	12.4	16.4
Debt-to-equity ratio (%)	45.3	57.3
Current ratio	2.8	1.1

Altium Limited

ASX code: ALU www.altium.com

Share price ($)	36.81
12-month high ($)	38.49
12-month low ($)	19.73
Market capitalisation ($mn)	4 804.1
Price-to-NTA-per-share ratio	25.3
5-year share price return (% p.a.)	65.2
Dividend reinvestment plan	No

Sector: Information technology	Company	Sector
Price/earnings ratio (times)	65.3	29.4
Dividend yield (%)	0.9	1.6

Sydney-based software company Altium was founded in Tasmania in 1985. It was originally named Protel. Its specialty is the provision of software that allows engineers to design printed circuit boards (PCBs). Its core product is Altium Designer. A much smaller division, Microcontrollers and Embedded Systems (formerly called Electronic Systems Solutions), is responsible for the Tasking-brand set of embedded tools for code development. An even smaller division, Electronic Parts, Search and Discovery (previously named Cloud Applications), provides an electronic parts search tool. Altium now has most of its operations abroad, but retains its Sydney headquarters and its ASX listing.

Latest business results (June 2019, full year)

Altium reported its eighth straight year of double-digit revenue and profit growth, thanks again to a strong product array and its impressive roster of global blue-chip customers. The core Boards and Systems division achieved a 22 per cent increase in sales, with another strong performance from China, where sales jumped by

37 per cent. But it was the company's two smaller divisions that were the stars. The Microcontrollers and Embedded Systems operation saw revenues up 37 per cent and the Electronic Parts, Search and Discovery business posted a 49 per cent surge in sales. Altium reports its finances in American dollars, so the weakness of the Australian dollar magnified the strong result. All figures in this book are converted to Australian dollars using prevailing exchange rates.

Outlook

Printed circuit boards are incorporated in most electronic devices, and demand for them continues to grow. The strong rise in smart electronic connected devices is partly behind this trend. It is expensive for a customer to switch once it makes a decision to employ Altium software, and the company has a high level of recurring subscription fee income. It has a strong reputation for its PCB design software, with high profit margins and a growth rate significantly higher than the industry average, and it has set itself a June 2020 target of US$200 million in total revenues, up from US$172.8 million in June 2019. Another target is for 100 000 subscribers to its Altium Designer services by 2025, compared with 43 698 at June 2019. China is becoming an important market and Altium has opened a new sales office in Beijing, while expanding its existing sales centres in Shenzhen and Shanghai. It expects its new Altium 365 cloud-based platform to become a significant driver of future growth. At June 2019 Altium had no debt and more than US$80 million in cash holdings.

Year to 30 June	2018	2019
Revenues ($mn)	184.7	239.9
Boards & systems (%)	78	77
Microcontrollers & embedded systems (%)	14	13
Electronic parts, search & discovery (%)	8	10
EBIT ($mn)	52.1	79.0
EBIT margin (%)	28.2	32.9
Profit before tax ($mn)	52.2	80.0
Profit after tax ($mn)	49.3	73.5
Earnings per share (c)	37.98	56.35
Cash flow per share (c)	43.34	62.57
Dividend (c)	27	34
Percentage franked	0	0
Net tangible assets per share ($)	1.07	1.46
Interest cover (times)	~	~
Return on equity (%)	25.4	31.3
Debt-to-equity ratio (%)	~	~
Current ratio	1.5	1.8

Alumina Limited

ASX code: AWC www.aluminalimited.com

Share price ($)	2.21
12-month high ($)	3.20
12-month low ($)	2.07
Market capitalisation ($mn)	6 364.5
Price-to-NTA-per-share ratio	2.3
5-year share price return (% p.a.)	13.1
Dividend reinvestment plan	No

Sector: Materials	Company	Sector
Price/earnings ratio (times)	7.5	13.2
Dividend yield (%)	14.7	4.4

Melbourne-based Alumina traces its origins back to the late 1950s and the mining of bauxite by WMC Limited. This led in 1961 to the establishment of a joint venture company between WMC and the Aluminium Company of America (Alcoa). In 2002 WMC spun off its interest in this business into a separate company, Alumina. Today Alumina's sole business activity is ownership of 40 per cent of the equity of Alcoa World Alumina and Chemicals (AWAC), in partnership with Alcoa, which holds the other 60 per cent. AWAC is an international business, responsible for about 10 per cent of global alumina production. It manages bauxite mines in Western Australia, Brazil, Saudi Arabia and Guinea. It also operates alumina refineries in Western Australia, Texas, Brazil, Saudi Arabia and Spain. Other businesses include the Alcoa Steamship operation and the Portland aluminium smelter in Victoria, in which it holds a 55 per cent equity share.

Latest business results (June 2019, half year)

Falling alumina prices sent revenues and profits down. The company divides its operations into three segments, bauxite mining, alumina refining and Portland aluminium smelting. The mining business produced 19.9 million tonnes of bauxite, up from 19.1 million in the June 2018 half, at an average cash cost of US$10.50 per tonne, down from US$11.70. Most production is for the company's own use, though there are also some third-party sales. It refined 6.2 million tonnes of alumina at its own refineries, up from 6.1 million in June 2018, at an average cash cost of US$218 per tonne, down from US$224. However, the average price received of US$375 per tonne was a big drop from US$424 in the June 2018 half. The Portland smelter produced 80 000 tonnes of aluminium, down from 82 000 in June 2018, with a 17 per cent decline in the average sales price. Note that Alumina reports its results in US dollars. The Australian dollar figures in this book — converted at prevailing exchange rates — are for guidance only.

Outlook

Alumina benefits from high-quality bauxite reserves and low-cost alumina refining operations. Its shares have attracted attention for a high dividend yield. However, its financial results are directly linked to global alumina and aluminium prices, which recently have been weak, due in part to increasing Chinese production and a resumption of full operations at the giant Alunorte refinery in Brazil. Prices in the longer term are tied to economic growth prospects, so the threat of trade wars and the possibility of global economic weakness could hurt prices further.

Year to 31 December	2017	2018
Revenues ($mn)	468.8	892.7
EBIT ($mn)	443.5	848.5
EBIT margin (%)	94.6	95.1
Profit before tax ($mn)	441.3	847.2
Profit after tax ($mn)	441.3	847.2
Earnings per share (c)	15.33	29.43
Cash flow per share (c)	15.34	29.44
Dividend (c)	17.31	32.43
Percentage franked	100	100
Interest cover (times)	200.9	636.4
Return on equity (%)	16.1	28.6
Half year to 30 June	2018	2019
Revenues ($mn)	384.2	311.5
Profit before tax ($mn)	371.9	297.0
Profit after tax ($mn)	371.9	297.0
Earnings per share (c)	13.20	9.86
Dividend (c)	11.17	6.29
Percentage franked	100	100
Net tangible assets per share ($)	0.86	0.96
Debt-to-equity ratio (%)	2.6	2.8
Current ratio	24.4	0.3

AMA Group Limited

ASX code: AMA

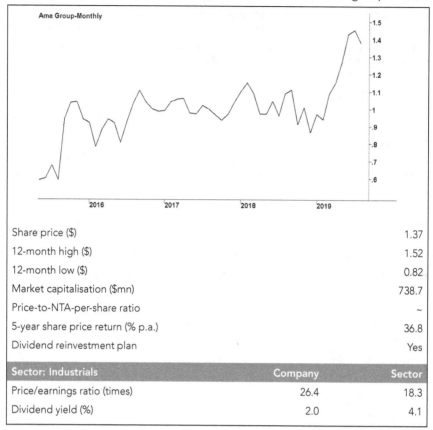

Share price ($)	1.37
12-month high ($)	1.52
12-month low ($)	0.82
Market capitalisation ($mn)	738.7
Price-to-NTA-per-share ratio	~
5-year share price return (% p.a.)	36.8
Dividend reinvestment plan	Yes

Sector: Industrials	Company	Sector
Price/earnings ratio (times)	26.4	18.3
Dividend yield (%)	2.0	4.1

Gold Coast–based AMA, formerly known as Allomak, specialises in vehicle maintenance and repairs. It has grown rapidly through acquisition, and operates through many subsidiaries. Its core business is vehicle panel repair. It also maintains an Automotive Components and Accessories division which is involved in a variety of auto-related businesses, including the manufacture and distribution of a range of car accessories, as well as automotive component remanufacturing.

Latest business results (June 2019, full year)

AMA continued to acquire new businesses, driving sales and profits higher. The Vehicle Panel Repair division represents about 86 per cent of business, and it completed 21 acquisitions during the year, including six in the heavy vehicle repair industry, as well as opening facilities at four greenfield sites. Revenues for the division rose 21 per cent, with EBITDA up 19 per cent. At June 2019 the division operated a total of 130 panel repair shops. The Automotive Components and Accessories division comprises four segments: manufacturing, distribution, remanufacturing and workshop. This division too enjoyed double-digit growth in sales and revenues. There was a good performance from the manufacturing segment, which specialises in the production of specialist auto protective accessories, thanks to a new production management team working closely with OEM customers to develop innovative products. The relocation of the corporate head office and support centre to new premises at Bundall on the Gold Coast is intended to set the company up for future growth.

Outlook

AMA continues its strong expansion with a steady series of acquisitions, as it works to consolidate Australia's $7 billion crash repair sector. With a well-regarded management team in place, it has become the dominant company in this business. Its own target is to reach $1 billion in annual revenues by the June 2021 year, with an EBITDA of $100 million (compared with $58.2 million in June 2019). It has placed a particular emphasis on New South Wales, where the number of panel repair shops has been growing sharply. It is also placing a new focus on the heavy vehicle repair business, which it regards as offering strong growth potential, with initially six businesses across three states. It has engaged in a major restructuring of its Automotive Components and Accessories division, which has been formed from many small businesses, and is realising some good growth and synergy benefits. However, parts of this division continue to underperform. The company's new digital, centralised estimating service is streamlining operations for insurers and fleet clients.

Year to 30 June	2018	2019
Revenues ($mn)	497.2	602.1
EBIT ($mn)	36.0	42.0
EBIT margin (%)	7.2	7.0
Profit before tax ($mn)	35.3	39.5
Profit after tax ($mn)	24.1	28.1
Earnings per share (c)	4.59	5.19
Cash flow per share (c)	7.13	8.17
Dividend (c)	2.5	2.75
Percentage franked	100	100
Net tangible assets per share ($)	~	~
Interest cover (times)	52.0	16.7
Return on equity (%)	14.4	15.5
Debt-to-equity ratio (%)	21.4	35.6
Current ratio	0.9	0.8

Ansell Limited

ASX code: ANN

www.ansell.com

Share price ($)	27.39
12-month high ($)	28.14
12-month low ($)	21.07
Market capitalisation ($mn)	3623.8
Price-to-NTA-per-share ratio	8.0
5-year share price return (% p.a.)	9.0
Dividend reinvestment plan	Yes

Sector: Health care	Company	Sector
Price/earnings ratio (times)	17.7	37.1
Dividend yield (%)	2.4	1.4

Melbourne-based Ansell has roots that stretch back to the manufacture of pneumatic bicycle tyres in the 19th century. It is today a global leader in a variety of safety and healthcare products. It makes a wide range of examination and surgical gloves for the medical profession. It also makes gloves and other hand and arm protective products for industrial applications, including for single use, along with household gloves. It has offices and production facilities in 55 countries, and more than 90 per cent of company revenues derive from abroad. Though still based in Australia, the company has its operational headquarters in the US.

Latest business results (June 2019, full year)

Ansell reports its results in US dollars, and sales and profits edged up, though the gains were magnified when converted to Australian dollars, as used in this book. The Healthcare division enjoyed a 4.8 per cent rise in sales, with especially solid demand in the life science and synthetic surgical categories. However, rising raw material costs, especially in the first half, forced profits down. The Industrial division saw revenues rise 1.5 per cent, which partially reflected a new corporate acquisition.

European demand was weak, especially in the automobile sector, though largely offset by strength in emerging markets. Nevertheless, thanks to lower costs and some price rises the division reported a solid rise in profits. The results in this book do not include the one-off costs for the company's transformation program, and on a statutory basis profits actually fell. Note that the figures in this book have been converted to Australian dollars using prevailing currency rates.

Outlook

Ansell has a strong portfolio of products, which gives it a degree of pricing power. It has achieved success in its research and development efforts, with a continuing stream of innovative and high-margin products. Thanks to a major company transformation program, which still continues, it has been able to lower its manufacturing costs. The acquisition in 2019 of US specialty gloves manufacturer Ringer Gloves has boosted the Industrial division, and the company is actively seeking further acquisitions. Its high exposure to the health sector gives it a degree of protection against volatile economic cycles that can hurt demand for its industrial products. Nevertheless, Ansell remains quite exposed to global economic trends, as well as to raw material prices and currency movements. The company's early forecast is for earnings per share in the June 2020 year of US$1.12 to US$1.22, compared with US$1.115 in June 2019.

Year to 30 June	2018	2019
Revenues ($mn)	1960.3	2081.9
Healthcare (%)	52	53
Industrial (%)	48	47
EBIT ($mn)	248.7	278.2
EBIT margin (%)	12.7	13.4
Gross margin (%)	39.1	39.0
Profit before tax ($mn)	237.6	262.8
Profit after tax ($mn)	193.0	209.6
Earnings per share (c)	134.23	154.90
Cash flow per share (c)	170.65	194.12
Dividend (c)	60.02	64.93
Percentage franked	24	0
Net tangible assets per share ($)	4.81	3.41
Interest cover (times)	22.5	18.0
Return on equity (%)	10.6	10.3
Debt-to-equity ratio (%)	~	10.5
Current ratio	3.9	3.1

APN Property Group Limited

ASX code: APD   www.apngroup.com.au

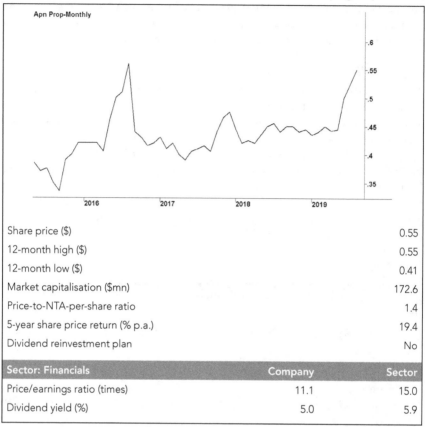

Share price ($)	0.55
12-month high ($)	0.55
12-month low ($)	0.41
Market capitalisation ($mn)	172.6
Price-to-NTA-per-share ratio	1.4
5-year share price return (% p.a.)	19.4
Dividend reinvestment plan	No

Sector: Financials	Company	Sector
Price/earnings ratio (times)	11.1	15.0
Dividend yield (%)	5.0	5.9

Melbourne company APN Property was established in 1996 as a funds management group specialising in real estate. Its funds are targeted at both institutional and retail investors. It established its flagship APN Property for Income Fund in 1998 and its first direct property fund, APN Retirement Properties Fund, in 1999. Today the company manages 12 funds, including domestic and international property securities, direct property and listed funds. It derives income from investing in its own funds, and profits are also affected by changes in the valuation of its properties.

Latest business results (June 2019, full year)

APN delivered its sixth straight year of higher recurring revenues, with profits also strong. Fund management fees of $15 million were up 6 per cent from the previous year, and co-investment income — from the company's own investments — grew 18 per cent to $8 million. The company classifies its operations into four broad categories, and all reported higher revenues and profits. The largest category, Real Estate Securities Funds, comprises five funds, with growth in value thanks to a positive investment performance, though partially offset by net fund outflows by investors. Two ASX-listed funds, the APN Industria REIT and the APN Convenience Retail REIT, comprise two further categories, and both these grew during the year. The fourth category, Direct Funds, comprises fixed-term unlisted direct property syndicates. During the year this division successfully launched the $24 million APN Nowra Property Fund. At June 2019 the company's total funds under management of $2.9 billion were up 5 per cent from a year earlier.

Outlook

APN's particular goal is to invest in properties that provide annuity-style income. It also hopes to gain from capital appreciation. With Australian interest rates low, and equity markets volatile, it sees great potential for its funds. The Real Estate Securities Funds division — the bulk of its business — has an income focus, with funds that are targeted at investors seeking stable superannuation, retirement and investment income, with some capital growth and lower-than-market volatility. This division has seen especially impressive growth in demand for its strongly performing APN Asian REIT. The company is seeking new distribution channels for these funds, particularly with independent financial advisers, and it is also planning new funds. Its Direct Funds division has a team that is an active participant in the commercial property market, and is seeking to buy additional packages of properties suitable for new syndicates. The company is also actively seeking out and acquiring appropriate new properties for its two ASX-listed funds.

Year to 30 June	2018	2019
Revenues ($mn)	25.9	26.7
EBIT ($mn)	19.3	20.2
EBIT margin (%)	74.7	75.5
Profit before tax ($mn)	18.9	20.1
Profit after tax ($mn)	13.6	14.5
Earnings per share (c)	4.61	4.94
Cash flow per share (c)	4.68	4.99
Dividend (c)	2.25	2.75
Percentage franked	100	70
Net tangible assets per share ($)	0.38	0.40
Interest cover (times)	41.6	229.4
Return on equity (%)	11.7	11.7
Debt-to-equity ratio (%)	1.3	~
Current ratio	2.7	2.5

ARB Corporation Limited

ASX code: ARB

www.arb.com.au

ARB Corporation-Monthly

Share price ($)	18.73
12-month high ($)	20.17
12-month low ($)	14.55
Market capitalisation ($mn)	1 493.3
Price-to-NTA-per-share ratio	4.7
5-year share price return (% p.a.)	9.7
Dividend reinvestment plan	Yes

Sector: Consumer discretionary	Company	Sector
Price/earnings ratio (times)	26.1	13.7
Dividend yield (%)	2.1	3.9

Melbourne-based ARB, founded in 1975, is a prominent manufacturer of specialty automotive accessories, and an international leader in the design and production of specialised equipment for four-wheel-drive vehicles. These include its Air Locker air-operated locking differential system. It also makes and distributes a wide range of other products, including bull bars, roof racks, tow bars, canopies, the Old Man Emu range of suspension products and a variety of touring and camping accessories. It operates a network of 66 ARB-brand stores throughout Australia, including 26 that are company-owned. It has established manufacturing facilities in Thailand, with distribution centres in the United States, the Czech Republic, Thailand and Dubai. It exports to more than 100 countries, and overseas business represents nearly 30 per cent of total company turnover.

Latest business results (June 2019, full year)

ARB enjoyed another good result, with rising sales and profits. Some 63 per cent of total income is from the Australian after-market, comprising ARB stores and other retailers, as well as vehicle dealers and fleet operators. Demand just edged up, hurt by a slowdown in domestic sales of SUVs and four-wheel-drive utilities, which are ARB's target market. However, exports grew by nearly 10 per cent, helped by the weaker dollar. Sales in the US represent about half of all overseas business, and profits there jumped 40 per cent, having doubled in the previous year, although this is from a low base, and profit margins remain low. Original equipment manufacturer sales to Australian vehicle makers recorded 17 per cent growth, thanks to some new contracts, although this business represents less than 8 per cent of total revenues.

Outlook

ARB continues to grow. It regards product development as a key element in helping it maintain a competitive edge, and research and development spending grew 37 per cent to $13 million in the June 2019 year. A new 20 000-square-metre warehouse in Thailand, opening in 2019, will provide increased warehousing and manufacturing capacity and will boost the efficiency of the company's global distribution network. The weak dollar has helped the company's export business. However, it has also raised some costs, as much of the company's production is manufactured at its plant in Thailand, and the dollar has fallen against the Thai currency. ARB-brand stores are an important generator of sales and the company is steadily rolling out new outlets, with three launched during the June 2019 year. At June 2019 ARB had no debt and more than $8 million in cash holdings.

Year to 30 June	2018	2019
Revenues ($mn)	422.7	443.9
EBIT ($mn)	74.6	77.9
EBIT margin (%)	17.7	17.6
Gross margin (%)	42.9	42.8
Profit before tax ($mn)	74.4	77.7
Profit after tax ($mn)	51.0	57.1
Earnings per share (c)	64.33	71.86
Cash flow per share (c)	80.61	89.31
Dividend (c)	37	39.5
Percentage franked	100	100
Net tangible assets per share ($)	3.50	3.98
Interest cover (times)	277.5	360.7
Return on equity (%)	17.7	17.6
Debt-to-equity ratio (%)	~	~
Current ratio	2.9	3.8

ASX Limited

ASX code: ASX
www.asx.com.au

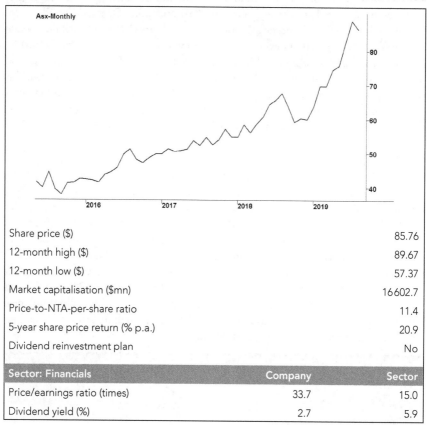

Asx-Monthly

Share price ($)	85.76
12-month high ($)	89.67
12-month low ($)	57.37
Market capitalisation ($mn)	16602.7
Price-to-NTA-per-share ratio	11.4
5-year share price return (% p.a.)	20.9
Dividend reinvestment plan	No

Sector: Financials	Company	Sector
Price/earnings ratio (times)	33.7	15.0
Dividend yield (%)	2.7	5.9

ASX (Australian Securities Exchange) was formed in 1987 through the amalgamation of six independent stock exchanges that formerly operated in the state capital cities. Each of those exchanges had a history of share trading dating back to the 19th century. Though originally a mutual organisation of stockbrokers, in 1998 ASX became a listed company, with its shares traded on its own market. It expanded in 2006 when it merged with the Sydney Futures Exchange. Today it provides primary, secondary and derivative market services, along with clearing, settlement and compliance services. It is also a provider of a range of comprehensive market data and technical services.

Latest business results (June 2019, full year)

ASX reported a solid result, with revenues and profits up and all divisions stronger. The best result came from the Trading Services division, with revenues up 9.4 per cent, thanks to an increased volume of equities trading. The largest division, Derivatives and OTC Markets, saw revenues rising by 7.8 per cent, thanks once again to growth in futures trading and a record year for the OTC clearing business. The Listings and Issuer Services division recorded 5.5 per cent revenue growth, with

111 new listings during the year worth \$37.4 billion, compared with 137 new listings worth \$25.7 billion in the previous year. The smallest division, Equity Post-Trade Services, achieved a 3.5 per cent increase in revenues, thanks to stronger cash market trading activity during the year.

Outlook

ASX's profits are highly geared to levels of market activity. Nevertheless, such is the diverse variety of instruments available to investors nowadays that even market weakness or turbulence does not necessarily lead to a decline in trading volumes, although a protracted bear market could dent the company's profitability. ASX also enjoys a high degree of protection in its operations, with little effective competition for many of its businesses. In line with its vision of becoming one of the world's most respected financial marketplaces, it boosted its capital spending to \$75.1 million in the June 2019 year, from \$54.1 million in the previous year, in order to upgrade its technology. Capital spending could rise further to \$80 million in June 2020. In particular, it plans to replace its CHESS equities clearing and settlement system with a major new platform using distributed ledger technology — also sometimes referred to as blockchain — to become operational by March 2021. It is also upgrading its secondary data centre and its ASX Net communications network, which connects its data centres to its customers.

Year to 30 June	2018	2019
Revenues ($mn)	822.7	863.8
Derivatives and OTC markets (%)	35	36
Trading services (%)	25	26
Listings and issuer services (%)	27	25
Equity post-trade services (%)	13	13
EBIT ($mn)	575.4	606.3
EBIT margin (%)	69.9	70.2
Profit before tax ($mn)	642.1	705.1
Profit after tax ($mn)	445.1	492.0
Earnings per share (c)	230.02	254.16
Cash flow per share (c)	254.62	278.86
Dividend (c)	216.3	228.7
Percentage franked	100	100
Net tangible assets per share ($)	7.79	7.53
Interest cover (times)	~	~
Return on equity (%)	11.3	12.5
Debt-to-equity ratio (%)	~	~
Current ratio	1.1	1.1

AUB Group Limited

ASX code: AUB   www.aubgroup.com.au

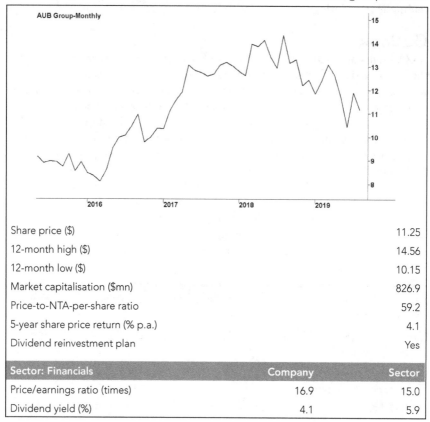

Share price ($)	11.25
12-month high ($)	14.56
12-month low ($)	10.15
Market capitalisation ($mn)	826.9
Price-to-NTA-per-share ratio	59.2
5-year share price return (% p.a.)	4.1
Dividend reinvestment plan	Yes

Sector: Financials	Company	Sector
Price/earnings ratio (times)	16.9	15.0
Dividend yield (%)	4.1	5.9

Sydney-based AUB Group, formerly known as Austbrokers Holdings, was established in 1985. It manages a network of insurance businesses throughout Australia and New Zealand. Its principal business is insurance broking, and it typically holds an equity stake of at least 50 per cent in each business, usually in partnership with the original owners. It also manages the SURA underwriting agency business, which operates agencies in many specialised areas of the insurance business. A third division provides risk services to insurers, brokers and corporate clients. It has announced plans to buy rival insurance broker Coverforce Holdings.

Latest business results (June 2019, full year)

Organic growth and acquisitions pushed sales and profits higher. The core Australian broking operation, representing more than 60 per cent of company business, benefited from some premium increases, and profits rose by 3.7 per cent.

Another excellent result came from AUB's New Zealand operation — about 14 per cent of total company turnover — which delivered a third straight year of double-digit profit growth. However, much of this came as the company moved from a 50 per cent stake to 100 per cent in one of New Zealand's largest insurance brokers, BrokerWeb Risk Services. The SURA underwriting business also prospered, with another year of double-digit profit growth. However, the risk services business saw profits tumble by 66 per cent, as the company's health and rehabilitation businesses experienced reduced demand.

Outlook

AUB has achieved success with its model of buying a stake in an insurance broking house but, in most cases, continuing to operate it with the original owners. This has allowed the businesses to preserve their local identity and management, while benefiting from the support of a large group. The company is able to help its members develop their businesses through growth initiatives, including the addition of new products, and sometimes through appropriate bolt-on acquisitions. Since entering the New Zealand market in 2014 it has become that country's largest broking management group and it is looking for further acquisitions there. It is a beneficiary of rising premiums, and expects this to continue, though at a slower rate than in recent years. In August 2019 it announced an agreement with the largest shareholder of rival insurance broker Coverforce Holdings to acquire that business for $150 million to $200 million. However, the deal is facing a court challenge. AUB's early forecast is for after-tax profit growth of 4 per cent to 6 per cent in the June 2020 year, in addition to the benefits of any acquisitions.

Year to 30 June	2018	2019
Revenues ($mn)	246.1	276.4
EBIT ($mn)	67.3	70.0
EBIT margin (%)	27.3	25.3
Profit before tax ($mn)	64.4	66.8
Profit after tax ($mn)	44.6	46.4
Earnings per share (c)	69.78	66.64
Cash flow per share (c)	81.21	82.89
Dividend (c)	45.5	46
Percentage franked	100	100
Net tangible assets per share ($)	0.37	0.19
Interest cover (times)	22.9	22.0
Return on equity (%)	15.7	13.1
Debt-to-equity ratio (%)	17.5	7.1
Current ratio	1.2	1.1

Australia and New Zealand Banking Group Limited

ASX code: ANZ

www.anz.com.au

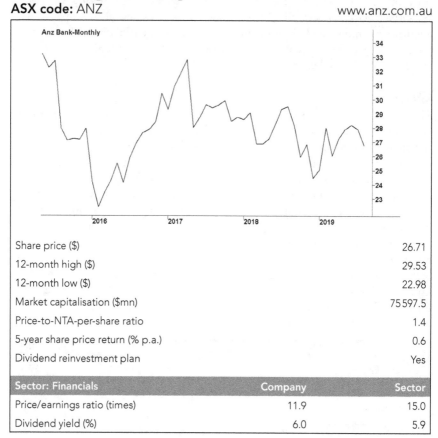

Share price ($)	26.71
12-month high ($)	29.53
12-month low ($)	22.98
Market capitalisation ($mn)	75597.5
Price-to-NTA-per-share ratio	1.4
5-year share price return (% p.a.)	0.6
Dividend reinvestment plan	Yes

Sector: Financials	Company	Sector
Price/earnings ratio (times)	11.9	15.0
Dividend yield (%)	6.0	5.9

Melbourne-based ANZ has its roots in the establishment of the Bank of Australasia in London in 1835. It is today one of the country's four banking giants and one of the largest companies. It is a market leader in New Zealand banking, and it is also active throughout Asia and the Pacific region. Altogether, it has a presence in more than 30 countries, including a major technology and back office operation in Bangalore, India, and minority stakes in a range of Asian banks.

Latest business results (March 2019, half year)

The after-tax profit rose modestly on a cash basis, which strips out one-off costs and asset sales, though on a statutory basis profits fell. Some of the increase came from favourable foreign exchange movements. The bank also achieved a decline in its operating costs, with a cut in staff numbers and a reduction in restructuring expenses. The best result came from the bank's institutional banking business, one of its traditional strengths, with profits up 32 per cent. A year earlier they had fallen by 26 per cent. However, the core Australian banking business saw profits down 13 per cent as the bank's net interest margin fell and its home loans business weakened. New Zealand banking is another of ANZ's strengths, representing more than 20 per cent of total company earnings, and profits were a little higher. But the Wealth division recorded a small loss.

Outlook

ANZ has initiated a restructuring of its operations, believing that Australian banks are set to face an increasing series of headwinds. It has divested itself of some underperforming businesses, and is backtracking on its ambitious moves into Asian banking. It has tightened its lending criteria, though has conceded that it may need to re-evaluate its new risk settings in order to boost market share. It believes it can continue to lower its cost base, and it expects its institutional banking business to remain buoyant. But like all the major banks it faces a rapidly changing financial environment, with higher compliance costs as a result of the recent Banking Royal Commission, and a plethora of challenges from new digital entrants to the banking industry. It will also suffer from any slowdown in the housing market or in the Australian economy. It maintains its strong position in New Zealand banking, but is concerned at signs of growing competition there and a slowing Auckland housing market.

Year to 30 September	2017	2018
Operating income ($mn)	19 816.0	19 214.0
Net interest income ($mn)	14 875.0	14 514.0
Operating expenses ($mn)	8 967.0	9 248.0
Profit before tax ($mn)	9 650.0	9 278.0
Profit after tax ($mn)	6 809.0	6 487.0
Earnings per share (c)	233.96	224.60
Dividend (c)	160	160
Percentage franked	100	100
Non-interest income to total income (%)	24.9	24.5
Cost-to-income ratio (%)	45.3	48.1
Return on equity (%)	11.7	11.0
Return on assets (%)	0.8	0.7
Half year to 31 March	2018	2019
Operating income ($mn)	9 870.0	9 746.0
Profit before tax ($mn)	4 989.0	4 988.0
Profit after tax ($mn)	3 493.0	3 564.0
Earnings per share (c)	98.30	123.00
Dividend (c)	80	80
Percentage franked	100	100
Net tangible assets per share ($)	18.28	18.94

Australian Ethical Investment Limited

ASX code: AEF www.australianethical.com.au

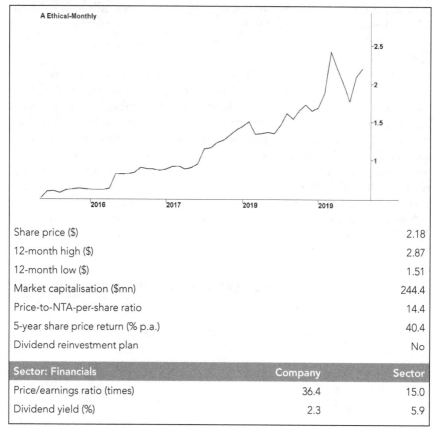

Share price ($)	2.18
12-month high ($)	2.87
12-month low ($)	1.51
Market capitalisation ($mn)	244.4
Price-to-NTA-per-share ratio	14.4
5-year share price return (% p.a.)	40.4
Dividend reinvestment plan	No

Sector: Financials	Company	Sector
Price/earnings ratio (times)	36.4	15.0
Dividend yield (%)	2.3	5.9

Australian Ethical, based in Sydney, was founded in 1986. It is a wealth management company that specialises in investments in corporations that meet a set of ethical criteria. It operates a range of wholesale and retail funds, incorporating Australian and international shares, emerging companies and fixed interest. It also manages the Australian Ethical Advocacy Fund, which seeks to engage directly with companies to pursue improved corporate behaviours. The company donates up to 10 per cent of its profits to charities and activist groups through its Australian Ethical Foundation.

Latest business results (June 2019, full year)

New money flowing into its funds and a solid investment performance delivered double-digit gains in revenues and profits. Net inflows totalled $330 million, down from $520 million in the previous year. There was a sharp reduction in managed fund and institutional fund inflows, with most of the new money coming from superannuation business, and the number of the company's superannuation members grew 11 per cent to 40 530. Management fees received by the company for the year rose 8 per cent to $28.7 million, despite a fee reduction during the year. Administration fees were up 30 per cent to $7.3 million, member and withdrawal fees increased by 12 per cent to $3.7 million and the company also received performance fees totalling $0.8 million, compared with nothing in the previous year, thanks to the strong outperformance of its Emerging Companies Fund. All but one of the company's funds achieved returns above their benchmarks. Funds under management at $3.4 billion at June 2019 were up 21 per cent from a year earlier.

Outlook

Australian Ethical is a small company but is one of the leaders in a growing trend towards ethical investment. One reason it has attracted attention for its funds is because of its perceived independence. Some rival ethical or green funds are actually managed by large institutional investors. The company's pledge is that it seeks out positive investments that support people, quality and sustainability, while avoiding investments that harm people, animals, society or the environment. Its Ethical Charter gives details of the criteria it uses for its investments, and it provides a public list of the companies in which it is prepared to invest. It also publishes position papers on a wide range of topical issues. The company is investing in a new digital platform to streamline operations and it plans to boost its promotional activity in order to increase investor awareness of its brand.

Year to 30 June	2018	2019
Revenues ($mn)	36.0	41.0
EBIT ($mn)	7.2	8.8
EBIT margin (%)	19.9	21.5
Profit before tax ($mn)	7.4	9.1
Profit after tax ($mn)	5.0	6.5
Earnings per share (c)	4.59*	5.99
Cash flow per share (c)	4.91*	6.32
Dividend (c)	4*	5
Percentage franked	100	100
Net tangible assets per share ($)	0.14*	0.15
Interest cover (times)	~	~
Return on equity (%)	34.2	40.5
Debt-to-equity ratio (%)	~	~
Current ratio	2.8	2.4

* adjusted for a 100-for-1 share split in December 2018

Australian Pharmaceutical Industries Limited

ASX code: API   www.api.net.au

Aust Pharm-Monthly

Share price ($)	1.31
12-month high ($)	1.94
12-month low ($)	1.25
Market capitalisation ($mn)	645.2
Price-to-NTA-per-share ratio	2.8
5-year share price return (% p.a.)	1.8
Dividend reinvestment plan	No

Sector: Health care	Company	Sector
Price/earnings ratio (times)	11.8	37.1
Dividend yield (%)	5.7	1.4

Melbourne-based Australian Pharmaceutical Industries (API) dates back to the 1910 establishment of the Chemists' Cooperative Company in New South Wales. It has steadily grown and is today one of Australia's largest pharmaceuticals wholesalers and retailers. Its brands include Priceline Pharmacy, Soul Pattinson Chemist, Pharmacist Advice, Club Premium and Pharmacy Best Buys. It also maintains a small Consumer Brands division, manufacturing a range of pharmaceutical, health and beauty products. In 2018 it acquired Clear Skincare Clinics. Washington H. Soul Pattinson owns 19 per cent of the company's equity.

Latest business results (February 2019, half year)

Revenues edged down, although the company reported that they rose by 6.6 per cent if sales of high-cost, low-margin hepatitis C medication are excluded. Profits marked time. Pharmacy distribution revenues rose to $1.4 billion, despite strong competition and some disruption from Pharmaceutical Benefits Scheme (PBS) reforms. Total network sales for Priceline Pharmacy—most of the 480 stores are owned on a franchise basis—edged up to $1.1 billion. Revenues for the Consumer

Brands division jumped 20.7 per cent to $34 million, with profits also strongly higher. The newly acquired Clear Skincare business saw a solid rise in sales. Debt levels rose substantially to fund the Clear Skincare acquisition and to take an equity stake in rival Sigma Healthcare.

Outlook

API is one of the three companies that dominate the wholesale pharmaceutical market in Australia. The other two are Sigma Healthcare and EBOS. An ageing population supports a slow increase in drugs demand. However, this business is heavily regulated by the PBS, and it is difficult to achieve much growth in profits. Consequently, the company is working to grow by other means, and to diversify into non-PBS product areas. Late in 2018 it made attempts to initiate a merger with Sigma, and it acquired nearly 13 per cent of Sigma's equity. However, Sigma eventually rejected the proposal. API views health and beauty products as offering significant long-term growth potential, and it is moving from its traditional focus on mass-market brands to selected niche and prestige ranges. Its Consumer Brands division is working to develop new health and beauty products that have few equivalents in the domestic market. Its $127 million acquisition in 2018 of Clear Skincare Clinics has provided API with an entry to the highly promising market for non-invasive aesthetic services such as laser hair removal, anti-ageing and acne treatments, and cosmetic injectables. This company operates 45 clinics in Australia and two in New Zealand.

Year to 31 August	2017	2018
Revenues ($mn)	4061.2	4026.3
EBIT ($mn)	89.3	88.9
EBIT margin (%)	2.2	2.2
Gross margin (%)	12.2	12.3
Profit before tax ($mn)	76.4	76.5
Profit after tax ($mn)	52.4	54.7
Earnings per share (c)	10.69	11.11
Cash flow per share (c)	16.54	16.84
Dividend (c)	7	7.5
Percentage franked	100	100
Interest cover (times)	6.9	7.2
Return on equity (%)	9.6	10.3
Half year to 28 February	2018	2019
Revenues ($mn)	2009.3	1977.1
Profit before tax ($mn)	36.0	36.3
Profit after tax ($mn)	26.8	26.8
Earnings per share (c)	5.45	5.44
Dividend (c)	3.5	3.75
Percentage franked	100	100
Net tangible assets per share ($)	0.75	0.46
Debt-to-equity ratio (%)	4.5	51.4
Current ratio	1.4	1.4

Bapcor Limited

ASX code: BAP   www.bapcor.com.au

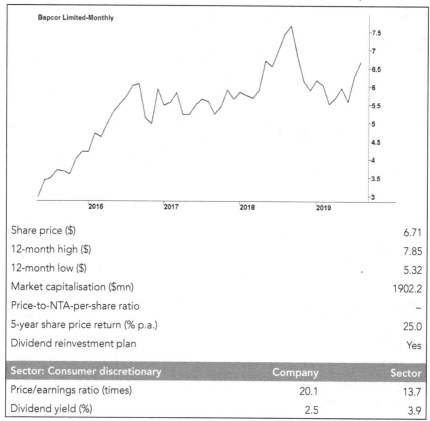

Share price ($)	6.71
12-month high ($)	7.85
12-month low ($)	5.32
Market capitalisation ($mn)	1902.2
Price-to-NTA-per-share ratio	~
5-year share price return (% p.a.)	25.0
Dividend reinvestment plan	Yes

Sector: Consumer discretionary	Company	Sector
Price/earnings ratio (times)	20.1	13.7
Dividend yield (%)	2.5	3.9

Melbourne company Bapcor started in 1971 as Burson Auto Parts, supplying a range of automotive products to workshops and service stations. It grew steadily, organically and by acquisition, opening stores throughout Australia, and taking its present name in 2016. It now services the automotive aftermarket under numerous brands, including Autobarn, Midas and ABS. It has extensive operations in Australia and New Zealand, and in 2018 it opened its first stores in Thailand, in partnership with a local auto specialist company. It operates from more than 950 locations in Australia, New Zealand and Thailand.

Latest business results (June 2019, full year)

Revenues and profits rose in a pleasing result. The Trade division, comprising the Burson Auto Parts and the Precision Automotive Equipment business units, is the largest of Bapcor's operating segments. It saw revenues up 4.6 per cent, including same-store growth of 2.2 per cent, with profits rising by 8.5 per cent. The Specialist Wholesale division comprises a range of small outlets that focus on sourcing replacement parts for the automotive aftermarket. This operation achieved double-digit revenues and profit growth, with a particularly strong performance from the auto electrical unit. The Retail division comprises company-owned and franchised stores and workshops under the Autobarn, Autopro, Sprint Auto Parts, Midas and ABS names. Sales were up but competitive pressures drove profits down. New Zealand businesses enjoyed a good year, with a double-digit rise in profits. The company reported a positive first year of business in Thailand.

Outlook

Bapcor is a leader in the supply of a huge range of auto parts to more than 30 000 auto workshop customers, and this business is expected to continue to grow as the population increases, even in the event of an economic slowdown. A worsening economy can actually help the company, as car owners tend to put off the purchase of a new car and instead spend money on maintaining their existing car, boosting the demand for more parts. The company is experiencing strong growth in online orders, including a trebling of digital business for Autobarn in the June 2019 year through its click and collect and its click and deliver initiatives. The move to Thailand takes Bapcor to a car market the size of Australia's but with a very fragmented auto parts sector. The company's long-term target is for more than 1500 stores in Australia, New Zealand and Asia. Its early forecast is that its after-tax profit will experience mid- to high-single-digit percentage growth in the June 2020 year.

Year to 30 June	2018	2019
Revenues ($mn)	1212.3	1296.6
Trade (%)	39	39
Specialist wholesale (%)	28	30
Retail (%)	19	19
Bapcor New Zealand (%)	14	12
EBIT ($mn)	131.5	145.9
EBIT margin (%)	10.8	11.3
Gross margin (%)	45.0	46.9
Profit before tax ($mn)	118.0	130.6
Profit after tax ($mn)	84.8	94.3
Earnings per share (c)	30.37	33.45
Cash flow per share (c)	35.95	39.52
Dividend (c)	15.5	17
Percentage franked	100	100
Net tangible assets per share ($)	~	~
Interest cover (times)	9.8	9.6
Return on equity (%)	13.9	13.9
Debt-to-equity ratio (%)	44.6	46.1
Current ratio	2.0	2.3

Beach Energy Limited

ASX code: BPT   www.beachenergy.com.au

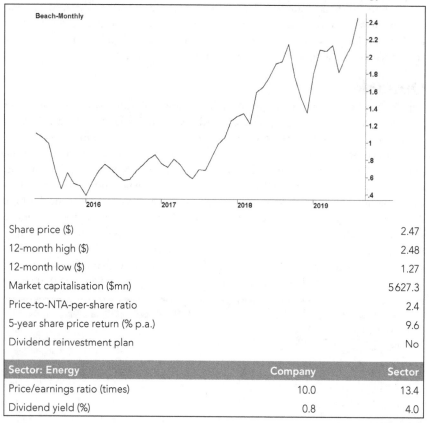

Share price ($)	2.47
12-month high ($)	2.48
12-month low ($)	1.27
Market capitalisation ($mn)	5 627.3
Price-to-NTA-per-share ratio	2.4
5-year share price return (% p.a.)	9.6
Dividend reinvestment plan	No

Sector: Energy	Company	Sector
Price/earnings ratio (times)	10.0	13.4
Dividend yield (%)	0.8	4.0

Adelaide-based Beach Energy, with a history dating back to 1961, is a major oil and gas producer. Since the acquisition of Lattice Energy its operations have been concentrated on five production hubs — the Cooper Basin region of South Australia and Queensland, the Bass Basin in the Bass Strait, the Otway Basin of Victoria and South Australia, the Perth Basin and the Taranaki Basin in New Zealand. It also maintains an active exploration and development program in other areas of Australia and New Zealand.

Latest business results (June 2019, full year)

A full year's contribution from Lattice Energy — acquired in January 2018 for $1.6 billion — helped deliver a big increase in revenues and profits. The company also benefited from higher Australian dollar energy prices. Total production of

29.4 million barrels of oil equivalent (boe) was up from 19 million barrels in the previous year. Operating costs of $9.30 per boe were down from $9.70. The average realised oil price of $101.80 per barrel was a 9 per cent rise from the previous year, thanks to dollar weakness. The average realised gas/ethane price rose 4 per cent. During the year the company drilled 134 wells, 40 per cent more than in the previous year, and with a success rate of 84 per cent. Also during the year the company repaid all its remaining debt, two years ahead of schedule.

Outlook

Beach continues with its plans to leverage its Lattice assets into a series of growth opportunities. With proved and probable reserves of 326 million boe at June 2019, it plans a major exploration program aimed at boosting production to between 34 million boe and 40 million boe annually within five years. It plans capital spending of $750 million to $850 million in the June 2020 year, up from $447 million in June 2019. One priority is the Black Watch onshore-to-offshore well in the Otway Basin, with the output needed to ensure continued supply to the Otway Gas Plant. The company also sees further good potential in the Perth Basin. However, with gas production expected to fall, it is forecasting a decline in total production in the June 2020 year of 27 million boe to 29 million boe. The company's financial results remain heavily dependent on its ability to find new oil and gas resources, as well as on oil prices and exchange rate trends. Having paid off all its debt, at June 2019 Beach had cash holdings of nearly $172 million, and it has expressed interest in acquisitions.

Year to 30 June	2018	2019
Revenues ($mn)	1267.4	2077.7
EBIT ($mn)	452.6	848.1
EBIT margin (%)	35.7	40.8
Gross margin (%)	38.9	41.9
Profit before tax ($mn)	416.0	790.0
Profit after tax ($mn)	301.5	560.0
Earnings per share (c)	13.89	24.59
Cash flow per share (c)	28.28	47.53
Dividend (c)	2	2
Percentage franked	100	100
Net tangible assets per share ($)	0.77	1.02
Interest cover (times)	12.4	14.6
Return on equity (%)	18.6	26.6
Debt-to-equity ratio (%)	33.4	~
Current ratio	1.5	1.0

Beacon Lighting Group Limited

ASX code: BLX   www.beaconlighting.com.au

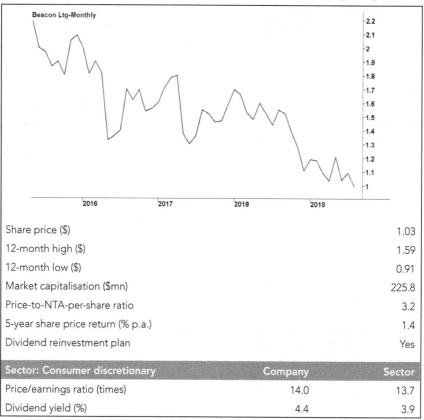

Share price ($)	1.03
12-month high ($)	1.59
12-month low ($)	0.91
Market capitalisation ($mn)	225.8
Price-to-NTA-per-share ratio	3.2
5-year share price return (% p.a.)	1.4
Dividend reinvestment plan	Yes

Sector: Consumer discretionary	Company	Sector
Price/earnings ratio (times)	14.0	13.7
Dividend yield (%)	4.4	3.9

Melbourne-based lighting specialist Beacon dates back to the launch of the first Beacon Lighting store in 1967. It steadily expanded throughout Australia, and today has more than 110 stores, supplying a wide range of lighting fixtures and light globes, as well as ceiling fans. Its Beacon Lighting Commercial division supplies many commercial projects, including volume residential developments, apartment complexes, aged care facilities, hotels and retail fit-outs. It also operates an international wholesale business, based in Hong Kong and with a showroom in China.

Latest business results (June 2019, full year)

A weak second half sent profits down, despite a modest rise in sales. A slowing housing market, the federal election and tightening credit conditions within the housing sector all affected business. In addition, with most of its products imported, the company is hurt by the weak dollar. During the year its stores enjoyed some strength in Queensland, but this was more than offset by weakness in New South Wales, Victoria and Western Australia. Online sales were up 22 per cent. The company opened five new stores, closed one and acquired two franchise stores. At June 2019 it operated 109 company stores and four franchise stores. Note that the latest result is for a 53-week period, compared with 52 weeks for the June 2018 year.

Outlook

Beacons's business is closely linked to trends in the housing market, and it is hopeful of a recovery in the June 2020 year. In addition, it has a variety of other strategies for expansion. It has launched a series of new businesses, and these are displaying strong growth, with a combined increase in sales in the June 2019 year of 43 per cent, and with profits up 59 per cent, though from a very low base, and with lower margins than the core lighting business. Its Light Source Solutions Roadway division supplies LED street lighting. Beacon Energy Solutions designs and installs energy-efficient lighting and power systems. Masson for Light works with architects to supply designer lights for prestige construction projects. Beacon International sells Beacon lighting products in the US, Europe and China, much of it through online channels. The company has introduced its Beacon Design Studio service, which now operates in 28 stores. A newly acquired distribution centre supplying Queensland and New South Wales stores is expected to deliver cost efficiencies. During the June 2020 year Beacon plans to close two stores and open at least two others, as well as converting one franchise store to a company store.

Year to 30 June*	2018	2019
Revenues ($mn)	237.6	247.6
EBIT ($mn)	29.3	25.1
EBIT margin (%)	12.3	10.1
Gross margin (%)	65.7	64.0
Profit before tax ($mn)	27.7	23.1
Profit after tax ($mn)	19.6	16.0
Earnings per share (c)	9.09	7.37
Cash flow per share (c)	10.89	9.44
Dividend (c)	5	4.55
Percentage franked	100	100
Net tangible assets per share ($)	0.30	0.33
Interest cover (times)	18.8	12.7
Return on equity (%)	27.9	20.1
Debt-to-equity ratio (%)	20.5	39.2
Current ratio	1.8	1.7

* 24 June 2018

Bell Financial Group Limited

ASX code: BFG   www.bellfg.com.au

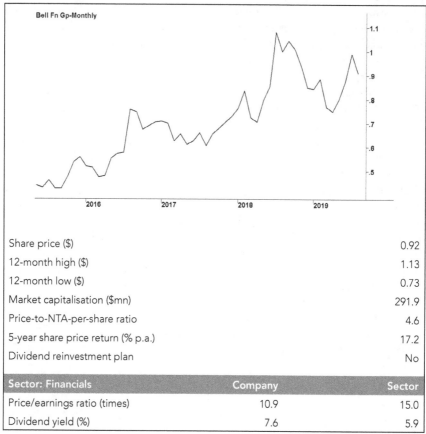

Share price ($)	0.92
12-month high ($)	1.13
12-month low ($)	0.73
Market capitalisation ($mn)	291.9
Price-to-NTA-per-share ratio	4.6
5-year share price return (% p.a.)	17.2
Dividend reinvestment plan	No

Sector: Financials	Company	Sector
Price/earnings ratio (times)	10.9	15.0
Dividend yield (%)	7.6	5.9

Melbourne-based Bell Financial has its origins in Bell Commodities, founded in 1970 by executive director Colin Bell. Today it divides its operations into three broad segments. Bell Potter Securities is a prominent provider of stockbroking, investment and financial advisory services to private, institutional and corporate clients. It incorporates the Bell Commodities and the Bell FX (foreign exchange) businesses. A second division, Bell Potter Capital, offers margin lending, superannuation lending and cash management services to its clients. Bell Direct provides an online share trading platform. It operates from 16 offices across Australia, and from offices in New York, London and Hong Kong.

Latest business results (June 2019, half year)

In a good period for the company, despite a slow start in January, revenues and profits rose by double-digit amounts. For reporting purposes Bell divides its operations into two segments, retail and wholesale. The latter, comprising equities brokerage and corporate fee income, generated most of the good result, with revenues up 66 per cent to $31.9 million and the after-tax profit more than trebling to $9.2 million. Corporate fee income was especially strong, rising by more than 140 per cent. By contrast, retail business—equities and futures brokerage, foreign exchange, corporate fee income, portfolio administration services, margin lending and deposits—saw the after-tax profit down, on a 4 per cent rise in revenues. The company had funds under advice of $54.8 billion at June 2019, up from $48.7 billion a year earlier.

Outlook

Financial brokerage comprises around 55 per cent of Bell Financial's income, and the company will be hurt by any prolonged bear market. However, while markets remain relatively buoyant its prospects are solid. It has been achieving some good results in equity capital markets, with 75 transactions in the June 2019 half, raising almost $1.25 billion in new equity capital, and a strong pipeline of work for the second half of the year. A new discovery and trade execution platform is being rolled out across the company's business network, and over time this will deliver a significant lowering of execution costs. It is also working to reduce contract note costs by upgrading the capability of its equity platform. In August 2019 its Bell Potter Capital business acquired two structured products from Macquarie Bank, Equity Lever and Geared Equity Investments. These offer investments that are aimed at self-managed superannuation funds wishing to add leverage to their equity portfolios. The acquisition almost doubled the size of Bell Potter Capital's existing loan book.

Year to 31 December	2017	2018
Revenues ($mn)	188.8	202.2
EBIT ($mn)	19.5	22.8
EBIT margin (%)	10.3	11.3
Profit before tax ($mn)	31.2	36.0
Profit after tax ($mn)	20.6	24.7
Earnings per share (c)	7.82	8.48
Cash flow per share (c)	8.40	8.98
Dividend (c)	7.5	7
Percentage franked	100	100
Interest cover (times)	~	~
Return on equity (%)	10.7	12.4
Half year to 30 June	2018	2019
Revenues ($mn)	91.1	106.4
Profit before tax ($mn)	14.7	22.6
Profit after tax ($mn)	9.8	15.9
Earnings per share (c)	3.70	5.00
Dividend (c)	2.75	3.5
Percentage franked	100	100
Net tangible assets per share ($)	0.22	0.20
Debt-to-equity ratio (%)	81.8	30.3

BHP Group Limited

ASX code: BHP

www.bhp.com

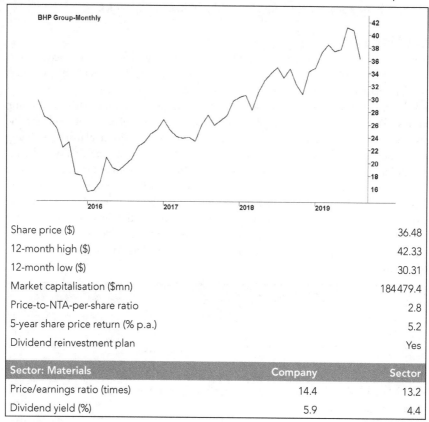

Share price ($)	36.48
12-month high ($)	42.33
12-month low ($)	30.31
Market capitalisation ($mn)	184479.4
Price-to-NTA-per-share ratio	2.8
5-year share price return (% p.a.)	5.2
Dividend reinvestment plan	Yes

Sector: Materials	Company	Sector
Price/earnings ratio (times)	14.4	13.2
Dividend yield (%)	5.9	4.4

BHP Group was formed in 2001 from the merger of BHP, which was founded as Broken Hill Proprietary in 1885, and Billiton, which dates back to 1851. With its headquarters in Melbourne, it is today one of the world's largest diversified resources companies, with a powerful portfolio of assets incorporating iron ore, copper, coal, nickel, potash, and oil and gas. It has operations in many countries.

Latest business results (June 2019, full year)

Higher iron ore prices lay behind a modest rise in profits for BHP. Profits for the company's iron ore business rose by 25 per cent, thanks to an 18 per cent increase in average prices for the company during the year. It also benefited from an increase in sales volumes, thanks especially to record production at its Jimblebar mine in Western Australia. Iron ore was responsible for less than 40 per cent of company revenues, but nearly 50 per cent of profit. By contrast, copper profits fell by

30 per cent, as prices fell and sales volumes declined. Coal profits also fell, with lower average thermal coal prices only partially offset by a rise in metallurgical coal prices. The petroleum business benefited from higher prices, and profits rose. Note that BHP reports its results in US dollars. The Australian dollar figures in this book — converted at prevailing exchange rates — are for guidance only.

Outlook

BHP has been working over some years to lower its cost base, and this should protect it to a degree in the event of weakening Chinese demand or a global economic slowdown. In particular, it claims that its Western Australian iron ore business now has the cheapest operating costs among all its rivals. It expects that its capital spending in both the June 2020 and June 2021 years will be around US$8 billion per year, up from US$7.6 billion in June 2019. Multi-billion-dollar projects under way include the Spence copper mine expansion project in Chile, the Mad Dog petroleum venture in the Gulf of Mexico, the South Flank iron ore project in Western Australia and the Jansen potash infrastructure project in Canada. In August 2019 it approved an investment of US$283 million for the development of the Ruby oil and gas project in Trinidad and Tobago. It is also carrying out feasibility studies on a major scheme to introduce autonomous (driverless) trucks to some of its Australian coal and iron ore sites. It is considering a sale of its thermal coal assets.

Year to 30 June	2018	2019
Revenues ($mn)	56 748.7	61 511.1
Iron ore (%)	34	39
Copper (%)	30	24
Coal (%)	20	21
Petroleum (%)	12	13
EBIT ($mn)	22 839.5	23 694.4
EBIT margin (%)	40.2	38.5
Profit before tax ($mn)	21 201.3	22 216.7
Profit after tax ($mn)	12 660.5	13 147.2
Earnings per share (c)	237.85	253.81
Cash flow per share (c)	393.28	417.36
Dividend (c)	159.13	215.11
Percentage franked	100	100
Net tangible assets per share ($)	13.92	13.15
Interest cover (times)	13.9	16.0
Return on equity (%)	16.9	18.4
Debt-to-equity ratio (%)	18.0	17.8
Current ratio	2.5	1.9

Blackmores Limited

ASX code: BKL
www.blackmores.com.au

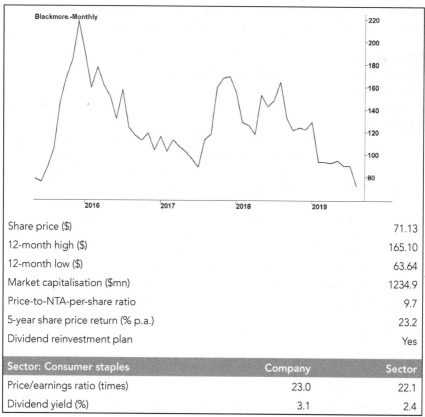

Share price ($)	71.13
12-month high ($)	165.10
12-month low ($)	63.64
Market capitalisation ($mn)	1234.9
Price-to-NTA-per-share ratio	9.7
5-year share price return (% p.a.)	23.2
Dividend reinvestment plan	Yes

Sector: Consumer staples	Company	Sector
Price/earnings ratio (times)	23.0	22.1
Dividend yield (%)	3.1	2.4

Founded in Queensland in the 1930s, and now based in Sydney, Blackmores is a leading manufacturer and distributor of a wide range of natural healthcare products, nutritional supplements and cosmetics, with high market shares. It has a buoyant export business, especially to China. Its BioCeuticals operation manufactures nutritional supplements for healthcare practitioners and its Pure Animal Wellbeing (PAW) business specialises in natural dietary supplements for dogs and cats. It also owns the Chinese herbal medicines manufacturer Global Therapeutics, which markets its products under the Fusion Health and Oriental Botanicals brands. It entered the weight loss sector in 2018 with the acquisition of the Impromy weight management portfolio of products.

Latest business results (June 2019, full year)

Revenues edged up but profits fell, as the company took a hit from its Chinese operations. Sales to China of $122 million were down 15 per cent from the previous year, with EBIT crashing 40 per cent. Sales in Australia and New Zealand were steady, though rising costs, including higher raw material prices, sent EBIT down.

A bright note came from the rest of Asia, with sales of $107 million up 30 per cent, and EBIT soaring 218 per cent, although from a low base, and profitability for this business remains low. The BioCeuticals division saw sales rise 4 per cent to $113 million, with EBIT up 10 per cent.

Outlook

Blackmores has been hurt by new Chinese regulations making it onerous for small entrepreneurs in Australia to buy up its products in Australia and ship them for resale in China. From around 2015 this business had been generating some strong sales for many of Blackmores' products. The company believes that difficulties with the Chinese market will continue until early in 2020. However, its other Asia businesses continue to grow, with Vietnamese sales up 157 per cent in the June 2019 year and South Korean sales up 28 per cent. The company has placed a particular emphasis on its joint venture company in the Indonesian market, and this moved into profit during the second half of the June 2019 year. It is now evaluating the prospects for an entry into the Indian market. Following some encouraging trials, the BioCeuticals division may begin marketing a medical cannabis product. In February 2019 Blackmores announced a major streamlining of its operations, with a target of $60 million in cost savings over three years. The move to a new Melbourne manufacturing facility in October 2019 is also expected to reduce costs.

Year to 30 June	2018	2019
Revenues ($mn)	601.1	609.5
EBIT ($mn)	101.6	80.5
EBIT margin (%)	16.9	13.2
Profit before tax ($mn)	97.7	75.5
Profit after tax ($mn)	70.0	53.5
Earnings per share (c)	406.38	309.15
Cash flow per share (c)	458.27	372.03
Dividend (c)	305	220
Percentage franked	100	100
Net tangible assets per share ($)	7.35	7.30
Interest cover (times)	25.9	16.1
Return on equity (%)	37.8	26.7
Debt-to-equity ratio (%)	25.6	45.5
Current ratio	1.7	2.0

BlueScope Steel Limited

ASX code: BSL   www.bluescope.com

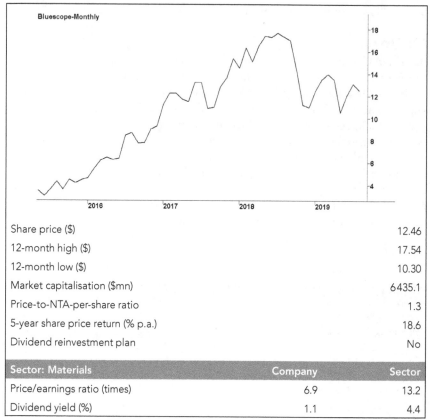

Share price ($)	12.46
12-month high ($)	17.54
12-month low ($)	10.30
Market capitalisation ($mn)	6435.1
Price-to-NTA-per-share ratio	1.3
5-year share price return (% p.a.)	18.6
Dividend reinvestment plan	No

Sector: Materials	Company	Sector
Price/earnings ratio (times)	6.9	13.2
Dividend yield (%)	1.1	4.4

Melbourne-based BlueScope Steel, originally a division of BHP, was established as an independent company in 2002. It is a major international producer of steel products for a wide variety of industrial applications. It is the world's third-largest manufacturer of painted and coated steel products, including Colorbond roofing materials. It is also a prominent supplier of engineered steel buildings. The company is structured into five businesses. Australian Steel Products operates the country's largest steelworks at Port Kembla, with a focus on the building and construction industry. Building Products Asia and North America comprises metal coating, painting and roll-forming businesses at 29 plants. North Star BlueScope Steel is a leading American producer of hot rolled coil. Buildings North America services low-rise non-residential customers in the US and Canada. The New Zealand and Pacific Islands business operates production facilities in New Zealand, Fiji, New Caledonia and Vanuatu.

Latest business results (June 2019, full year)

With some two-thirds of its income derived from abroad, BlueScope was a significant beneficiary of the weak dollar. It was also helped by another excellent performance from its North Star steel business, and reported a solid rise in revenues and profits. North Star was able to raise prices at a faster rate than increases in the cost of raw materials, and EBIT surged 52 per cent from the previous year. Though only 19 per cent of company revenues, this business alone contributed nearly 45 per cent of total EBIT, and other divisions were weak. The largest division, Australian Steel Products, saw EBIT down 9 per cent, due to some weakening domestic demand and higher costs. The three remaining divisions, Building Products Asia and North America, Buildings North America, and New Zealand and Pacific Steel, each reported EBIT declines of 27 per cent to 28 per cent, generally due to rising costs and reduced despatch volumes.

Outlook

BlueScope occupies a solid position within the Australian economy, and to a lesser extent within the economies of the US and Asia. Its fortunes will be greatly affected by economic trends in these countries. It is also influenced by currency rate trends and raw material prices. The company has announced a $1 billion expansion of its North Star steel mill, to be operational by 2023. North Star is based in Ohio and supplies the automotive and construction industries. However, with raw material costs continuing to rise and global steel prices falling, BlueScope expects profits in the December 2019 half to fall.

Year to 30 June	2018	2019
Revenues ($mn)	11 497.8	12 532.8
Australian steel products (%)	44	43
Building products Asia & North America (%)	22	22
North Star Bluescope Steel (%)	17	19
Buildings North America (%)	10	9
New Zealand & Pacific Steel (%)	7	7
EBIT ($mn)	1 301.0	1 348.3
EBIT margin (%)	11.3	10.8
Profit before tax ($mn)	1 197.3	1 310.5
Profit after tax ($mn)	826.0	966.3
Earnings per share (c)	148.34	180.65
Cash flow per share (c)	215.73	257.80
Dividend (c)	14	14
Percentage franked	6	0
Net tangible assets per share ($)	8.63	9.95
Interest cover (times)	12.5	35.7
Return on equity (%)	14.4	14.6
Debt-to-equity ratio (%)	~	~
Current ratio	1.7	1.8

Brambles Limited

ASX code: BXB
www.brambles.com

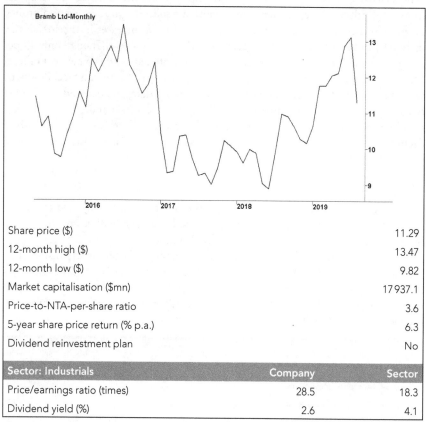

Share price ($)	11.29
12-month high ($)	13.47
12-month low ($)	9.82
Market capitalisation ($mn)	17937.1
Price-to-NTA-per-share ratio	3.6
5-year share price return (% p.a.)	6.3
Dividend reinvestment plan	No

Sector: Industrials	Company	Sector
Price/earnings ratio (times)	28.5	18.3
Dividend yield (%)	2.6	4.1

Sydney-based Brambles has a history that dates back to 1875, when Walter Bramble opened a butcher's business, later expanding into transportation and logistics. Today, following a long series of acquisitions, it is the global leader in pallet, crates and container pooling services under the brand name CHEP (Commonwealth Handling Equipment Pool, a term used by the Australian government to designate pallets and other assets left in Australia by the US Army after World War II). It owns approximately 330 million pallets, crates and containers through a network of more than 750 service centres in 60 countries. In 2019 it sold its IFCO reusable plastic containers business.

Latest business results (June 2019, full year)

In a mixed result, sales rose, thanks to growth in new business and some price increases. Higher revenues and supply chain efficiencies offset rising costs, and profits too edged up. However, a higher tax rate meant that the after-tax profit fell, as in the previous year the company had received a one-off benefit associated with US tax reform. Volume growth of 4 per cent was driven by new customers in Europe and the US, and the company was able to raise its average prices by 3 per cent. But the result was hurt by inefficiencies associated with US network capacity constraints and higher costs in Latin America. The sale, completed in May 2019, of its IFCO reusable plastic containers business for US$2.5 billion led to a sharp increase in the company's cash holdings and a big decline in net debt levels. Note that Brambles reports its results in US dollars. The Australian dollar figures in this book — converted at prevailing exchange rates — are for guidance only.

Outlook

Brambles is heavily influenced by trends in global trade and, more generally, the global economy. Consequently, it could suffer from trade wars or political instability, and it has already noted a slowing of business in core European markets. It is also greatly affected by currency trends. With half its revenues coming from the Americas, it has been a beneficiary of a strong US economy. Nevertheless, American operations have been suffering from high costs, with profit margins that are substantially below those prevailing elsewhere. The company is working to drive down costs and believes that over time it can boost American margins. It expects customer numbers to continue to rise, while it also expands into new markets. Its early forecast is for mid-single-digit percentage growth for sales and profits in the June 2020 year.

Year to 30 June	2018	2019
Revenues ($mn)	5882.0	6382.4
CHEP Americas (%)	49	50
CHEP EMEA (%)	40	40
CHEP Asia-Pacific (%)	11	10
EBIT ($mn)	1024.6	1029.0
EBIT margin (%)	17.4	16.1
Profit before tax ($mn)	888.6	906.1
Profit after tax ($mn)	728.3	630.7
Earnings per share (c)	45.77	39.58
Cash flow per share (c)	84.16	81.80
Dividend (c)	29	29
Percentage franked	30	48
Net tangible assets per share ($)	1.49	3.17
Interest cover (times)	7.5	8.4
Return on equity (%)	19.7	13.7
Debt-to-equity ratio (%)	83.1	13.4
Current ratio	0.7	1.6

Breville Group Limited

ASX code: BRG   www.brevillegroup.com

Share price ($)	16.25
12-month high ($)	19.66
12-month low ($)	10.13
Market capitalisation ($mn)	2114.0
Price-to-NTA-per-share ratio	11.3
5-year share price return (% p.a.)	19.7
Dividend reinvestment plan	No

Sector: Consumer discretionary	Company	Sector
Price/earnings ratio (times)	31.4	13.7
Dividend yield (%)	2.3	3.9

Sydney-based Breville Group traces its origins to the production of the first Breville radio in 1932. It later moved into the home appliance business and was subsequently acquired by Housewares International. In 2008 Housewares changed its name to Breville Group, and today the company is a leading designer and distributor of kitchen home appliances under the Breville, Kambrook and Ronson brands. Its subsidiary in the UK distributes Breville products under the Sage brand. Breville is active in 65 countries, and international business is responsible for around 80 per cent of company turnover.

Latest business results (June 2019, full year)

Continuing strong overseas demand for its products helped deliver the company's fourth consecutive increase in profits. Breville segments its operations into two broad divisions, Global Product and Distribution. The former, responsible for the sale of products designed and developed by Breville, generated more than 80 per cent of company turnover, with revenues up 17.2 per cent and EBIT rising 7.5 per cent, although these figures were magnified by dollar weakness. North America was once again strong but the star was Europe, with 35.1 per cent growth in sales on a constant currency basis, thanks to a first full year's contribution from Germany, successful expansion into Switzerland and the Benelux countries and continuing strong demand from the UK. The Distribution division achieved an excellent 36 per cent jump in EBIT, on 18.8 per cent sales growth, with particularly strong US demand for Nespresso products.

Outlook

Breville has been achieving great success with its strategy of developing its own lines of premium home appliances for the North American, European and Australia/ New Zealand markets. North America alone now represents 58 per cent of company revenues, thanks to a continuing series of attractive, high-margin products. The company is now working to replicate its North American success in Europe, where sales are still only about 15 per cent of turnover. It has achieved particular success in the UK, with Germany also gaining strength. It plans to launch sales in Spain and France during the June 2020 year, with Portugal and Italy likely to follow. However, there are fears the company's growing European business could be hurt by Brexit uncertainties, while American tariffs on Chinese-made goods could hurt sales in the US market, as many of the company's products are manufactured in China. This has already forced it to raise prices in the US. Operations are also influenced by currency fluctuations and by trends in consumer sentiment.

Year to 30 June	2018	2019
Revenues ($mn)	646.8	760.0
EBIT ($mn)	86.9	97.3
EBIT margin (%)	13.4	12.8
Gross margin (%)	35.9	35.7
Profit before tax ($mn)	84.4	94.3
Profit after tax ($mn)	58.5	67.4
Earnings per share (c)	44.98	51.80
Cash flow per share (c)	55.21	64.57
Dividend (c)	33	37
Percentage franked	60	60
Net tangible assets per share ($)	1.31	1.44
Interest cover (times)	34.3	32.1
Return on equity (%)	21.6	22.7
Debt-to-equity ratio (%)	~	~
Current ratio	2.9	2.6

Brickworks Limited

ASX code: BKW

www.brickworks.com.au

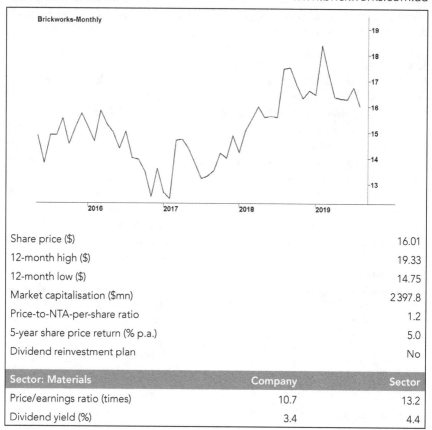

Share price ($)	16.01
12-month high ($)	19.33
12-month low ($)	14.75
Market capitalisation ($mn)	2 397.8
Price-to-NTA-per-share ratio	1.2
5-year share price return (% p.a.)	5.0
Dividend reinvestment plan	No

Sector: Materials	Company	Sector
Price/earnings ratio (times)	10.7	13.2
Dividend yield (%)	3.4	4.4

Sydney-based Brickworks, founded in 1934, is one of Australia's largest manufacturers of building products used especially in the home construction sector. Its brands include Austral Bricks, Austral Masonry, Austral Precast, Bristile Roofing, Auswest Timber, Bowral Bricks, Nubrik, GB Masonry and UrbanStone. It also manages an extensive land portfolio, based on surplus and redundant building products sites, and it operates an industrial property trust in a joint venture with Goodman. In November 2018 it acquired America's fourth-largest brick manufacturer, Glen-Gery. In a cross-shareholding arrangement, it owns 39 per cent of the equity of Washington H. Soul Pattinson, while Soul Pattinson owns 44 per cent of the equity in Brickworks.

Latest business results (January 2019, half year)

Brickworks announced a double-digit jump in revenues and profits, thanks to a strong performance from its property business. Property EBIT of $132 million—more than 60 per cent of total company EBIT for the period—soared 167 per cent, thanks especially to the sale of a major Punchbowl property and a large revaluation profit from its joint venture property trust. EBIT from investments—essentially the returns from the company's holdings in Washington H. Soul Pattinson—was steady at

$61 million. By contrast, the Building Products division, though responsible for 85 per cent of company revenues, saw EBIT fall 35 per cent to $26 million. The core Austral Bricks business was especially weak, with sales down and margins hit by higher energy expenses and maintenance costs. The newly acquired $151 million Glen-Gery business in the US contributed revenues of $26 million in its first 10 weeks of Brickworks ownership, which the company said was ahead of internal forecasts.

Outlook

Brickworks is pessimistic about the near-term outlook for its domestic building products operations. Higher energy prices have added about $12 million to its cost base for the July 2019 year, at a time when demand for new homes is softening. The company has also expressed concerns about the longer-term outlook for Australian manufacturing businesses, with rising energy costs a particular worry. It is now looking to the US for growth and over the coming three to five years plans to develop a strong brick-making operation there with new acquisitions, new products, plant upgrades, the rationalisation of facilities and the establishment of a new design studio. It may also invest in a new state-of-the-art plant. Domestically, it sees especially bright prospects for its joint venture industrial property trust, as online shopping boosts demand for well-located warehouse facilities.

Year to 31 July	2017	2018
Revenues ($mn)	839.7	818.9
EBIT ($mn)	246.1	279.5
EBIT margin (%)	29.3	34.1
Gross margin (%)	33.4	30.8
Profit before tax ($mn)	233.9	265.3
Profit after tax ($mn)	196.4	223.7
Earnings per share (c)	131.79	149.80
Cash flow per share (c)	150.48	169.48
Dividend (c)	51	54
Percentage franked	100	100
Interest cover (times)	20.1	19.7
Return on equity (%)	10.3	11.1
Half year to 31 January	2018	2019
Revenues ($mn)	376.2	441.6
Profit before tax ($mn)	138.5	200.9
Profit after tax ($mn)	116.9	159.7
Earnings per share (c)	78.31	106.75
Dividend (c)	18	19
Percentage franked	100	100
Net tangible assets per share ($)	12.03	13.04
Debt-to-equity ratio (%)	15.8	11.3
Current ratio	2.4	1.2

Caltex Australia Limited

ASX code: CTX

www.caltex.com.au

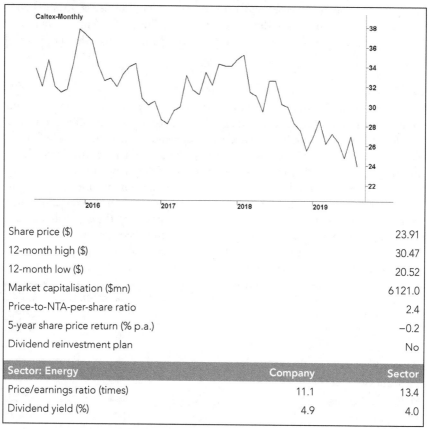

Share price ($)	23.91
12-month high ($)	30.47
12-month low ($)	20.52
Market capitalisation ($mn)	6121.0
Price-to-NTA-per-share ratio	2.4
5-year share price return (% p.a.)	−0.2
Dividend reinvestment plan	No

Sector: Energy	Company	Sector
Price/earnings ratio (times)	11.1	13.4
Dividend yield (%)	4.9	4.0

Sydney-based Caltex Australia formally got its start in 1941, although it has roots dating back to 1900 and the initial marketing of Texaco products in this country. It operates the Lytton refinery in Brisbane, which produces petrol, diesel and jet fuel, along with small amounts of fuel oil, liquid petroleum gas and other gases. Caltex supplies customers through a network of terminals, depots, pipelines and a large transportation fleet. Its retail network incorporates around 2000 petrol stations, including some in New Zealand. It has launched The Foodary chain of cafés at many of its petrol stations.

Latest business results (June 2019, half year)

Revenues rose but profits fell sharply, as demand eased and higher fuel costs hurt refining margins. Caltex also presents what it calls a replacement cost of sales operating profit, which excludes the impact of volatile crude oil prices, and uses replacement costs, rather than historical costs. On this basis — which the company says is a fairer measure of its performance — its after-tax profit slumped from $296 million to $135 million. Total Australian fuel demand fell 2.2 per cent from the June 2018 half, driven especially by weakness in agriculture and construction, and the company's total sales volume fell 6 per cent to 9.6 billion litres. Lytton refinery profits plummeted as the Caltex Refiner Margin, a key measure of profitability, dropped from an average of US$10.06 per barrel in the 2018 first half to US$7.50. The refinery was also hit by unplanned power outages. The company's Convenience Retail division — its petrol station network — saw profits fall for another year, due to a decline in petrol sales and reduced margins.

Outlook

Caltex has been looking to transform its operations and stimulate growth through a makeover of its Convenience Retail division. In 2018 it announced an important new arrangement with Woolworths, with the two companies to launch the new Foodary convenience store chain at approximately 250 Caltex petrol stations. They also entered into a new 15-year fuel supply agreement. At June 2019 Caltex had opened 63 Foodary outlets. However, it has now conceded that it is unlikely to meet its original target of annual EBIT from Foodary outlets of between $120 million and $150 million by 2024. It is working to cut expenses, with the target of lowering its cost base by $100 million annually by the end of 2020. It will move its head office out of the Sydney CBD and also sell about 50 of its Sydney and Melbourne petrol stations.

Year to 31 December	2017	2018
Revenues ($mn)	16 285.8	21 731.3
EBIT ($mn)	930.3	830.1
EBIT margin (%)	5.7	3.8
Gross margin (%)	13.3	9.8
Profit before tax ($mn)	863.4	780.9
Profit after tax ($mn)	619.1	560.4
Earnings per share (c)	237.20	214.72
Cash flow per share (c)	325.00	312.58
Dividend (c)	121	118
Percentage franked	100	100
Interest cover (times)	13.9	16.9
Return on equity (%)	21.0	17.3
Half year to 30 June	2018	2019
Revenues ($mn)	10 185.6	10 308.7
Profit before tax ($mn)	541.2	221.0
Profit after tax ($mn)	382.5	155.4
Earnings per share (c)	146.70	60.60
Dividend (c)	57	32
Percentage franked	100	100
Net tangible assets per share ($)	10.72	9.94
Debt-to-equity ratio (%)	31.2	69.4
Current ratio	1.3	1.3

Cedar Woods Properties Limited

ASX code: CWP   www.cedarwoods.com.au

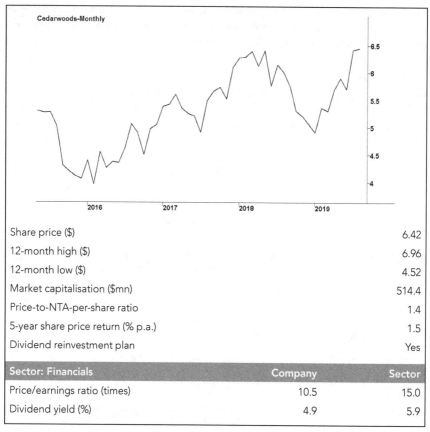

Share price ($)	6.42
12-month high ($)	6.96
12-month low ($)	4.52
Market capitalisation ($mn)	514.4
Price-to-NTA-per-share ratio	1.4
5-year share price return (% p.a.)	1.5
Dividend reinvestment plan	Yes

Sector: Financials	Company	Sector
Price/earnings ratio (times)	10.5	15.0
Dividend yield (%)	4.9	5.9

Perth-based Cedar Woods, founded in 1987, is a prominent property developer. Its main interests are in urban land subdivision for residential, commercial and industrial purposes. Its work includes apartment projects, integrated housing developments, business parks, mixed-use developments, large-scale master-planned communities and a growing number of commercial projects. Its original focus was on its home state, but it has also become very active in Melbourne and has recently entered the Brisbane and Adelaide markets.

Latest business results (June 2019, full year)

Cedar Woods overcame a weak housing market to post a solid gain in profits, rebounding from the decline of the previous year. Nevertheless, with some discounting necessary to achieve sales, as well as a change in the product mix, the rise in revenues substantially outpaced the increase in profits, and margins were down.

The Ariella estate at Brabham in Perth was its biggest selling development, although the company also completed and settled a growing number of Melbourne townhouses, and it finalised work on the $58 million Target head office building at Williams Landing in Melbourne. In Adelaide the initial residents moved into the Glenside townhouses, and the company reported that for the first time all four states in which it operates contributed to sales.

Outlook

Cedar Woods has a strategy of targeting high-growth urban corridors in close proximity to transport infrastructure for its developments, and it continues to build up its land bank. At June 2019 it had presales of $330 million on its books, up from $320 million a year earlier, with two-thirds of these due to be settled in the June 2020 year. However, with the market still weak, the company is forecasting that June 2020 profits will be down. Looking further ahead, it expects that a firm economy, low interest rates and population growth will all contribute to continuing growth, although much will also depend on how much finance is available to home buyers. It has 9600 lots in its development pipeline across four states, with 34 projects, and is able to move quickly to ramp up development work should market conditions improve. A number of projects are expected to contribute to earnings from the June 2021 year, including Huntington Apartments in Victoria, Ariella and Solaris in Western Australia, and Wooloowin in Queensland. Cedar Woods also continues to take advantage of a depressed market to buy more development land. This includes the $15 million acquisition, announced in August 2019, of a 1.4 hectare high-potential site at Subiaco in Perth.

Year to 30 June	2018	2019
Revenues ($mn)	239.8	375.1
EBIT ($mn)	64.5	71.3
EBIT margin (%)	26.9	19.0
Gross margin (%)	40.5	29.7
Profit before tax ($mn)	61.1	68.9
Profit after tax ($mn)	42.6	48.6
Earnings per share (c)	53.93	60.86
Cash flow per share (c)	56.48	63.71
Dividend (c)	30	31.5
Percentage franked	100	100
Net tangible assets per share ($)	4.44	4.70
Interest cover (times)	19.3	30.2
Return on equity (%)	12.5	13.3
Debt-to-equity ratio (%)	30.9	28.0
Current ratio	2.0	3.2

CIMIC Group Limited

ASX code: CIM   www.cimic.com.au

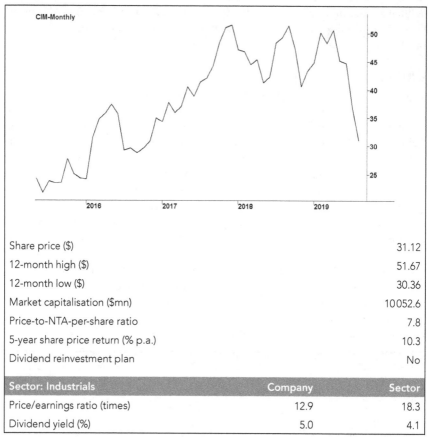

CIM-Monthly

Share price ($)	31.12
12-month high ($)	51.67
12-month low ($)	30.36
Market capitalisation ($mn)	10052.6
Price-to-NTA-per-share ratio	7.8
5-year share price return (% p.a.)	10.3
Dividend reinvestment plan	No

Sector: Industrials	Company	Sector
Price/earnings ratio (times)	12.9	18.3
Dividend yield (%)	5.0	4.1

CIMIC, based in Sydney, was founded in 1949, and until 2015 it was named Leighton Holdings. Its new name derives from its main businesses, Construction, Infrastructure, Mining and Concessions. It is one of Australia's largest contractors, with particular strengths in construction, mining, mineral processing, engineering and a wide range of services. Offshore work contributes about a quarter of revenues. Around 72 per cent of the company's shares are owned by German construction company Hochtief, which itself is majority-owned by Spanish construction giant ACS Group.

Latest business results (June 2019, half year)

Profits just edged up in a result that disappointed the market and sent the shares sharply lower. Construction work is responsible for more than half of company turnover, and revenues fell 7 per cent, with profits down 15 per cent. Strength in large-scale transport infrastructure projects in Australia was more than offset by a sharp decline in the Hong Kong construction market. By contrast, the mining and minerals processing business enjoyed an excellent half, with revenues up 16 per cent and profits jumping by 26 per cent. As well as some major work at Australian mines, the company was involved with several mines in Indonesia, and also with significant mine and processing plant projects in Mongolia, the United States, Chile and Botswana. Though representing less than 30 per cent of company revenues, mining and minerals processing contributed more than 40 per cent of profits. CIMIC's third main area of activity is maintenance and servicing work for railways and major engineering and infrastructure projects around Australia, with revenues and profits for this business largely in line with the June 2018 half.

Outlook

CIMIC is a leading participant in the Australian infrastructure construction market, and will benefit as investment increases. During the June 2019 half it received new orders of $8.3 billion and at the end of the period had an order backlog of $36.8 billion, up 6 per cent from a year earlier. For 2020 and beyond it sees a pipeline of some $400 billion in possible new work. It is bidding for major projects that include road and rail infrastructure work around Australia, a copper mine project in Chile and the North–South Corridor expressway in Singapore. CIMIC is known for its strong balance sheet, with more than $1.3 billion in net cash holdings at June 2019. It forecasts a December 2019 after-tax profit of $790 million to $840 million.

Year to 31 December	2017	2018
Revenues ($mn)	13 429.5	14 670.2
EBIT ($mn)	1 002.4	1 142.6
EBIT margin (%)	7.5	7.8
Profit before tax ($mn)	959.2	1 074.7
Profit after tax ($mn)	702.1	780.6
Earnings per share (c)	216.53	240.74
Cash flow per share (c)	374.21	413.19
Dividend (c)	135	156
Percentage franked	100	100
Interest cover (times)	23.2	16.8
Return on equity (%)	21.2	27.7
Half year to 30 June	2018	2019
Revenues ($mn)	6937.4	6955.1
Profit before tax ($mn)	503.0	503.6
Profit after tax ($mn)	363.0	366.7
Earnings per share (c)	111.90	113.10
Dividend (c)	70	71
Percentage franked	100	100
Net tangible assets per share ($)	3.11	4.00
Debt-to-equity ratio (%)	~	~
Current ratio	0.9	0.9

The Citadel Group Limited

ASX code: CGL www.citadelgroup.com.au

Share price ($)	3.91
12-month high ($)	9.30
12-month low ($)	3.63
Market capitalisation ($mn)	192.6
Price-to-NTA-per-share ratio	~
5-year share price return (% p.a.)	14.6
Dividend reinvestment plan	No

Sector: Information technology	Company	Sector
Price/earnings ratio (times)	17.7	29.4
Dividend yield (%)	2.8	1.6

Founded in 2007, Canberra-based Citadel is a software and technology company with a specialty in the provision of secure information management. Its main clients are in the health, national security and defence spheres. It operates Australia's largest laboratory information system, supporting over 60 laboratories nationwide, and also manages an extensive range of digital health systems. It operates from offices in Canberra, Sydney, Melbourne, Brisbane and Adelaide. In June 2019 it acquired the systems integration and engineering specialist Noventus.

Latest business results (June 2019, full year)

Sales and profits fell in a disappointing result for the company. Timing issues were to blame for much of the bad news. Some project extensions, expected to begin during the year, were instead delayed until early in the June 2020 year, as government departments postponed spending initiatives until after the general election. Payments on a major project were also delayed. In addition, the company has begun the transition from high-margin consulting and managed services to software-as-a-service (SaaS) operations. The latter provide reduced margins in the short term, though higher margins over the medium term. In response to shareholder concerns about the need for improved transparency in its financial reporting, the company provided a breakdown of its revenues and profits into three segments — knowledge, technology and health. It was the first category, knowledge, that suffered a sharp decline in sales and profits, hit by government spending delays. By contrast, the health category, which provides software products for diagnostic laboratories and clinical applications, saw sales up and profits steady. The low-margin technology business, which specialises in data, video and voice technology management, actually enjoyed a solid increase in sales, but with profits down.

Outlook

Citadel believes that it is set to return to growth, and it forecasts that its revenues and profits will rise by low double-digit amounts in the June 2020 year. The $5.7 million acquisition of Noventus has boosted its exposure to the defence, government, telecommunications and transportation sectors, and is expected to contribute around $18 million in revenues and $2 million in EBITDA in June 2020. The company is developing new SaaS products that it believes will broaden its revenues base, and is experiencing strong growth for SaaS business. It believes that it can use its intellectual property to expand into overseas markets. It has been enjoying particular success with its CHARM oncology information management system, acquired in 2017, which now has a 28 per cent share of the medical oncology e-health market.

Year to 30 June	2018	2019
Revenues ($mn)	105.4	98.2
Knowledge (%)	55	44
Technology (%)	27	35
Health (%)	18	21
EBIT ($mn)	26.6	15.2
EBIT margin (%)	25.2	15.5
Gross margin (%)	51.5	44.6
Profit before tax ($mn)	25.3	14.3
Profit after tax ($mn)	14.3	10.9
Earnings per share (c)	29.42	22.08
Cash flow per share (c)	44.53	38.30
Dividend (c)	13.8	10.8
Percentage franked	100	100
Net tangible assets per share ($)	0.06	~
Interest cover (times)	21.2	16.8
Return on equity (%)	18.7	13.1
Debt-to-equity ratio (%)	~	~
Current ratio	1.6	1.4

Clover Corporation Limited

ASX code: CLV www.clovercorp.com.au

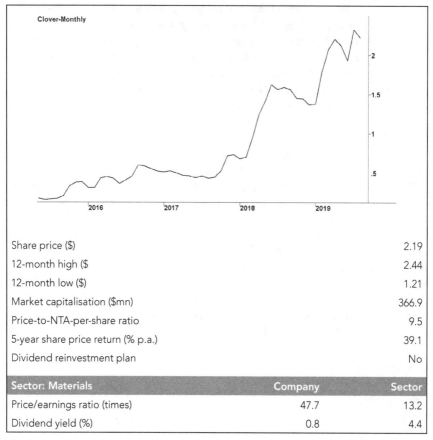

Share price ($)	2.19
12-month high ($	2.44
12-month low ($)	1.21
Market capitalisation ($mn)	366.9
Price-to-NTA-per-share ratio	9.5
5-year share price return (% p.a.)	39.1
Dividend reinvestment plan	No

Sector: Materials	Company	Sector
Price/earnings ratio (times)	47.7	13.2
Dividend yield (%)	0.8	4.4

Melbourne-based Clover, founded in 1988 as a family-owned company, develops value-added nutrients for use in foods or as nutritional supplements. Its key product is DHA, a form of omega 3. It sells this under the Nu-Mega and Ocean Gold range of tuna oils. It also markets nutritional oil powders, based on technology developed by the Commonwealth Scientific and Industrial Research Organisation. In addition, the company has developed technology that allows nutritional oils to be added to infant formula, foods and beverages. Overseas customers account for about half of company sales.

Latest business results (January 2019, half year)

Clover reported another excellent result, with expansion into new markets helping deliver a solid jump in profits. The infant formula market was especially strong, although the company reported that some customers were limiting their purchases in anticipation of legislative changes regarding the addition of DHA to infant products. Domestic sales actually fell. However, this was more than offset by surging demand elsewhere, with Asian sales up 39 per cent, European sales rising 53 per cent and American sales ahead by 42 per cent.

Outlook

Thanks to its excellent technology, Clover is now experiencing strong demand for its DHA products, especially from the infant formula market. It is a beneficiary of fast-growing Chinese demand for foreign-produced formula, and Asian sales are now more than a third of total turnover. European sales remain low but have the potential to increase significantly as new EU legislation goes into force in 2020, requiring a minimum DHA content in infant formula. China too may introduce similar legislation. The company has established a warehouse in the Netherlands, with a full-time sales agent, in readiness for growth in Europe. It is also developing new products, aimed especially at the American health and sports nutrition markets. Developments include a new vegan encapsulated product, organic products, powdered drinks and health bars. Clover has taken a 35 per cent stake in Melody Dairies, a New Zealand company that is planning to build a new spray dryer facility at Hamilton, New Zealand, for converting liquids into powders. When completed, late in 2020 or early in 2021, Clover will have the right to access 35 per cent of the operational time of this facility, which is expected to lower production costs for selected products and boost profit margins. It has also raised capacity at its Melbourne plant. With exports growing strongly the company is a beneficiary of a weak dollar.

Year to 31 July	2017	2018
Revenues ($mn)	47.9	63.0
EBIT ($mn)	5.0	10.8
EBIT margin (%)	10.4	17.2
Gross margin (%)	24.2	29.0
Profit before tax ($mn)	5.0	10.6
Profit after tax ($mn)	3.6	7.6
Earnings per share (c)	2.20	4.59
Cash flow per share (c)	2.55	5.02
Dividend (c)	1	1.75
Percentage franked	100	100
Interest cover (times)	~	57.2
Return on equity (%)	11.6	21.5
Half year to 31 January	2018	2019
Revenues ($mn)	31.0	34.3
Profit before tax ($mn)	4.4	6.2
Profit after tax ($mn)	3.2	4.5
Earnings per share (c)	1.93	2.71
Dividend (c)	0.5	0.63
Percentage franked	100	100
Net tangible assets per share ($)	0.19	0.23
Debt-to-equity ratio (%)	~	3.1
Current ratio	4.6	4.2

Cochlear Limited

ASX code: COH www.cochlear.com

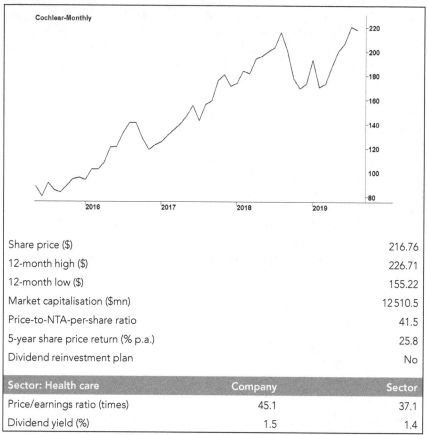

Share price ($)	216.76
12-month high ($)	226.71
12-month low ($)	155.22
Market capitalisation ($mn)	12 510.5
Price-to-NTA-per-share ratio	41.5
5-year share price return (% p.a.)	25.8
Dividend reinvestment plan	No

Sector: Health care	Company	Sector
Price/earnings ratio (times)	45.1	37.1
Dividend yield (%)	1.5	1.4

Sydney-based Cochlear, founded in 1981, has around 65 per cent of the world market for cochlear bionic-ear implants, which are intended to assist the communication ability of people suffering from severe hearing impediments. It also sells the Baha bone-anchored hearing implant, as well as a range of acoustic products. With manufacturing facilities and technology centres in Australia, Sweden, Belgium and the US, it has sales in over 100 countries, and overseas business accounts for more than 90 per cent of revenues and profits.

Latest business results (June 2019, full year)

The company notched up another solid result, despite a small decline in implant demand. Cochlear implant revenues rose 2 per cent, though were down 3 per cent on a constant currency basis, with unit sales also down 3 per cent, to 34 083. Both the US and Germany lost market share, although the company reported a sales recovery towards the end of the financial year with the launch of the new Nucleus Profile Plus Series implant. Services revenues rose by 20 per cent, or 14 per cent on a constant currency basis, thanks mainly to existing customers upgrading their sound processors. The small Acoustics division saw revenues up by 5 per cent, although they edged down on a constant currency basis, with a decline in upgrade sales.

Outlook

Cochlear continues to launch new products at an impressive rate, with research and development spending up 10 per cent in the June 2019 year to $184 million, and this is helping it maintain its leadership position. It is already seeing a rise in sales following the launch of its Nucleus Profile Plus Series implants. These are the world's thinnest implants with the benefit that they enable the implant recipient to undergo a magnetic resonance imaging scan without the need to remove the internal magnet. The company is also working to expand its markets. It views hearing-impaired adults in developed countries as offering great potential, thanks to a current penetration rate of only around 3 per cent. In recent years this has become the fastest-growing market segment for the company. Cochlear is building a $50 million implant production facility in China, aimed especially at servicing fast-growing emerging markets. This will be its first implant manufacturing facility outside Australia, and will boost total company production capacity by 50 per cent when it is completed in 2020. The company's early forecast is for a June 2020 after-tax profit of $290 million to $300 million, though much will depend on currency movements.

Year to 30 June	2018	2019
Revenues ($mn)	1363.7	1426.7
Cochlear implants (%)	62	58
Services (%)	26	30
Acoustics (%)	12	12
EBIT ($mn)	348.4	370.1
EBIT margin (%)	25.5	25.9
Gross margin (%)	73.0	74.8
Profit before tax ($mn)	340.5	365.6
Profit after tax ($mn)	245.8	276.7
Earnings per share (c)	427.27	480.82
Cash flow per share (c)	486.72	547.72
Dividend (c)	300	330
Percentage franked	100	100
Net tangible assets per share ($)	4.61	5.22
Interest cover (times)	44.1	82.2
Return on equity (%)	42.6	41.4
Debt-to-equity ratio (%)	14.1	14.2
Current ratio	2.0	1.8

Codan Limited

ASX code: CDA

www.codan.com.au

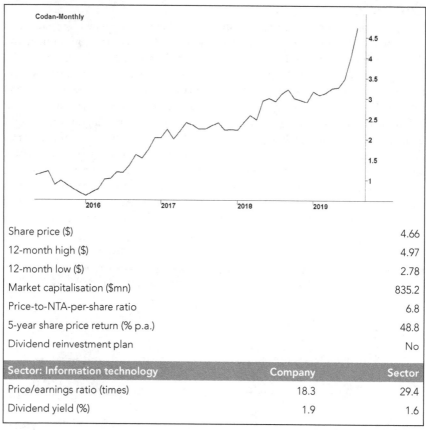

Share price ($)	4.66
12-month high ($)	4.97
12-month low ($)	2.78
Market capitalisation ($mn)	835.2
Price-to-NTA-per-share ratio	6.8
5-year share price return (% p.a.)	48.8
Dividend reinvestment plan	No

Sector: Information technology	Company	Sector
Price/earnings ratio (times)	18.3	29.4
Dividend yield (%)	1.9	1.6

Adelaide electronics company Codan was founded in 1959. It is a leading world manufacturer of metal-detecting products, including metal detectors for hobbyists, gold detectors for small-scale miners and landmine detectors for humanitarian applications. A second division produces high-frequency communication radios for military and humanitarian use. A smaller business, the company's Perth-based Minetec subsidiary, provides electronic productivity and safety devices and services for the mining industry. Codan sells to more than 150 countries, and overseas sales represent more than 85 per cent of company revenues.

Latest business results (June 2019, full year)

Profits rebounded, after falling in the previous year, with revenues also up, as all three of the company's businesses achieved growth. The core Metal Detection division saw sales up 11 per cent, with profits rising by 5 per cent. There was strong demand from new gold markets in the Middle East, as well as the first full year's contribution from the innovative Equinox coin and treasure detector. However, the best result came from the Communications division, with sales up 37 per cent and profits more than doubling. The company attributed this to its strategy of forming strategic partnerships with key suppliers and expanding into the global military market. It has also been targeting larger projects. The small Tracking Solutions division, incorporating the Minetec business, saw some delays in securing orders, but nevertheless boosted sales by 19 per cent, though it recorded a loss for the year.

Outlook

Codan is a significant force in three niche high-tech product areas. When demand is high, and the company can get the product mix right, there is the potential for strong profit growth. Its metal detectors dominate the African artisanal gold mining market, with the Middle East a growing market. The company has opened a new office in Brazil to boost Latin American sales. In the coin and treasure market it believes its new Vanquish model will boost its market share. Its Communications division has a strong order book and expects continued growth. The new Sentry Military Manpack radio system will strengthen its position in the land mobile radio sector. The company is targeting militaries in the Middle East, Africa, Asia, Eastern Europe and Latin America, and in July 2019 announced a $15 million contract with the government of Kenya to supply a tactical communications network system. The Minetec business has concluded a global licensing, technology development and marketing agreement with US construction equipment giant Caterpillar, and expects this to generate strong growth for its mine productivity and safety devices.

Year to 30 June	2018	2019
Revenues ($mn)	229.9	270.8
Metal detection (%)	71	67
Communications (%)	25	28
EBIT ($mn)	53.7	63.4
EBIT margin (%)	23.4	23.4
Gross margin (%)	57.3	56.6
Profit before tax ($mn)	53.2	63.3
Profit after tax ($mn)	41.6	45.7
Earnings per share (c)	23.36	25.51
Cash flow per share (c)	32.73	34.03
Dividend (c)	8.5	9
Percentage franked	100	100
Net tangible assets per share ($)	0.57	0.69
Interest cover (times)	105.7	918.4
Return on equity (%)	23.5	22.9
Debt-to-equity ratio (%)	~	~
Current ratio	1.6	1.9

Collins Foods Limited

ASX code: CKF   www.collinsfoods.com

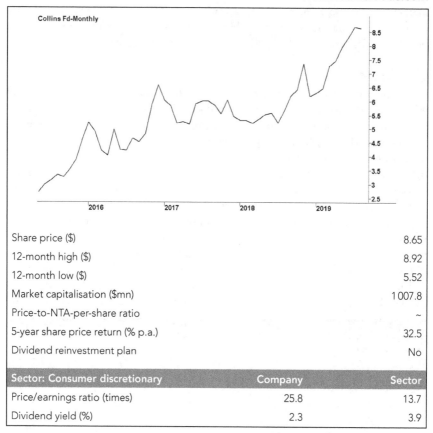

Share price ($)	8.65
12-month high ($)	8.92
12-month low ($)	5.52
Market capitalisation ($mn)	1 007.8
Price-to-NTA-per-share ratio	~
5-year share price return (% p.a.)	32.5
Dividend reinvestment plan	No

Sector: Consumer discretionary	Company	Sector
Price/earnings ratio (times)	25.8	13.7
Dividend yield (%)	2.3	3.9

Collins Foods, based in Brisbane, dates back to 1968 when it obtained the KFC fried chicken franchise for Queensland. Today it owns and operates KFC outlets across Australia, and is the country's largest KFC franchisee. It also owns KFC stores in Germany and the Netherlands. It operates the Sizzler restaurant business, with company-owned restaurants in Australia and a growing number of franchise outlets in Thailand, China and Japan. It has launched the Taco Bell Mexican restaurant brand in Australia.

Latest business results (April 2019, full year)

Sales and profits rose again, thanks to organic growth and new-store business. KFC Australia saw sales rise by nearly 16 per cent, thanks to impressive same-store sales growth of 3.7 per cent, along with the opening of seven new restaurants. But European same-store sales fell by 3.7 per cent, as key promotional campaigns were less successful than in previous years. Four new restaurants, two each in Germany and the Netherlands, were opened during the year, and European revenues were up, although profits fell. In Australia, the company opened three new Taco Bell outlets and closed two Sizzler restaurants. At the end of the period the company operated 231 franchised KFC restaurants in Australia, 20 in the Netherlands and 17 in Germany. It owned and operated 12 Sizzler restaurants in Australia, with 77 franchised stores in Asia, mainly in Thailand. It also operated four franchised Taco Bell outlets in Australia.

Outlook

Collins has been achieving solid success in its KFC business with new product offerings, effective cost controls and margin improvement, and it continues to expand. It expects to open as many as 10 further KFC outlets in Australia during the April 2020 year. It is also moving strongly into home delivery, together with Deliveroo and Menulog. It is reviewing its European restaurant portfolio, with a view to closing some underperforming businesses. But at the same time it is working to upgrade others and open new ones. It has opened its first four Taco Bell restaurants in Queensland and reports that these are trading in line with expectations. It plans to expand to a total of around 50 Taco Bells within three years, including 10 new ones in the April 2020 year. It regards its domestic Sizzler operation as non-core, and does not have growth plans for this business. Rather, it is working to maintain margins, and is ready to close further outlets if performance starts to deteriorate and as leases expire. However, Sizzler Asia continues to grow.

Year to 28 April*	2018	2019
Revenues ($mn)	770.9	901.2
KFC restaurants Australia (%)	81	80
KFC restaurants Europe (%)	12	14
Sizzler restaurants (%)	7	5
EBIT ($mn)	59.0	70.1
EBIT margin (%)	7.7	7.8
Gross margin (%)	52.4	52.4
Profit before tax ($mn)	48.5	59.3
Profit after tax ($mn)	32.5	39.1
Earnings per share (c)	28.28	33.57
Cash flow per share (c)	54.65	69.95
Dividend (c)	17	19.5
Percentage franked	100	100
Net tangible assets per share ($)	~	~
Interest cover (times)	5.6	6.5
Return on equity (%)	10.8	11.4
Debt-to-equity ratio (%)	67.8	60.3
Current ratio	0.9	0.9

* 29 April 2018

Commonwealth Bank of Australia

ASX code: CBA   www.commbank.com.au

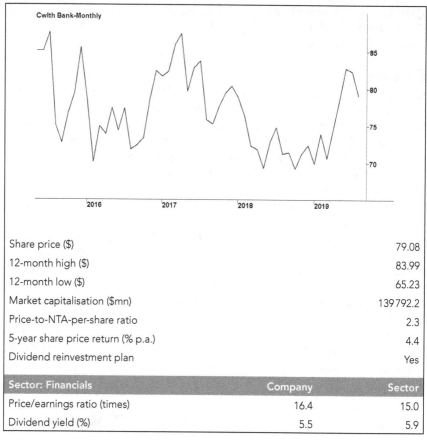

Share price ($)	79.08
12-month high ($)	83.99
12-month low ($)	65.23
Market capitalisation ($mn)	139792.2
Price-to-NTA-per-share ratio	2.3
5-year share price return (% p.a.)	4.4
Dividend reinvestment plan	Yes

Sector: Financials	Company	Sector
Price/earnings ratio (times)	16.4	15.0
Dividend yield (%)	5.5	5.9

The Commonwealth Bank, based in Sydney, was founded in 1911. It is today one of Australia's largest banks, and one of the country's top providers of home loans, personal loans and credit cards, as well as the largest holder of deposits. Commonwealth Securities is Australia's largest online stockbroker. It has significant interests in New Zealand, through ASB Bank, and a network of businesses in Asia. It owns Bankwest in Western Australia. It has sold its Colonial First State wealth management business.

Latest business results (June 2019, full year)

Revenues were down and the cash profit slipped for the second consecutive year, as the bank was hit by falling interest rates, a slowing economy and higher customer compensation fees. The decline in official interest rates led to a contraction in the net interest margin — although it steadied in the second half — forcing revenues down. During the year the bank spent $2.2 billion in customer remediation payments or provisions, following revelations of wrongful conduct at the recent Banking Royal Commission. This amount was up from $1.2 billion in the previous year. In addition, operating expenses rose, with the addition of some 600 risk and compliance staff, in response to concerns from bank regulators. The weakness was spread across all of the bank's domestic operations. The core Retail Banking Services division — which includes the home loans and retail deposit businesses, and generates around half of the bank's earnings — saw profits down 12 per cent, despite a 4 per cent increase in home lending. Profits for the Business and Private Banking division were down 7 per cent, although business lending rose by 4 per cent. The Institutional Banking and Markets division saw profits down 8 per cent. By contrast, New Zealand operations were once again strong.

Outlook

Commonwealth Bank occupies a powerful position in the domestic economy as well as in the local banking industry. Thanks to a large branch network, offering many cross-selling opportunities, it has pricing power that has generally enabled it to maintain a cost advantage over some of its rivals. It is working to streamline its operations. It has sold Colonial First State Global Asset Management for $4.2 billion and is divesting itself of most of its insurance and financial planning businesses. It has spent heavily on new technology, which sometimes now gives it an edge over its main domestic rivals. It has announced a US$100 million investment in the Swedish bank Klarna, and will introduce Klarna's credit payment products to Australia.

Year to 30 June	2018	2019
Operating income ($mn)	24 914.0	24 407.0
Net interest income ($mn)	18 342.0	18 120.0
Operating expenses ($mn)	10 995.0	11 269.0
Profit before tax ($mn)	12 848.0	11 941.0
Profit after tax ($mn)	8 915.0	8 492.0
Earnings per share (c)	510.60	481.13
Dividend (c)	431	431
Percentage franked	100	100
Non-interest income to total income (%)	26.4	25.8
Net tangible assets per share ($)	33.14	34.86
Cost-to-income ratio (%)	44.1	46.2
Return on equity (%)	13.7	12.4
Return on assets (%)	0.9	0.9

Corporate Travel Management Limited

ASX code: CTD

investor.travelctm.com.au

Corp Trav-Monthly

Share price ($)	17.88
12-month high ($)	33.87
12-month low ($)	17.30
Market capitalisation ($mn)	1 939.8
Price-to-NTA-per-share ratio	31.4
5-year share price return (% p.a.)	20.5
Dividend reinvestment plan	No

Sector: Consumer discretionary	Company	Sector
Price/earnings ratio (times)	22.5	13.7
Dividend yield (%)	2.2	3.9

Brisbane-based Corporate Travel Management was established in 1994 as a specialist business travel service. Thanks to a series of acquisitions it is now servicing clients in more than 70 countries, and overseas business represents more than 70 per cent of total company turnover.

Latest business results (June 2019, full year)

Corporate Travel enjoyed another strong year, with all regions reporting double-digit gains in revenues and underlying profits. The best growth came from Asia, the smallest of the company's reporting regions, with sales jumping by 49 per cent and underlying EBITDA up by nearly 27 per cent, although this to a large degree reflected the $60 million acquisition, completed in October 2018, of a majority stake in Hong Kong–based Lotus Travel Group. The largest region, North America, enjoyed another good year, though with a slowing of client activity in the second half. North American profit margins remained lower than those prevailing in other regions. Europe overcame Brexit uncertainties to post another good result, with very high profit margins. Australia/New Zealand also did well, with gains in market share, despite a slowdown in business before the federal election. During the year the company recorded a total transaction value — the actual value of all tickets and other items sold — of $6.48 billion, up 30 per cent from the June 2018 year.

Outlook

Corporate Travel Management has grown into a global company, able to manage clients in any part of the world. It has established technology hubs in Sydney, Hong Kong, Los Angeles and Manchester, and believes that these give it a growing edge in the highly fragmented global market for corporate travel. It estimates the worldwide corporate travel market as worth US$1.4 trillion annually, with no single company enjoying much more than a 1 per cent share, and it sees enormous scope for growth. Employee expenses account for approximately 70 per cent of the company's cost base, so as it steadily automates its processes it expects to achieve gains in productivity. With its acquisition of a majority stake of Lotus Travel Group, it believes that Chinese business will become a significant generator of increasing company profits, although it could be affected by political turmoil in the region. However, during the year some activist financial analysts challenged the company's business model, and this had the effect of driving the share price lower. Corporate Travel's early forecast is for EBITDA for the June 2020 year of between $165 million and $175 million, up from $150.1 million in June 2019.

Year to 30 June	2018	2019
Revenues ($mn)	371.0	446.7
Travel services North America (%)	34	33
Travel services Australia & NZ (%)	29	27
Travel services Europe (%)	22	22
Travel services Asia (%)	15	18
EBIT ($mn)	106.8	123.4
EBIT margin (%)	28.8	27.6
Profit before tax ($mn)	103.7	120.9
Profit after tax ($mn)	76.7	86.2
Earnings per share (c)	72.41	79.64
Cash flow per share (c)	89.24	98.43
Dividend (c)	36	40
Percentage franked	71	73
Net tangible assets per share ($)	0.03	0.57
Interest cover (times)	34.5	49.9
Return on equity (%)	18.3	16.9
Debt-to-equity ratio (%)	~	~
Current ratio	1.2	1.3

Credit Corp Group Limited

ASX code: CCP   www.creditcorpgroup.com.au

Share price ($)	29.29
12-month high ($)	29.36
12-month low ($)	17.71
Market capitalisation ($mn)	1 608.5
Price-to-NTA-per-share ratio	3.5
5-year share price return (% p.a.)	26.9
Dividend reinvestment plan	No

Sector: Financials	Company	Sector
Price/earnings ratio (times)	20.6	15.0
Dividend yield (%)	2.5	5.9

Sydney-based Credit Corp was formed in 1992, although it has its origins in companies that started in the early 1970s. It provides debt collection services to companies in numerous industries, including the finance, insurance, legal and government sectors, though with a specialty in consumer credit card debt. It has operations in the United States and in New Zealand. It also runs the Credit Corp Financial Services consumer lending business. In August 2019 it acquired rival debt collection company Baycorp for $65 million.

Latest business results (June 2019, full year)

For a second straight year continuing growth in the company's consumer lending business and in its American activities helped generate a solid rise in revenues and profits. The company's core business—representing nearly 60 per cent of turnover—is its Australia/New Zealand debt collection operations, and revenues and the after-tax profit both edged down. By contrast, US debt collection business surged again, with revenues up 70 per cent—following an 84 per cent jump in the previous year—and with profits nearly trebling, though from a low base. The Australia/New Zealand consumer lending operation saw revenues rise 19 per cent and the after-tax profit increase by 25 per cent, with the consumer loan book 16 per cent higher than a year earlier, at $212 million.

Outlook

Credit Corp's main business effectively involves buying consumer debt at a discount to its face value, then seeking to recover an amount in excess of the purchase price. Often this recovery takes the form of phased payments over an extended period, and Credit Corp thus has substantial recurring income. Setting an appropriate price for the acquisition of parcels of debt is one of the keys to success, and Credit Corp has acquired considerable expertise in this. However, this has become a competitive business, and, as the market leader in Australia, Credit Corp has limited scope for expansion. It is now looking to America and to its consumer lending operations for growth. It has been steadily boosting its profile in the large and growing US market, and operations there moved into profit during the June 2018 year. It believes American revenues could grow in the medium term to become as large as its Australia/New Zealand business, with the potential for robust profit margins. Its consumer lending business has also been progressing strongly, and now represents nearly 30 per cent of revenues and profit. However, this activity is subject to stringent regulatory control. Following the acquisition of debt collection company Baycorp, Credit Corp plans to undertake a restructuring of its businesses. It expects a June 2020 after-tax profit of $81 million to $83 million.

Year to 30 June	2018	2019
Revenues ($mn)	286.8	313.8
EBIT ($mn)	101.2	112.5
EBIT margin (%)	35.3	35.8
Profit before tax ($mn)	92.0	100.5
Profit after tax ($mn)	64.3	70.3
Earnings per share (c)	135.11	141.92
Cash flow per share (c)	139.54	146.67
Dividend (c)	67	72
Percentage franked	100	100
Net tangible assets per share ($)	5.99	8.43
Interest cover (times)	11.0	9.4
Return on equity (%)	24.1	18.7
Debt-to-equity ratio (%)	69.8	25.9
Current ratio	5.8	7.5

CSR Limited

ASX code: CSR

www.csr.com.au

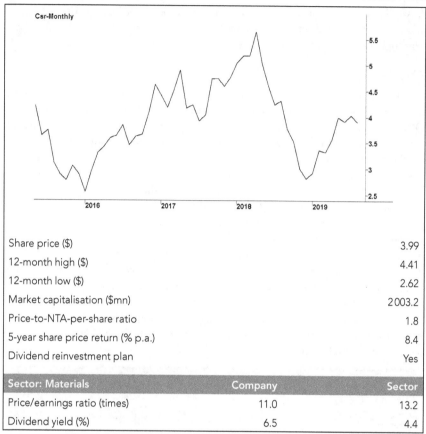

Share price ($)	3.99
12-month high ($)	4.41
12-month low ($)	2.62
Market capitalisation ($mn)	2 003.2
Price-to-NTA-per-share ratio	1.8
5-year share price return (% p.a.)	8.4
Dividend reinvestment plan	Yes

Sector: Materials	Company	Sector
Price/earnings ratio (times)	11.0	13.2
Dividend yield (%)	6.5	4.4

Sydney-based CSR, founded in 1855 as a sugar refiner, is now a leading manufacturer of building products for residential and commercial construction, with distribution throughout Australia and New Zealand. Its brands include Gyprock plasterboard, Bradford insulation, Monier roof tiles and Hebel concrete products. It is also a joint venture partner in Australia's second-largest aluminium smelter at Tomago, and it has established a brick-making joint venture with Boral, named PGH Bricks and Pavers. In addition, it operates a residential and industrial property development business, based on former industrial sites. It has sold its Viridian Glass business.

Latest business results (March 2019, full year)

Profits for continuing operations fell, after five consecutive annual rises, with many areas of business showing weakness. The core Building Products division saw revenues edge up, but EBIT was down by 4 per cent, although higher prices and an improved product mix offset a modest decline in sales in the second half. The Hebel business had a good year and Bradford insulation products and Rediwall wall systems were strong, but most other products experienced weakness. The company's aluminium business benefited from higher sales prices. However, EBIT plunged by

54 per cent as a result of rising electricity prices. In addition, a weaker dollar boosted the price of imported raw materials. Property sales achieved EBIT of $38.8 million, which was 19 per cent down on the previous year. When Viridian Glass — now sold — is included in the result, the company reported a big loss.

Outlook

CSR has been a major beneficiary of the strength of the Australian house construction and renovation market, but is now being hurt by weakness in this industry. Nevertheless, with the Australian population continuing to grow, it is optimistic about the long-term outlook for its building products operations, and it is working to boost capacity. It has completed a $75 million expansion of its Hebel facility in New South Wales, and is also boosting its construction systems production capacity at both New South Wales and Victoria. It has acquired a new site in Western Australia for the Bradford insulation operation. An extensive hedging program will help stabilise profits for the aluminium business, but the company remains concerned about rising energy costs. Its property division remains active, with new residential and industrial projects in western Sydney and continuing work at Chirnside Park in Melbourne. A series of major projects is expected to underpin property earnings for the coming 10 years.

Year to 31 March	2018	2019
Revenues ($mn)	2237.7	2322.8
Building products (%)	75	73
Aluminium (%)	25	27
EBIT ($mn)	310.6	264.3
EBIT margin (%)	13.9	11.4
Gross margin (%)	33.4	29.9
Profit before tax ($mn)	301.1	256.4
Profit after tax ($mn)	210.6	181.7
Earnings per share (c)	41.86	36.11
Cash flow per share (c)	55.73	49.03
Dividend (c)	27	26
Percentage franked	63	75
Net tangible assets per share ($)	2.15	2.19
Interest cover (times)	32.7	33.5
Return on equity (%)	17.7	15.1
Debt-to-equity ratio (%)	1.1	~
Current ratio	1.6	2.1

Data#3 Limited

ASX code: DTL

www.data3.com

Share price ($)	2.54
12-month high ($)	2.70
12-month low ($)	1.31
Market capitalisation ($mn)	391.1
Price-to-NTA-per-share ratio	12.7
5-year share price return (% p.a.)	29.3
Dividend reinvestment plan	No

Sector: Information technology	Company	Sector
Price/earnings ratio (times)	21.6	29.4
Dividend yield (%)	4.2	1.6

Brisbane-based IT consultant Data#3 was formed in 1984 from the merger of computer software consultancy Powell, Clark and Associates with IBM typewriter dealer Albrand Typewriters and Office Machines. Today it operates from offices around Australia and in Fiji, providing information and communication technology services — notably software licensing and software asset management — to a wide range of businesses that include banking and finance, mining, tourism and leisure, legal, health care, manufacturing, distribution, government and utilities.

Latest business results (June 2019, full year)

Profits bounced back from the previous year's decline in an excellent result that the company attributed to digital transformation — the drive by Australian companies and public bodies to place increasing amounts of their operations onto digital platforms. Data#3 divides its activities broadly into two segments, products and services, and both were strong. The product segment boosted revenues by 21 per cent, with profits up by 17 per cent and solid demand for both infrastructure and software products. The services segment saw revenues increase by 13 per cent, with all parts of this business — support services, project services, recruitment and management consulting — reporting stronger sales. However, a change in the sales mix, due to the company decommissioning its own cloud service in favour of a public cloud offering, led to lower margins, and profits just edged up. There was a significant expansion of public cloud-based offerings, with revenues jumping 35 per cent to $362 million, having surged 58 per cent in the previous year. The 77-per-cent-owned subsidiary Discovery Technology, which provides wi-fi-based IT location and analytical services, once again reported sharply lower sales.

Outlook

Data#3 has adopted a three-year strategic plan with three key long-term objectives — to deliver sustained profit growth, to boost its services revenues, with enhanced margins, and to expand its cloud services revenues. The company is a major reseller for Microsoft products, and stands to benefit as Microsoft becomes a global leader in public cloud services. In 2018 Data#3 was selected by the federal government's Digital Transformation Agency as its sole provider of Microsoft licensing services, extending the existing nine-year relationship for a further three years. It believes its Discovery Technology subsidiary is set for a recovery and will become a significant participant in the fast-moving data and analytics market. However, the company sees the retention of skilled staff as a growing challenge. At June 2019 Data#3 had net cash holdings of more than $121 million, and it continues to seek out expansion opportunities.

Year to 30 June	2018	2019
Revenues ($mn)	1180.3	1414.4
EBIT ($mn)	19.5	25.7
EBIT margin (%)	1.7	1.8
Profit before tax ($mn)	20.4	26.6
Profit after tax ($mn)	14.1	18.1
Earnings per share (c)	9.14	11.76
Cash flow per share (c)	11.65	14.01
Dividend (c)	8.2	10.7
Percentage franked	100	100
Net tangible assets per share ($)	0.18	0.20
Interest cover (times)	~	~
Return on equity (%)	32.7	39.6
Debt-to-equity ratio (%)	~	~
Current ratio	1.1	1.1

DWS Limited

ASX code: DWS

www.dws.com.au

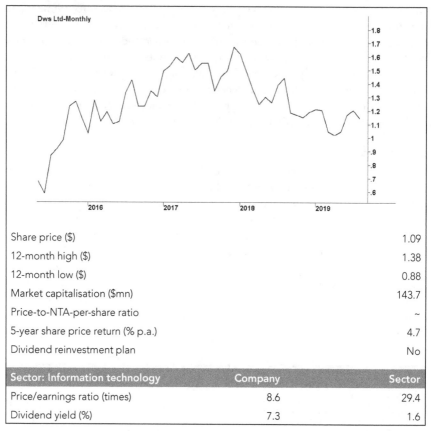

Share price ($)	1.09
12-month high ($)	1.38
12-month low ($)	0.88
Market capitalisation ($mn)	143.7
Price-to-NTA-per-share ratio	~
5-year share price return (% p.a.)	4.7
Dividend reinvestment plan	No

Sector: Information technology	Company	Sector
Price/earnings ratio (times)	8.6	29.4
Dividend yield (%)	7.3	1.6

Melbourne-based DWS is an IT services company established in 1991. It specialises in the design, development and maintenance of software for a range of clients across many industries. It also manages the IT services and consultancy businesses Phoenix and Symplicit, and in July 2018 it acquired the Canberra-based strategic management and IT consulting business Projects Assured. It operates from offices in Melbourne, Sydney, Adelaide, Canberra and Brisbane. The DWS founder and chief executive officer, Danny Wallis, owns 42 per cent of the company equity.

Latest business results (June 2019, full year)

The acquisition of Projects Assured led to a big jump in revenues and a smaller increase in normalised profits. It also generated a substantial rise in contracts with the government and defence sector, which rose from 14 per cent of company turnover in the June 2018 year to 35 per cent. By contrast, the banking and finance sector fell from 44 per cent to 34 per cent, and the information technology and communications sector fell from 20 per cent to 9 per cent. A change in senior management at the Symplicit business generated an improved performance in the second half, after first-half weakness. With demand rising for the company's services, the number of billable consultants rose from 704 at June 2018 to 751 at June 2019. Borrowings to finance the Projects Assured acquisition generated an increase in interest payments from $0.8 million in the June 2018 year to $3.1 million, and depreciation charges also rose sharply. In addition, the company reported one-off acquisition costs, and on a statutory basis its profits fell.

Outlook

The acquisition of Projects Assured for approximately $43 million has greatly diversified DWS's operations. It now has more than 130 staff members in Canberra with experience at government departments that include Health, Defence and Human Services, as well as the Australian Taxation Office. It has also worked with most state governments and with many local councils. The company is now working to leverage the benefits of its new businesses, with the aim of further diversifying its operations. Nevertheless, despite the acquisition, Victoria continues to generate more than half the company's turnover, and the company's fortunes remain dependent to a large degree on economic trends in that state. It is working to boost IT-related consulting work, which slumped from $24.8 million in June 2018 to $15.4 million in June 2019. In the absence of further merger and acquisition opportunities, DWS will place a focus on shareholder returns and on paying down debt.

Year to 30 June	2018	2019
Revenues ($mn)	126.1	163.5
EBIT ($mn)	22.5	25.9
EBIT margin (%)	17.9	15.8
Profit before tax ($mn)	21.9	22.9
Profit after tax ($mn)	15.9	16.8
Earnings per share (c)	12.07	12.74
Cash flow per share (c)	12.37	14.22
Dividend (c)	10	8
Percentage franked	100	100
Net tangible assets per share ($)	0.03	~
Interest cover (times)	34.5	8.6
Return on equity (%)	22.5	23.5
Debt-to-equity ratio (%)	2.6	46.9
Current ratio	1.5	1.3

Fiducian Group Limited

ASX code: FID   www.fiducian.com.au

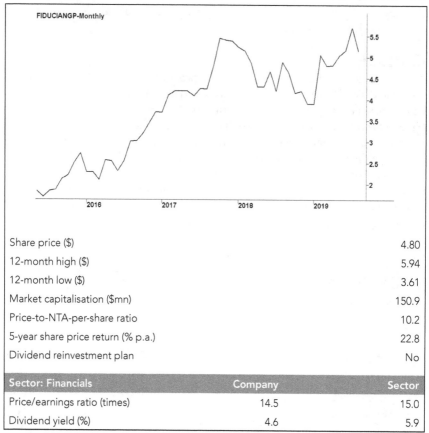

Share price ($)	4.80
12-month high ($)	5.94
12-month low ($)	3.61
Market capitalisation ($mn)	150.9
Price-to-NTA-per-share ratio	10.2
5-year share price return (% p.a.)	22.8
Dividend reinvestment plan	No

Sector: Financials	Company	Sector
Price/earnings ratio (times)	14.5	15.0
Dividend yield (%)	4.6	5.9

Sydney financial services company Fiducian Group was founded in 1996 by executive chairman Indy Singh. Initially it specialised in the provision of masterfund, client administration and financial planning services to financial advisory groups. It has since expanded and is now a holding company with five divisions — Fiducian Portfolio Services is in charge of trustee and superannuation services; Fiducian Investment Management Services operates the company's managed funds; Fiducian Service is the administration service provider for all the company's products; Fiducian Financial Services manages the company's financial planning businesses; and Fiducian Business Services provides accounting and business services. In 2019 the company acquired the financial planning business of Tasmanian financial services group MyState.

Latest business results (June 2019, full year)

Revenues and profits were up again, in another solid result for the company. For reporting purposes the company divides its operations into three broad segments. The largest of these is now the company's successful funds management business, with revenues up 12 per cent and the pre-tax profit rising by 13 per cent. Financial planning revenues rose by 8 per cent, but this business remained in the red, as the company invested to grow, as well as to boost its compliance monitoring procedures in the wake of the Banking Royal Commission. The corporate and administration segment incorporates all the company's other businesses, and profits edged down on a small rise in revenues. Funds under management, advice and administration grew 10 per cent to $7.4 billion.

Outlook

Fiducian managed nine company-owned financial planning offices at June 2019, as well as 32 franchised offices, with a total of 67 authorised representatives across Australia. It is continually boosting these numbers as new offices join the group and it has also been achieving solid organic growth. Its $3.5 million acquisition of MyState's retail financial planning business, effective from July 2019, delivers a team of financial planners and more than $340 million in funds under advice. Under the acquisition agreement, MyState will in future refer customers seeking financial planning guidance to Fiducian. The funds management business offers 15 funds, and the company believes that its method of choosing fund managers with differing investment styles delivers greater diversification with reduced risks. Fiducian management have stated that they expect profits to continue to grow in the June 2020 year. However, the company is vulnerable to any major downturn in financial markets. At June 2019 it had no debt and cash holdings of more than $11 million.

Year to 30 June	2018	2019
Revenues ($mn)	45.4	48.9
Funds management (%)	34	36
Financial planning (%)	35	35
Corporate and administration (%)	31	29
EBIT ($mn)	13.0	13.8
EBIT margin (%)	28.6	28.2
Profit before tax ($mn)	13.4	14.3
Profit after tax ($mn)	9.2	10.4
Earnings per share (c)	29.42	33.03
Cash flow per share (c)	33.89	38.73
Dividend (c)	20	22.3
Percentage franked	100	100
Net tangible assets per share ($)	0.49	0.47
Interest cover (times)	~	~
Return on equity (%)	31.3	31.4
Debt-to-equity ratio (%)	~	~
Current ratio	2.5	2.4

Flight Centre Travel Group Limited

ASX code: FLT

www.fctgl.com

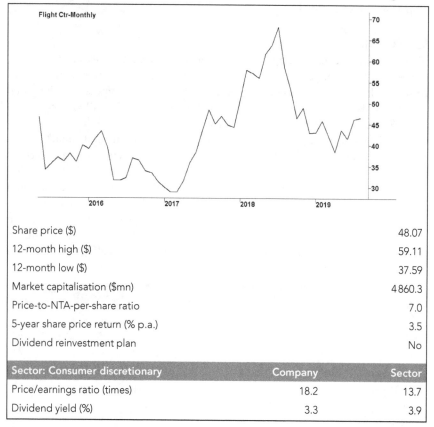

Share price ($)	48.07
12-month high ($)	59.11
12-month low ($)	37.59
Market capitalisation ($mn)	4 860.3
Price-to-NTA-per-share ratio	7.0
5-year share price return (% p.a.)	3.5
Dividend reinvestment plan	No

Sector: Consumer discretionary	Company	Sector
Price/earnings ratio (times)	18.2	13.7
Dividend yield (%)	3.3	3.9

Brisbane-based Flight Centre is the largest independent retail travel agency in Australia and New Zealand. It operates under numerous brands, including Student Flights, Universal Traveller, Travel Associates, Travel Managers, Topdeck Travel, Liberty Travel and Infinity Group. Its flagship corporate travel management network, FCM Travel Solutions, has operations and partnership agreements in numerous countries. Overseas revenues represent approximately half of total company turnover.

Latest business results (June 2019, full year)

Revenues rose but the underlying profit was down, hurt by weakened domestic business. The Australia and New Zealand segment, responsible for a little over half of company turnover, saw EBIT drop 34 per cent on a small decline in revenues, as leisure travel demand weakened. By contrast, the other main regional segments were positive, with notable contributions in most countries from the company's corporate business and benefits from the weaker dollar. The Americas now represent more than 20 per cent of turnover, and revenues and profits rose by double-digit amounts. The Europe/Middle East/Africa segment saw excellent profit growth on a small rise in sales as it succeeded in reducing operating costs. The Asia segment also enjoyed solid profit growth. During the year the company recorded total transactions — the actual value of all tickets and other items sold — of $23.7 billion, up 8.8 per cent from the previous year.

Outlook

In an environment of low-cost air travel that provides only modest profit margins, Flight Centre is engaged in a substantial overhaul of its operations. It is enjoying excellent growth for its corporate activities, which now generate 37 per cent of total transaction value, and the company has been actively making acquisitions in many countries aimed at boosting this business. It also now views American business as a key earnings driver, with strong future growth expected. Already corporate business is stronger in the Americas than in Australia/New Zealand. It is also seeking further geographical expansion, with European markets a key focus. It has been closing or downsizing underperforming operations, particularly in the leisure sector, while increasing its investment in technology. However, it remains heavily dependent on the mature Australian market for much of its business, with heavy costs from its large network of stores, at a time when travel bookings are increasingly moving online. The domestic travel sector is also vulnerable to the weakening dollar and trends in consumer spending. At June 2019 Flight Centre had net cash holdings of a massive $987 million, and it expects to make further acquisitions to boost its businesses.

Year to 30 June	2018	2019
Revenues ($mn)	2923.0	3055.3
EBIT ($mn)	384.9	344.6
EBIT margin (%)	13.2	11.3
Profit before tax ($mn)	384.7	343.1
Profit after tax ($mn)	283.0	266.6
Earnings per share (c)	280.36	264.39
Cash flow per share (c)	357.43	346.08
Dividend (c)	167	158
Percentage franked	100	100
Net tangible assets per share ($)	9.53	6.86
Interest cover (times)	2264.2	236.7
Return on equity (%)	19.0	17.9
Debt-to-equity ratio (%)	~	~
Current ratio	1.4	1.3

Fortescue Metals Group Limited

ASX code: FMG

www.fmgl.com.au

Fortescue-Monthly

Share price ($)	7.87
12-month high ($)	9.55
12-month low ($)	3.51
Market capitalisation ($mn)	24 231.5
Price-to-NTA-per-share ratio	1.6
5-year share price return (% p.a.)	20.6
Dividend reinvestment plan	Yes

Sector: Materials	Company	Sector
Price/earnings ratio (times)	5.5	13.2
Dividend yield (%)	5.5	4.4

Perth-based Fortescue was founded in 2003. It has been responsible for discovering and developing some of the largest iron ore mines in the world. It is today one of the world's largest iron ore producers, with operations that are centred on three mine sites in the Pilbara region. It also operates its own heavy-haul railway between its mines and its Herb Elliott Port at Port Hedland. More than 90 per cent of its sales are to China.

Latest business results (June 2019, full year)

Higher iron ore prices generated an excellent result for Fortescue, with a big jump in revenues and profits. Sales of 167.7 million tonnes were slightly less than in the previous year, but the average price of US$65 per tonne was 48 per cent higher. Average production costs of US$13.11 per tonne were up 6 per cent, with a series of productivity and efficiency initiatives only partially offsetting the impact of longer haul distances, higher fuel prices and increased staffing costs. Net debt — borrowings minus cash holdings — fell from US$3.1 billion to US$2.1 billion, and there was a sharp reduction in interest expenses. Note that Fortescue reports its results in US dollars. The Australian dollar figures in this book — converted at prevailing exchange rates — are for guidance only.

Outlook

Its heavy debt burden brought Fortescue near to collapse in 2012, and since then it has been devoting enormous effort into making itself more financially stable. In 2012 its basic production costs were as high as US$50 a tonne, but they have since fallen substantially and are now among the lowest in the world. It maintains an active exploration and development program at its Pilbara properties. Its massive US$1.3 billion Eliwana Mine and Rail project is expected to begin production of iron ore from December 2020. Its other major development is the US$2.6 billion Iron Bridge Magnetite project, which is targeted at beginning production in mid 2022. The company is optimistic that Chinese demand will remain strong, thanks to continuing urbanisation and industrialisation, although it also continues working to enlarge its presence in Japan, South Korea and other markets. Nevertheless, its fortunes are tied intimately to the price of iron ore, which can be volatile, and it is also influenced by currency fluctuations. In addition, its ore tends to be of a lower grade than that being produced by some rivals. It forecasts iron ore shipments in the June 2020 year of 170 million to 175 million tonnes.

Year to 30 June	2018	2019
Revenues ($mn)	9061.8	13840.3
EBIT ($mn)	2464.5	6697.2
EBIT margin (%)	27.2	48.4
Gross margin (%)	28.4	48.7
Profit before tax ($mn)	1638.2	6345.8
Profit after tax ($mn)	1155.3	4426.4
Earnings per share (c)	37.12	143.23
Cash flow per share (c)	91.11	196.98
Dividend (c)	23	43
Percentage franked	100	100
Net tangible assets per share ($)	4.22	4.91
Interest cover (times)	3.0	19.1
Return on equity (%)	9.0	31.3
Debt-to-equity ratio (%)	32.0	19.6
Current ratio	1.3	1.4

GR Engineering Services Limited

ASX code: GNG

www.gres.com.au

Share price ($)	0.93
12-month high ($)	1.44
12-month low ($)	0.75
Market capitalisation ($mn)	142.9
Price-to-NTA-per-share ratio	3.1
5-year share price return (% p.a.)	10.1
Dividend reinvestment plan	No

Sector: Materials	Company	Sector
Price/earnings ratio (times)	21.9	13.2
Dividend yield (%)	6.5	4.4

Perth-based GR Engineering, founded in 1986, is an engineering consulting and contracting company with a specialty in the construction of processing plants for the gold and base metal industries. Its subsidiary Upstream Production Solutions is a specialist provider of engineering services to the oil and gas industry. GR Engineering has offices in Perth, Brisbane and Indonesia, as well as operations in Europe and Africa.

Latest business results (June 2019, full year)

Project delays sent business tumbling, with steep falls in revenues and profits. In particular, little more than preliminary engineering design and procurement activities were undertaken at the major Thunderbird mineral sands project in Western Australia, and consequently revenue receipts were substantially below the company's expectations. In addition, the company has reported delays to the start of other projects that it was expecting to begin during the year. As a result, its Mineral Processing division reported revenues more than halving to $93.8 million, and with the pre-tax profit plunging from $15.7 million to $3.7 million. By contrast, the other division, Oil and Gas, enjoyed a good year, mainly from the provision of coal seam gas services in Queensland and offshore and onshore operations and maintenance work in Western Australia. This division's revenues rose 9 per cent to $88.4 million, with the pre-tax profit nearly quadrupling to $5.1 million. In the previous year this division's profits had fallen 77 per cent.

Outlook

GR Engineering has a strong reputation in its fields of operation. In particular, it has a strong weighting to the gold industry, and it would be a significant beneficiary of any new gold boom, which could lead to the reopening of many gold mines and the construction of new processing facilities. It is also working to diversify into new commodities, and has been involved in strategic studies associated with uranium and some other minerals. During the June 2019 year the company procured four important engineering contracts, including a $46 million contract for the Sandy Ridge Kaolin Mine project in Western Australia and a $24 million contract for the construction of a paste production facility at the Fosterville gold operation near Bendigo, Victoria. The Oil and Gas division continues to manage and execute maintenance services on more than 3500 coal seam gas wells in Queensland. It is also involved in operations and maintenance work for oil and gas production facilities in the Perth Basin. At June 2019 GR Engineering had net cash holdings of nearly $31 million, and it is seeking further growth opportunities.

Year to 30 June	2018	2019
Revenues ($mn)	283.6	182.3
EBIT ($mn)	15.7	8.4
EBIT margin (%)	5.5	4.6
Profit before tax ($mn)	16.2	8.8
Profit after tax ($mn)	11.6	6.5
Earnings per share (c)	7.59	4.25
Cash flow per share (c)	8.49	5.19
Dividend (c)	11	6
Percentage franked	55	67
Net tangible assets per share ($)	0.34	0.30
Interest cover (times)	~	~
Return on equity (%)	23.0	13.2
Debt-to-equity ratio (%)	~	~
Current ratio	2.5	2.1

GUD Holdings Limited

ASX code: GUD　　　　　　　　　　　　　　　www.gud.com.au

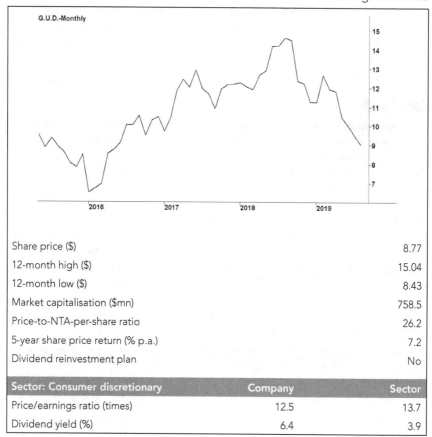

G.U.D.-Monthly

Share price ($)	8.77
12-month high ($)	15.04
12-month low ($)	8.43
Market capitalisation ($mn)	758.5
Price-to-NTA-per-share ratio	26.2
5-year share price return (% p.a.)	7.2
Dividend reinvestment plan	No

Sector: Consumer discretionary	Company	Sector
Price/earnings ratio (times)	12.5	13.7
Dividend yield (%)	6.4	3.9

GUD, based in Melbourne and founded in 1940, is a manufacturer and distributor of a diversified range of auto and industrial products. Following a series of acquisitions and divestments, its main automotive brands now include Ryco, Wesfil, Goss, BWI—incorporating the Narva and Projecta brands—Griffiths Equipment, IM Group, AA Gaskets and Disc Brakes Australia. The company also manufactures and distributes Davey water pumps and water treatment products.

Latest business results (June 2019, full year)

Revenues and profits rose once more, despite a slowdown in the second half. The Automotive division saw sales up by nearly 12 per cent, though only 1 per cent of this was attributed to organic growth, with the remainder due to recent acquisitions. Underlying EBIT rose by 5 per cent. This division contributes about three-quarters of company sales, but is responsible for more than 90 per cent of profit. Wesfil and Ryco enjoyed another good year, and there was a particularly strong performance from Disc Brakes Australia, which was acquired in July 2018. But AA Gaskets, IM Group and BWI were hurt by disappointing sales and some rising costs, although the company was generally able to implement price increases to offset the increasing expense of imported products. The Davey water products business reported a 3 per cent increase in sales and underlying EBIT, with growth in all key geographic regions.

Outlook

Having divested itself of a series of businesses that included Sunbeam home appliances, Oates cleaning products, Dexion storage products and Lock Focus locking systems, GUD is now focused on the steadily growing Australian automotive after-market sector. It continues to broaden the product ranges for its various brands and it is also seeking to expand exports. It hopes to secure further acquisitions and has developed a set of new acquisition criteria that it believes will boost profitability. It has also nurtured a pool of potential managers for newly acquired businesses. Nevertheless, a concern is the rise of private-label brands among some of its customers. The company estimates that this reduced June 2019 revenues by around $4 million. It has also expressed concern about growing competition for its important Ryco filtration business. It has developed a new strategic plan to boost profitability at its low-margin Davey business, and expects to see progress in this division over the coming two years. GUD forecasts just modest growth for all its businesses in the June 2020 year, though it believes the long-term outlook is rosy.

Year to 30 June	2018	2019
Revenues ($mn)	396.7	434.1
Automotive (%)	75	76
Davey (%)	25	24
EBIT ($mn)	83.8	89.4
EBIT margin (%)	21.1	20.6
Gross margin (%)	49.4	48.6
Profit before tax ($mn)	76.8	82.1
Profit after tax ($mn)	55.2	60.9
Earnings per share (c)	64.09	70.39
Cash flow per share (c)	68.61	74.21
Dividend (c)	52	56
Percentage franked	100	100
Net tangible assets per share ($)	0.35	0.33
Interest cover (times)	11.9	12.2
Return on equity (%)	23.7	22.4
Debt-to-equity ratio (%)	34.8	47.6
Current ratio	2.8	2.9

GWA Group Limited

ASX code: GWA   www.gwagroup.com.au

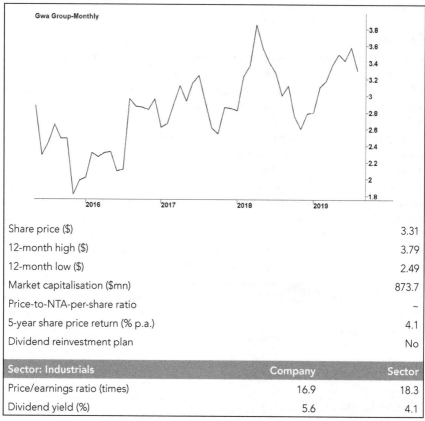

Share price ($)	3.31
12-month high ($)	3.79
12-month low ($)	2.49
Market capitalisation ($mn)	873.7
Price-to-NTA-per-share ratio	~
5-year share price return (% p.a.)	4.1
Dividend reinvestment plan	No

Sector: Industrials	Company	Sector
Price/earnings ratio (times)	16.9	18.3
Dividend yield (%)	5.6	4.1

Brisbane-based GWA is a prominent designer, importer and distributor of residential and commercial bathroom and kitchen products, marketed under brands that include Caroma, Dorf, Fowler, Stylus and Clark. In July 2018 it sold its GWA Door and Access Systems business and in April 2019 it acquired the New Zealand company Methven, which designs and manufactures showers, taps and valves.

Latest business results (June 2019, full year)

For a third successive year sales and profits rose by single-digit amounts. This was a good result, as the company reported that the overall bathroom and fixtures market declined by 1.4 per cent during the year, meaning that GWA was able to boost market share for the fourth consecutive year. The market slowdown was driven mainly by a decline in new home construction, although the home renovation business was also weak. Housing-related sales contribute about 84 per cent of the company's revenues. The remaining 16 per cent derives from commercial building activity, and this market edged up during the year. Victorian sales were especially strong, with New South Wales, South Australia and New Zealand also positive. But weakness continued in Queensland and Western Australia. Strong demand continued for the company's Caroma Cleanflush range of rimless toilets, with Cleanflush sales up 24 per cent, having jumped by 73 per cent in the previous year. Nearly 12 weeks of income from the Methven acquisition contributed to the good result, although revenues and profits edged up even without this benefit.

Outlook

After a long series of restructurings GWA is now almost completely exposed to a bathroom and kitchen fixtures market that is worth around $1.4 billion annually. It claims market shares as high as 50 per cent for some of its products. It has targeted three sectors — renovations and replacements, commercial construction and detached housing — and is developing new, high-margin products specifically for these markets. It sees excellent potential from its $112 million acquisition of Methven, which is the New Zealand leader in the taps and showers market, with a strong presence in Australia, as well as operations in the United Kingdom and Asia. Methven owns significant intellectual property, which GWA expects to leverage for its own products. It also expects annual cost synergies of at least $4.8 million by 2021. GWA hopes to implement price increases during the June 2020 year. Nevertheless, it does not expect a significant housing recovery in the near term. It is also vulnerable to growing competition and to the dollar weakness.

Year to 30 June	2018	2019
Revenues ($mn)	358.6	381.7
EBIT ($mn)	76.2	77.4
EBIT margin (%)	21.3	20.3
Gross margin (%)	43.0	42.6
Profit before tax ($mn)	71.4	73.6
Profit after tax ($mn)	50.1	51.8
Earnings per share (c)	19.00	19.61
Cash flow per share (c)	19.77	20.97
Dividend (c)	18	18.5
Percentage franked	100	100
Net tangible assets per share ($)	0.18	~
Interest cover (times)	15.8	20.6
Return on equity (%)	15.3	14.6
Debt-to-equity ratio (%)	29.1	37.0
Current ratio	3.2	2.7

Hansen Technologies Limited

ASX code: HSN

www.hansencx.com

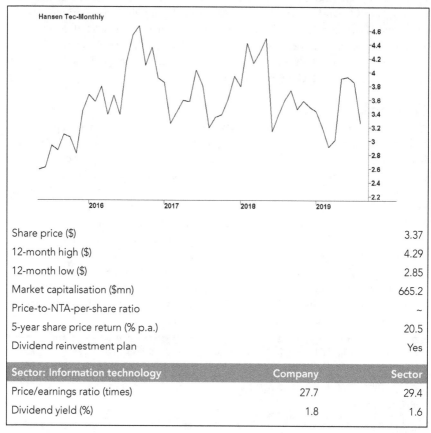

Share price ($)	3.37
12-month high ($)	4.29
12-month low ($)	2.85
Market capitalisation ($mn)	665.2
Price-to-NTA-per-share ratio	~
5-year share price return (% p.a.)	20.5
Dividend reinvestment plan	Yes

Sector: Information technology	Company	Sector
Price/earnings ratio (times)	27.7	29.4
Dividend yield (%)	1.8	1.6

Melbourne company Hansen Technologies dates back to an IT business launched in 1971. It later moved into the development of billing software systems and is today a major global provider of these services, specialising in the electricity, gas, water, pay television and telecommunications sectors. It also provides outsourced facilities management and IT services from its purpose-built data centres in Melbourne. Hansen has offices around the world, and overseas business represents more than 80 per cent of company turnover. In June 2019 it acquired Canadian software developer Sigma Systems.

Latest business results (June 2019, full year)

Sales edged up, although this reflected one month of revenues from the Sigma acquisition. Otherwise, sales and profits were down, due to a drop in one-off licence fees and some reduced project work, following the ending in the previous year of a major project. More than 60 per cent of income was represented by recurring revenues. During the year the company won some important new contracts, including a major deal to deliver a next-generation meter data management system in Sweden and a large contract to supply its second billing system in Finland.

Outlook

Though a small company, Hansen has developed a high reputation for its services. Once it does business with a customer it stands to benefit further from a long-term stream of recurring revenue. It has made 10 important acquisitions over 11 years and is seeking to make more. In particular, it is aiming at acquisitions that own intellectual property and with recurring revenue streams that will help Hansen expand to new regions or market segments. Its July 2017 acquisition of Enoro has given it significant strength in the Scandinavian energy billing sector and in June 2019 Hansen completed by far its largest-ever acquisition, Toronto-based Sigma Systems, bought for $164 million. This business is a leading global provider of catalogue-driven software products for telecommunications, media and technology companies, and Hansen believes it will provide many cross-selling opportunities as well as substantial synergy benefits. The Enoro and Sigma businesses together have added significant depth and diversity to Hansen's offerings, and the company expects them to drive future growth. To help reduce costs it has opened a new development centre in Vietnam, and the Sigma acquisition has delivered another large development centre, in India. Hansen's early forecast is for revenues in the June 2020 year of around $305 million to $310 million with EBITDA of $70 million to $76 million, up from $55.8 million in June 2019.

Year to 30 June	2018	2019
Revenues ($mn)	230.8	231.3
EBIT ($mn)	39.6	32.6
EBIT margin (%)	17.2	14.1
Profit before tax ($mn)	37.7	30.6
Profit after tax ($mn)	29.5	24.0
Earnings per share (c)	15.10	12.19
Cash flow per share (c)	25.53	23.74
Dividend (c)	6	6
Percentage franked	100	93
Net tangible assets per share ($)	~	~
Interest cover (times)	20.2	16.4
Return on equity (%)	15.5	10.0
Debt-to-equity ratio (%)	1.7	59.6
Current ratio	1.3	1.9

Harvey Norman Holdings Limited

ASX code: HVN　　　　　　　　　www.harveynormanholdings.com.au

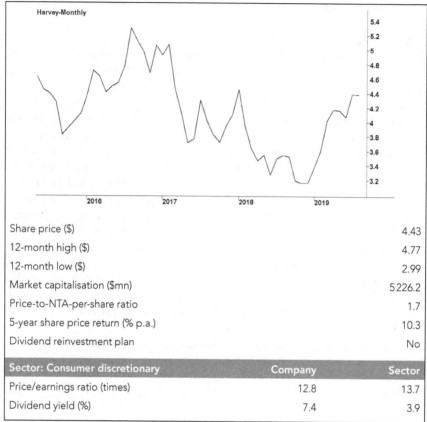

Share price ($)	4.43
12-month high ($)	4.77
12-month low ($)	2.99
Market capitalisation ($mn)	5 226.2
Price-to-NTA-per-share ratio	1.7
5-year share price return (% p.a.)	10.3
Dividend reinvestment plan	No

Sector: Consumer discretionary	Company	Sector
Price/earnings ratio (times)	12.8	13.7
Dividend yield (%)	7.4	3.9

Sydney-based Harvey Norman, established in 1982, operates a chain of 285 retail stores specialising in electrical and electronic goods, home appliances, furniture, flooring, carpets and manchester, throughout Australia, New Zealand, Ireland, Northern Ireland, Singapore, Malaysia, Slovenia and Croatia, under the Harvey Norman, Domayne and Joyce Mayne banners. The Australian stores are independently held as part of a franchise operation, from which Harvey Norman receives income for advisory and advertising services. It also receives a considerable amount of income from its own stores, from its $2.99 billion property portfolio and from the provision of finance to franchisees and customers.

Latest business results (June 2019, full year)

Buoyant business at many of the company's 90 overseas stores, bolstered by the weak dollar, offset soft conditions at home, and Harvey Norman reported a positive result. All overseas regions recorded higher sales. The Singapore and Malaysia segment was especially strong, with sales up 16 per cent to $568 million and the pre-tax profit jumping 48 per cent. The Ireland and Northern Ireland segment was also strong, with sales rising 18 per cent to $378 million and profits surging more than five-fold, though from a low base. New Zealand, the largest overseas contributor, recorded higher sales, but profits were down. By contrast, total sales by Harvey Norman's Australian franchisees of $5.7 billion were down 2 per cent. Franchise income received by Harvey Norman fell 2 per cent to $839 million, with franchise profits falling 12 per cent. Property profits rose 8.5 per cent.

Outlook

For the second straight year, Harvey Norman's overseas operations have recorded robust growth, at a time when domestic sales are weak. The company attributes this in part to its policy of establishing a premium flagship store in each of its countries of operation, raising brand awareness among local consumers and contributing to stronger business. Consequently, Harvey Norman plans further offshore expansion, and expects to open 21 new overseas stores by June 2021. Singapore and Malaysia have become particularly buoyant markets, and 17 of the stores will be in those countries. The company has also reported that its Australian stores have made a positive start to the new financial year, and that with interest rates low and the economy firm, and with indications of a housing recovery, the signs were positive for a good year domestically. Its stores operate with high levels of fixed costs, so a modest rise in sales can deliver a much bigger rise in profits, although the reverse is also true.

Year to 30 June	2018	2019
Revenues ($mn)	3156.1	3404.9
Retail (%)	62	65
Franchising operations (%)	28	24
Property (%)	9	10
EBIT ($mn)	549.3	598.1
EBIT margin (%)	17.4	17.6
Gross margin (%)	33.5	32.4
Profit before tax ($mn)	530.2	574.6
Profit after tax ($mn)	375.4	402.3
Earnings per share (c)	33.21	34.70
Cash flow per share (c)	40.72	42.05
Dividend (c)	30	33
Percentage franked	100	100
Net tangible assets per share ($)	2.55	2.63
Interest cover (times)	28.6	25.4
Return on equity (%)	13.2	13.2
Debt-to-equity ratio (%)	25.7	19.6
Current ratio	1.6	1.6

Infomedia Limited

ASX code: IFM   www.infomedia.com.au

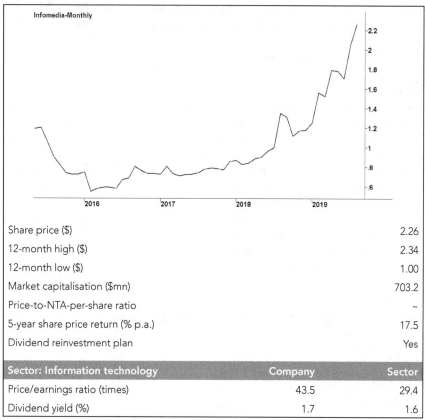

Share price ($)	2.26
12-month high ($)	2.34
12-month low ($)	1.00
Market capitalisation ($mn)	703.2
Price-to-NTA-per-share ratio	~
5-year share price return (% p.a.)	17.5
Dividend reinvestment plan	Yes

Sector: Information technology	Company	Sector
Price/earnings ratio (times)	43.5	29.4
Dividend yield (%)	1.7	1.6

Sydney electronic data company Infomedia was formed in 1990, and has grown into a world leader in the development of specialised electronic catalogues. Its main product is the Microcat electronic parts catalogue for the automotive industry, with versions for most leading car companies. Sold to customers in 186 countries, the catalogue enables service personnel in a motor dealership to identify the correct replacement parts for a vehicle. The company also produces the Superservice data management product, which provides automotive dealers with a range of service, repair and warranty management tools. In December 2018 Infomedia acquired the Australian automotive data analytics company Nidasu.

Latest business results (June 2019, full year)

Infomedia posted an excellent result, with double-digit gains in sales and profits. With the rise in earnings outstripping revenue gains, the company achieved a solid boost to its profit margins. A new global electronic parts contract with Nissan made a strong contribution, but the company also enjoyed good organic growth in all regions, as well as benefits from the Nidasu acquisition. Infomedia reports its results on a regional basis. The best growth in earnings came from the Americas region, with the pre-tax profit up 34 per cent on a 9 per cent gain in sales. The other two regions, Asia Pacific and Europe/Middle East/Africa, both achieved double-digit increases in sales and profits.

Outlook

In a fiercely competitive automobile market, car dealerships now generally make more profit from the supply of parts and service than they do from actual car sales. It is the fast-growing parts and service sector that is the target market for Infomedia. The company has identified a series of trends that it believes will drive change in this market, including increased digitisation and moves to electric and hybrid vehicles, and believes these will mean more complex parts in the average car. Its acquisition of Nidasu has greatly enhanced its data analytics capability and it believes this will help its clients reduce their operating costs and retain customers. With recurring revenues representing more than 95 per cent of turnover, Infomedia has a consistent and highly predictable revenue stream. It continues to invest heavily in research and development, and has a pipeline of new products for gradual release. However, with 85 per cent of its sales abroad, it is highly exposed to currency fluctuations. At June 2019 Infomedia had no debt and cash holdings of more than $15 million, and it continues to seek out further small-scale acquisitions.

Year to 30 June	2018	2019
Revenues ($mn)	72.9	84.6
EBIT ($mn)	16.2	22.2
EBIT margin (%)	22.2	26.2
Profit before tax ($mn)	15.7	21.1
Profit after tax ($mn)	12.9	16.1
Earnings per share (c)	4.16	5.19
Cash flow per share (c)	8.27	10.60
Dividend (c)	3.1	3.9
Percentage franked	100	0
Net tangible assets per share ($)	0.01	~
Interest cover (times)	28.8	20.2
Return on equity (%)	24.8	27.3
Debt-to-equity ratio (%)	~	~
Current ratio	1.9	1.5

Insurance Australia Group Limited

ASX code: IAG

www.iag.com.au

Share price ($)	8.04
12-month high ($)	8.74
12-month low ($)	6.53
Market capitalisation ($mn)	18 580.4
Price-to-NTA-per-share ratio	5.6
5-year share price return (% p.a.)	7.7
Dividend reinvestment plan	Yes

Sector: Financials	Company	Sector
Price/earnings ratio (times)	21.5	15.0
Dividend yield (%)	4.0	5.9

Sydney-based Insurance Australia Group (IAG), formerly NRMA Insurance, dates back to 1925, when the National Roads and Motorists' Association began providing insurance to its members in New South Wales and the Australian Capital Territory. It subsequently demutualised and listed on the ASX. It has grown through acquisition, and is now a major presence in Australia and New Zealand. Its brands include NRMA Insurance, CGU, SGIO, SGIC, WFI and Swann Insurance, all in Australia, as well as NZI, State, Lumley Insurance and AMI in New Zealand. In Victoria it provides general insurance products under the RACV brand through a distribution and underwriting relationship with RACV, and it underwrites the Coles Insurance brand nationally through a distribution agreement with Coles. It maintains operations in India and Malaysia, but has sold its businesses in Thailand, Indonesia and Vietnam.

Latest business results (June 2019, full year)

Profits fell, although they were up when the financial results from discontinued businesses were included. This was mainly the profit from the sale of the company's Thai operations. Net claim costs of $627 million from natural disasters were responsible for much of the profit decline, along with significantly reduced reserve releases. Premium revenues rose 3.1 per cent, thanks mainly to insurance rate increases. The underlying insurance margin — insurance and investment profits as a percentage of premiums, a key measure of profitability — rose from 14.1 per cent in the June 2018 year to 16.6 per cent. New Zealand business — representing 22 per cent of total company premium revenues — was once again especially strong. Net natural disaster costs there were sharply down, and the company continued to raise its rates, generating a substantial rise in profits.

Outlook

IAG, together with Suncorp, occupies a strong position in the Australian and New Zealand personal insurance business, giving it considerable pricing power. But the insurance business is inherently volatile, and any unforeseen major natural disaster has the capacity to take a big chunk from the company's earnings. IAG was previously intent on expansion throughout Asia. However, following an evaluation of these operations it has sold its Thai, Indonesian and Vietnamese subsidiaries, and is reviewing its holdings in India and Malaysia. The company believes it can achieve a premium revenue increase in the low single digits for the June 2020 year, based especially on further rate increases. However, it sees profits being affected by higher regulatory costs and lower investment returns, as well as by the company's accelerated investment in new technologies.

Year to 30 June	2018	2019
Premium revenues ($mn)	11 522.0	11 942.0
Profit before tax ($mn)	1 410.0	1 332.0
Profit after tax ($mn)	947.0	871.0
Earnings per share (c)	40.08	37.45
Cash flow per share (c)	47.06	44.75
Dividend (c)	34	32
Percentage franked	100	81
Net tangible assets per share ($)	1.47	1.43
Return on equity (%)	14.3	13.3
Debt-to-equity ratio (%)	21.8	23.0

Integrated Research Limited

ASX code: IRI

www.ir.com

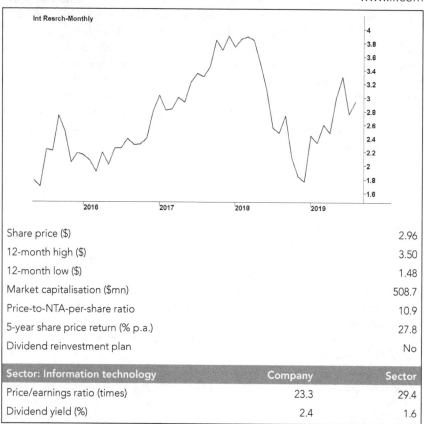

Share price ($)	2.96
12-month high ($)	3.50
12-month low ($)	1.48
Market capitalisation ($mn)	508.7
Price-to-NTA-per-share ratio	10.9
5-year share price return (% p.a.)	27.8
Dividend reinvestment plan	No

Sector: Information technology	Company	Sector
Price/earnings ratio (times)	23.3	29.4
Dividend yield (%)	2.4	1.6

Sydney-based Integrated Research, founded in 1988, is a software developer. Its main product, Prognosis, provides performance monitoring, diagnostics and reporting functions for an organisation's IT systems. It has particular application for high-volume environments, including ATM and EFTPOS systems, telecommunications networks, IT server infrastructure and internet services such as online banking and travel booking services. The company maintains offices in Australia, Britain, Germany, Singapore and the United States, and exports to more than 60 countries, with overseas business accounting for more than 95 per cent of company turnover. Customers include many of the world's largest organisations, such as stock exchanges, banks, credit card companies, airlines and universities, as well as government departments.

Latest business results (June 2019, full year)

Revenues and profits rose in a good result, driven by 19 per cent growth in licence fees to $62.8 million, and greatly enhanced by the weakness of the dollar. Maintenance fee revenues fell 3 per cent to $25 million. Testing service revenues also fell, down 4 per cent to $5 million. Consulting services were flat from the previous year, at $7.4

million. The company segments its sales into three broad product lines. The largest of these, communications, saw sales down 7 per cent to $51 million, with growth from Cisco customers offset by lower licence sales for Avaya and Microsoft Skype for Business customers. By contrast, sales to infrastructure customers rose 28 per cent to $26.3 million, as existing customers added extra modules to their purchases. The payments segment achieved the best result, with revenues soaring 92 per cent, with nine new customers during the year, and existing customers buying more. The company maintained its high level of research and development spending, up 17 per cent to $17.9 million.

Outlook

Integrated Research supplies software that monitors IT systems and thereby enables clients to improve customer service as well as avoid the risks associated with computer outages. Thanks to strong relationships with key hardware suppliers and the high reputation of its products it is experiencing steady growth in demand, with a long-term recurring revenue base of licence fees that will underpin future expansion. Renewal rates for its services remain at around 95 per cent. The company also finds that though a customer's initial purchase may be small, subsequent purchases will often include additional modules. It is introducing a new Software-as-a-Service business, with the launch of a cloud-based platform. At June 2019 Integrated Research had no debt and more than $9 million in cash holdings.

Year to 30 June	2018	2019
Revenues ($mn)	91.2	100.8
EBIT ($mn)	25.8	28.9
EBIT margin (%)	28.3	28.7
Profit before tax ($mn)	26.3	29.6
Profit after tax ($mn)	19.2	21.9
Earnings per share (c)	11.19	12.72
Cash flow per share (c)	17.36	19.32
Dividend (c)	6.5	7.25
Percentage franked	100	100
Net tangible assets per share ($)	0.21	0.27
Interest cover (times)	~	~
Return on equity (%)	36.1	34.2
Debt-to-equity ratio (%)	~	~
Current ratio	1.5	1.8

IPH Limited

ASX code: IPH

www.iphltd.com.au

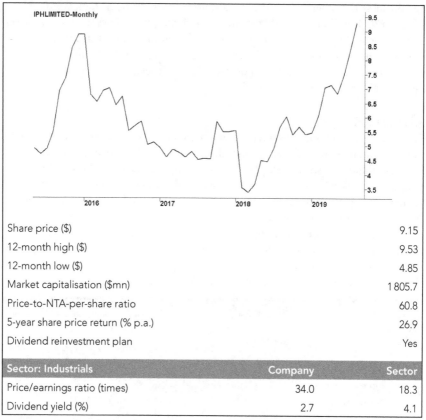

Share price ($)	9.15
12-month high ($)	9.53
12-month low ($)	4.85
Market capitalisation ($mn)	1 805.7
Price-to-NTA-per-share ratio	60.8
5-year share price return (% p.a.)	26.9
Dividend reinvestment plan	Yes

Sector: Industrials	Company	Sector
Price/earnings ratio (times)	34.0	18.3
Dividend yield (%)	2.7	4.1

Sydney-based IPH, with roots that stretch back to 1887, is a holding company for a group of businesses offering a wide range of intellectual property services and products. These include the filing, prosecution, enforcement and management of patents, designs, trademarks and other intellectual property. The company also develops data analytics software through its subsidiary Practice Insight. IPH operates from offices in Australia, New Zealand, Singapore, Malaysia, China, Indonesia, Thailand and Hong Kong. In August 2019 it acquired its listed rival Xenith IP Group.

Latest business results (June 2019, full year)

Organic growth, acquisitions and the weaker dollar all contributed to an excellent result. For reporting purposes the company segments its operations into Australian and New Zealand businesses and Asian businesses. The former represent about 65 per cent of total turnover, with revenues up by more than 10 per cent for the year. Total Australian patent filings increased by nearly 1 per cent. Australia/ New Zealand profits at the EBITDA level were up 14 per cent, thanks especially to cost efficiencies from the merger of several of the company's businesses, as well as a continuing improved performance from its AJ Park business in New Zealand, which was acquired in 2017. Asian operations achieved a 24 per cent jump in profits, with revenues up by 20 per cent, and an increase in patent filing activity in most countries. The company's very small data analytics software operation, Practice Insight, sold several of its businesses, and revenues were down, with another loss for the year.

Outlook

IPH has established itself as one of the leaders in Australia, New Zealand and South-East Asia in the intellectual property business. It has grown steadily, through organic growth and acquisition, and now operates through eight subsidiary companies. As it grows it achieves economies of scale that boost margins. It has become the largest filer of patents in Singapore, where it opened an office in 1997. It classifies the US, Western Europe, Japan and South Korea as the primary markets in its business, and its expressed aim is to establish itself in other regions. Its $192 million acquisition of Xenith has boosted its share of the domestic intellectual property market from around 20 per cent to more than 30 per cent and is also expected to deliver cost synergies over three years that will further boost margins. It is now actively seeking further acquisitions. Having divested itself of much of its activities, the Practice Insight software business will now focus solely on its autonomous time-keeping tool WiseTime.

Year to 30 June	2018	2019
Revenues ($mn)	222.0	252.5
EBIT ($mn)	54.8	73.2
EBIT margin (%)	24.7	29.0
Profit before tax ($mn)	53.3	70.6
Profit after tax ($mn)	40.7	53.1
Earnings per share (c)	20.79	26.91
Cash flow per share (c)	27.48	33.33
Dividend (c)	22.5	25
Percentage franked	45	55
Net tangible assets per share ($)	0.01	0.15
Interest cover (times)	36.4	28.5
Return on equity (%)	16.0	19.2
Debt-to-equity ratio (%)	5.2	10.6
Current ratio	2.7	3.9

IRESS Limited

ASX code: IRE   www.iress.com

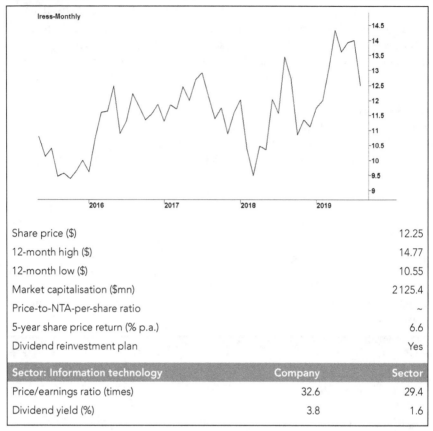

Share price ($)	12.25
12-month high ($)	14.77
12-month low ($)	10.55
Market capitalisation ($mn)	2 125.4
Price-to-NTA-per-share ratio	~
5-year share price return (% p.a.)	6.6
Dividend reinvestment plan	Yes

Sector: Information technology	Company	Sector
Price/earnings ratio (times)	32.6	29.4
Dividend yield (%)	3.8	1.6

Melbourne-based IRESS was founded in 1993. It produces the IRESS (Integrated Real-time Equity System) share market information system, used widely throughout the Australian investment community. Within the IRESS system it offers a portfolio of information and trading products with numerous applications for stockbrokers, fund managers and other financial professionals. It is also active in wealth management services, with its Xplan financial planning software. A third activity is the Mortgages division, which provides mortgage processing software. The company has expanded its operations to New Zealand, Europe, North America, Singapore, Hong Kong and South Africa. In May 2019 it acquired international market data provider QuantHouse.

Latest business results (June 2019, half year)

Revenues rose, and profits were up at the EBITDA level, but increases in depreciation charges and interest payments drove down the pre-tax and after-tax results. The core domestic business saw sales and profits edge up, with increasing demand for Xplan financial planning software in the wake of the Banking Royal Commission. There was also continuing strong demand from fund managers for investment management software products. British business was robust, with strong demand for Xplan software and a contribution from the QuantHouse acquisition. Australia/Pacific and Europe together generate more than 80 per cent of company turnover. Other smaller operations in South Africa and North America delivered revenue growth.

Outlook

IRESS's businesses are strongly geared to levels of financial market activity, which can lead to volatility in its operations. It is also vulnerable to structural changes in the financial sector, with automated systems to a degree displacing active fund managers. Nevertheless, its products are widely used in Australia, and the company reports high levels of customer loyalty. It benefits from the steady growth of superannuation assets. It has been enjoying success with its new Xplan Prime product for the financial planning industry. Its acquisition of QuantHouse for 39 million euros has given it a highly complementary business. QuantHouse provides clients around the world with more than 145 data feeds of financial information, with an emphasis on Europe, North America and Asia. IRESS has been placing an increasing focus on data provision, and the acquisition will provide opportunities to achieve cost synergies and scale. It is enjoying some good growth in the UK, particularly for its private wealth software, along with a strong pipeline of growth opportunities for its mortgage software. The company's forecast is for 2019 full-year profit growth of 6 per cent to 11 per cent, although much will depend on currency rate trends.

Year to 31 December	2017	2018
Revenues ($mn)	430.0	464.6
EBIT ($mn)	82.2	91.1
EBIT margin (%)	19.1	19.6
Profit before tax ($mn)	77.8	85.0
Profit after tax ($mn)	59.8	64.1
Earnings per share (c)	35.40	37.60
Cash flow per share (c)	50.25	53.31
Dividend (c)	44	46
Percentage franked	60	47
Interest cover (times)	18.5	14.9
Return on equity (%)	14.8	15.5
Half year to 30 June	2018	2019
Revenues ($mn)	229.7	241.8
Profit before tax ($mn)	41.8	41.5
Profit after tax ($mn)	32.0	30.4
Earnings per share (c)	18.90	17.70
Dividend (c)	16	16
Percentage franked	60	10
Net tangible assets per share ($)	~	~
Debt-to-equity ratio (%)	46.4	47.4
Current ratio	1.5	1.1

JB Hi-Fi Limited

ASX code: JBH

investors.jbhifi.com.au

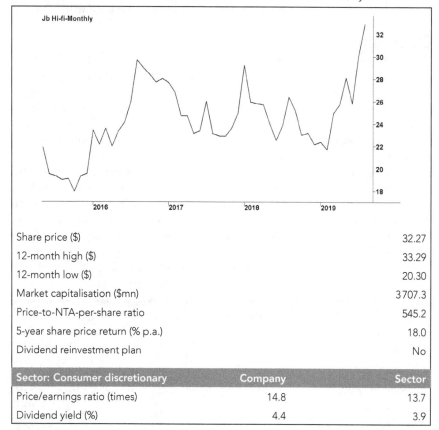

Share price ($)	32.27
12-month high ($)	33.29
12-month low ($)	20.30
Market capitalisation ($mn)	3707.3
Price-to-NTA-per-share ratio	545.2
5-year share price return (% p.a.)	18.0
Dividend reinvestment plan	No

Sector: Consumer discretionary	Company	Sector
Price/earnings ratio (times)	14.8	13.7
Dividend yield (%)	4.4	3.9

Melbourne-based JB Hi-Fi dates back to the opening in 1974 of a single recorded music store in the Melbourne suburb of East Keilor. It has since grown into a nationwide chain of home electronic and home appliance products outlets, and it has also expanded to New Zealand. In 2016 it acquired The Good Guys chain of home appliance stores. Its JB Hi-Fi Solutions division sells to the commercial, educational and insurance sectors. The company also maintains a growing online presence. At the end of June 2019 it operated 196 JB Hi-Fi and JB Hi-Fi Home stores in Australia, 14 JB Hi-Fi stores in New Zealand and 105 The Good Guys stores in Australia.

Latest business results (June 2019, full year)

In a challenging retail environment, JB Hi-Fi posted a good result, with increases in sales and profits. Domestic sales for JB Hi-Fi rose by 4.1 per cent, or 2.8 per cent on a same-store basis, driven by the communications, audio, fitness, games hardware and connected technology categories. By contrast, movie and music software sales again fell sharply. Online sales grew 23 per cent to $258 million. The Good Guys recorded sales growth of 2.2 per cent, or 0.9 per cent on a same-store basis, with particular strength in refrigeration, laundry, dishwashers, televisions, communications equipment and computers. Profits rose solidly for The Good Guys, although margins remained substantially lower than prevailing at the JB Hi-Fi Australia stores. New Zealand sales rose 2 per cent, though on a same-store basis the rise was 8.2 per cent. During the year the company opened five new JB Hi-Fi stores in Australia. It closed two in Australia and one in New Zealand. It also opened two new The Good Guys stores.

Outlook

JB Hi-Fi has a strong brand image throughout Australia and great customer loyalty. It has shown an impressive ability to contain costs. It continues to open new stores, though at a slower pace than in previous years. It is boosting floor space at its stores for growth categories such as mobile phones, gaming and connected technology, and is trialling new services such as television installation. Its JB Hi-Fi Solutions division delivered double-digit sales growth in the June 2019 year, and is expected eventually to generate around $500 million in annual sales. Nevertheless, the company operates in a fast-evolving and highly competitive business environment. It is also quite vulnerable to changes in consumer sentiment. Its early forecast is for June 2020 sales of approximately $7.25 billion.

Year to 30 June	2018	2019
Revenues ($mn)	6854.3	7095.3
JB Australia (%)	66	67
The Good Guys (%)	31	30
JB New Zealand (%)	3	3
EBIT ($mn)	350.6	372.9
EBIT margin (%)	5.1	5.3
Gross margin (%)	21.4	21.5
Profit before tax ($mn)	334.5	359.3
Profit after tax ($mn)	233.2	249.8
Earnings per share (c)	203.14	217.41
Cash flow per share (c)	256.36	266.32
Dividend (c)	132	142
Percentage franked	100	100
Net tangible assets per share ($)	~	0.06
Interest cover (times)	21.8	27.4
Return on equity (%)	25.9	25.1
Debt-to-equity ratio (%)	41.9	30.6
Current ratio	1.3	1.4

Jumbo Interactive Limited

ASX code: JIN www.jumbointeractive.com

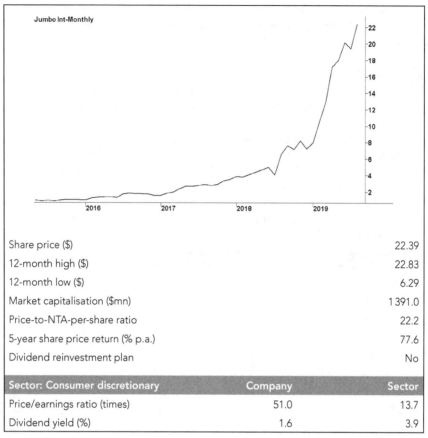

Share price ($)	22.39
12-month high ($)	22.83
12-month low ($)	6.29
Market capitalisation ($mn)	1391.0
Price-to-NTA-per-share ratio	22.2
5-year share price return (% p.a.)	77.6
Dividend reinvestment plan	No

Sector: Consumer discretionary	Company	Sector
Price/earnings ratio (times)	51.0	13.7
Dividend yield (%)	1.6	3.9

Jumbo Interactive was founded in Brisbane in 1995 as an internet service provider, but has since evolved into a major operator of internet services for lotteries. Its core business, Oz Lotteries, involves the sale of lottery services for Tabcorp at its ozlotteries.com website. These lotteries include OzLotto, Powerball, Lotto and Lucky Lotteries. It also manages lotteries for charitable organisations.

Latest business results (June 2019, full year)

Jumbo reported a superb result, with profits more than doubling on a 65 per cent rise in revenues. A new Powerball format has become a key marketing tool, with two $100 million Powerball jackpots in August 2018 and January 2019. Altogether there were 49 large jackpots during the year, with an average value of $38.4 million, up from 32, with an average value of $28.4 million, in the June 2018 year. The total transaction value during the year of all Jumbo's business was $320.7 million, a big jump from $183.1 million in the June 2018 year. The company reported that it had 761 863 active customers during the year, up from 437 540 in the previous year, with an average spend per active customer of $385.44, up from $371.13. It gained 444 004 new accounts, compared with 214 908 in the June 2018 year.

Outlook

Jumbo is a significant beneficiary of the Australian love of gambling. A new software platform and a vigorous marketing campaign have helped stimulate its recent growth. It is also enjoying success with new apps for mobile devices, and reports that these have succeeded in attracting a new demographic of younger customers. Consequently, 23.5 per cent of Australian lottery ticket sales are now online, up from 16.8 per cent in the June 2018 year, and this ratio is expected to grow. However, the company's sales and profits are driven to a certain degree by large jackpot activity, and the number of these can vary from year to year. Jumbo has expressed interest in exporting its software technology to overseas markets, and notes that the global lottery ticket market is worth some $445 billion per year, with only about 7 per cent of the tickets sold online. However, an earlier German venture was not successful and has been closed. Jumbo also expects continuing strong growth from the charity market. Its own target is for a total of at least $1 billion in ticket sales by 2022. At June 2019 the company had no debt and more than $84 million in cash holdings.

Year to 30 June	2018	2019
Revenues ($mn)	39.8	65.2
EBIT ($mn)	16.2	36.8
EBIT margin (%)	40.8	56.4
Profit before tax ($mn)	17.1	38.2
Profit after tax ($mn)	11.8	26.4
Earnings per share (c)	22.67	43.86
Cash flow per share (c)	28.79	49.56
Dividend (c)	18.5	36.5
Percentage franked	100	100
Net tangible assets per share ($)	0.63	1.01
Interest cover (times)	~	~
Return on equity (%)	26.1	42.4
Debt-to-equity ratio (%)	~	~
Current ratio	3.2	3.6

Lifestyle Communities Limited

ASX code: LIC www.lifestylecommunities.com.au

Share price ($)	7.33
12-month high ($)	7.49
12-month low ($)	4.81
Market capitalisation ($mn)	766.3
Price-to-NTA-per-share ratio	3.0
5-year share price return (% p.a.)	32.3
Dividend reinvestment plan	No

Sector: Financials	Company	Sector
Price/earnings ratio (times)	13.9	15.0
Dividend yield (%)	0.8	5.9

Melbourne company Lifestyle Communities, founded in 2003, develops and maintains residential and retirement communities throughout Victoria, in growth areas of Melbourne and in regional centres. These are aimed at over-50s and retirees. At June 2019 it had completed eight communities, with 2284 homes under management. Six more communities were under development and a further four were awaiting commencement.

Latest business results (June 2019, full year)

Revenues and profits continued to rise, in line with the steady roll-out of new communities. During the year the company settled 337 new homes, up from 321 in the previous year. These were at the Bittern, Berwick Waters, Ocean Grove, Shepparton and Geelong communities. It sold 209 homes, down from 293, with an average sales price of $401 000, up from $343 000. At June 2019 it had 239 homes sold but not settled. The result included non-cash property revaluations. Excluding these, the underlying after-tax profit rose from $33.8 million to $41.1 million.

Outlook

Lifestyle Communities operates on a model that differs from many retirement facilities, in that its residents own their homes but pay a rental charge to the company for the land, on a 90-year lease. It thus has a growing annuity-style income. It promotes its communities to active seniors, and the average age of new residents is around 67, which is about 10 years younger than the average age for new residents of retirement homes generally in Australia. Its goal is to buy two new sites each year, focused on Melbourne's growth corridors and on key Victorian regional centres. Projects still under development at June 2019 were at Shepparton, Geelong, Berwick Waters, Bittern, Ocean Grove and Mount Duneed. New communities awaiting commencement were at Kaduna Park, Wollert, Plumpton and Tyabb. The company noted that a competitive property market during 2018 and 2019 meant that it could not buy all the land it needed, and so would be launching one less project than earlier planned. In addition, it has experienced delays in receiving planning permits for its Kaduna Park and Wollert communities. Consequently it forecasts that home settlements for the June 2020 year will fall to between 270 and 310. Nevertheless, as the company grows, the number of resales — sales of established homes — increases, and Lifestyle Communities charges a deferred management fee for these. This will become a growing part of the company's income, and for the June 2020 year it forecasts sales of 60 to 80 established homes, up from 53 in the June 2019 year.

Year to 30 June	2018	2019
Revenues ($mn)	121.5	144.0
EBIT ($mn)	75.8	81.1
EBIT margin (%)	62.4	56.3
Gross margin (%)	20.3	24.8
Profit before tax ($mn)	75.5	79.7
Profit after tax ($mn)	52.7	55.1
Earnings per share (c)	50.39	52.67
Cash flow per share (c)	50.91	53.34
Dividend (c)	4.5	5.5
Percentage franked	100	100
Net tangible assets per share ($)	1.96	2.44
Interest cover (times)	256.0	57.9
Return on equity (%)	29.3	24.0
Debt-to-equity ratio (%)	15.4	37.3
Current ratio	0.7	1.1

Macquarie Group Limited

ASX code: MQG

www.macquarie.com.au

Macq Group-Monthly

Share price ($)	123.67
12-month high ($)	136.84
12-month low ($)	103.30
Market capitalisation ($mn)	42 095.1
Price-to-NTA-per-share ratio	2.7
5-year share price return (% p.a.)	20.3
Dividend reinvestment plan	Yes

Sector: Financials	Company	Sector
Price/earnings ratio (times)	13.4	15.0
Dividend yield (%)	4.6	5.9

Sydney-based Macquarie Group was established in 1969 as Hill Samuel Australia, a subsidiary of a British merchant bank. It is now Australia's leading locally owned investment bank, with a wide spread of activities and boasting special expertise in specific industries that include resources and commodities, energy, financial institutions, infrastructure and real estate. It has offices in 30 markets around the world, and international business accounts for around two-thirds of total company income.

Latest business results (March 2019, full year)

Macquarie posted a double-digit rise in profits for the second straight year, in an excellent result. The bank classifies its operations into five operating groups, and two of these made especially strong contributions. Macquarie Capital achieved an 89 per cent surge in profits thanks to asset realisations and increased fee and commission income. There was a particular contribution from the sale of the bank's stake in Quadrant Energy. The Commodities and Global Markets division saw profits up 65 per cent, thanks to a strong performance in commodities, as well as improved results in foreign exchange, interest rates and credit. A smaller division, Banking and Financial Services, reached a 3 per cent rise in profits, with growth in most areas of domestic banking. However, one of the company's core businesses, Macquarie Asset Management, saw profits down 4 per cent, as operating expenses rose and investment-related income fell. Profits fell 10 per cent at the Corporate and Asset division, due to higher provisions and impairments and a reduction in some investment-related income.

Outlook

With markets remaining uncertain, Macquarie is cautious about the near-term outlook. It has said that it expects its March 2020 profit to be slightly down, in part reflecting some substantial one-off income receipts in the March 2019 year. Nevertheless, it believes its expertise in major markets, its diversity, the ongoing benefits of continued cost initiatives, its risk management strengths and its ability to adapt its portfolio mix to changing market conditions have all positioned it well to deliver a superior performance in the medium term. More than half its profits are in the form of stable, annuity-style earnings, which reduces risk. In particular, its Macquarie Infrastructure and Real Assets business has become a global leader in infrastructure investment. In addition, with two-thirds of its income from abroad, the bank benefits from a weaker dollar. Nevertheless, Macquarie is also exposed to any downturn in the global economy and capital markets.

Year to 31 March	2018	2019
Operating income ($mn)	10 920.0	12 754.0
Net interest income ($mn)	1 986.0	1 760.0
Operating expenses ($mn)	7 456.0	8 887.0
Profit before tax ($mn)	3 464.0	3 867.0
Profit after tax ($mn)	2 557.0	2 982.0
Earnings per share (c)	792.93	920.36
Dividend (c)	525	575
Percentage franked	45	45
Non-interest income to total income (%)	81.8	86.2
Net tangible assets per share ($)	45.14	46.21
Cost-to-income ratio (%)	68.3	69.7
Return on equity (%)	16.0	17.5
Return on assets (%)	1.4	1.5

Magellan Financial Group Limited

ASX code: MFG   www.magellangroup.com.au

Share price ($)	50.91
12-month high ($)	62.60
12-month low ($)	22.55
Market capitalisation ($mn)	9015.5
Price-to-NTA-per-share ratio	14.8
5-year share price return (% p.a.)	33.7
Dividend reinvestment plan	No

Sector: Financials	Company	Sector
Price/earnings ratio (times)	24.7	15.0
Dividend yield (%)	3.0	5.9

Sydney-based Magellan is a specialist investment management company that evolved in 2006 from the ASX-listed Pengana Hedgefunds Limited. Its main business is Magellan Asset Management, which offers managed funds to retail and institutional investors, with particular specialties in global equities and infrastructure. In 2018 it acquired Airlie Funds Management.

Latest business results (June 2019, full year)

In volatile market conditions, Magellan posted an excellent result, with a big increase in revenues and profits. Management and services fees rose 22 per cent to $473 million. Performance fees more than doubled to $83.6 million, having soared 83 per cent in the previous year. The company achieved great success in containing costs, which increased by only 3 per cent, with staff costs up, as the average number of employees during the year rose from 116 to 125, but with marketing expenses down. At June 2019 Magellan had funds under management of $86.7 billion, up from $69.5 billion a year earlier, thanks to the strong investment performance and net inflows of $4.4 billion.

Outlook

Magellan continues to expand impressively, and funds under management exceed those of two rivals, Platinum Asset Management and Perpetual. It has a record of strong, long-term performance in global — and particularly, American — equities, and has become a significant beneficiary of moves by Australian investors to diversify into overseas markets. It also benefits from the reputation and stock-picking prowess of its Chairman and Chief Investment Officer, Hamish Douglass. Nevertheless, it remains heavily dependent on the state of financial markets, and it would suffer from any big sell-off in equities, or from a prolonged bear market. In addition, as its funds swell in size it becomes increasingly difficult for their fund managers to find the new investments needed to continue outperforming their benchmarks. The acquisition of Airlie Funds Management has provided Magellan with a new platform for growth. Airlie is a specialist Australian equities fund manager with over $6 billion of funds under management, mainly for institutional and high-net-worth clients. In August 2019 Magellan launched its new Magellan High Conviction Trust, which aims at investing in a concentrated portfolio of around 8 to 12 global stocks weighted towards Magellan's best ideas. In addition, the company is developing a major new fund aimed at retirees seeking income from their assets and is also actively planning other new funds. Magellan's stated target is that it should generate annual shareholder returns — profit growth plus dividends — in the low to mid teens annually over the medium term. At August 2019 funds under management had risen to $92.1 billion.

Year to 30 June	2018	2019
Revenues ($mn)	426.8	559.1
EBIT ($mn)	349.2	510.9
EBIT margin (%)	81.8	91.4
Profit before tax ($mn)	351.6	513.4
Profit after tax ($mn)	268.9	364.2
Earnings per share (c)	154.94	205.93
Cash flow per share (c)	156.03	208.72
Dividend (c)	119.6	151.8
Percentage franked	100	75
Net tangible assets per share ($)	2.92	3.44
Interest cover (times)	~	~
Return on equity (%)	50.4	53.8
Debt-to-equity ratio (%)	~	~
Current ratio	5.5	6.2

McMillan Shakespeare Limited

ASX code: MMS

www.mcms.com.au

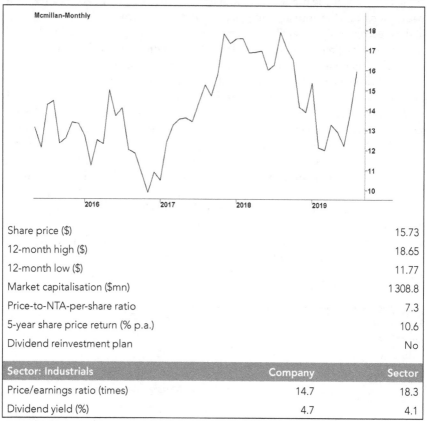

Share price ($)	15.73
12-month high ($)	18.65
12-month low ($)	11.77
Market capitalisation ($mn)	1 308.8
Price-to-NTA-per-share ratio	7.3
5-year share price return (% p.a.)	10.6
Dividend reinvestment plan	No

Sector: Industrials	Company	Sector
Price/earnings ratio (times)	14.7	18.3
Dividend yield (%)	4.7	4.1

Melbourne-based McMillan Shakespeare, founded in 1988, is a specialist provider of salary packaging, and vehicle leasing and finance services. It operates under three broad categories. The Group Remuneration Services division provides administrative services for salary packaging. It also arranges motor vehicle novated leases — three-way agreements between an employer, employee and financier to lease a vehicle — as well as providing related ancillary services such as insurance. The Asset Management division arranges financing and provides related management services for motor vehicles, commercial vehicles and equipment. The third division, Retail Financial Services, manages financial services for motor vehicles. McMillan Shakespeare has operations in New Zealand and the United Kingdom.

Latest business results (June 2019, full year)

Sales edged up but underlying profits weakened in a mixed year for the company. The Group Remuneration Services division performed well, with revenues and profits higher, thanks to a 2.5 per cent increase in salary packages and a 7.4 per cent rise in novated leasing volumes. This division is responsible for 40 per cent of company revenues but contributes nearly three-quarters of company profit. The Asset Management division also saw revenues up, but profits fell in both the Australia/New Zealand and the UK segments, with particular weakness in the second half of the year. In the previous year the UK business had recorded a 43 per cent jump in profits. The Retail Financial Services division was hit by falling sales of new cars and by regulatory uncertainty, and profits were down by more than 25 per cent, having fallen by more than 30 per cent in the previous year. The new Plan Partners business delivered an initial profit.

Outlook

The Group Remuneration Services division is responsible for taking advantage of complex laws to help employees, especially in the public and non-profit sectors, gain tax benefits. It occupies a strong position in Australia, with high profit margins and continuing growth from a strong pipeline of prospective business. The company's three-year Beyond 2020 transformational program has begun to reduce its cost base. It has initiated a strategic review of its UK operations, following a weak performance from that business. It is optimistic about the potential for its new initiative Plan Partners, which is designed to provide participants in the government's National Disability Insurance Scheme with greater choice, less complexity and more control over their management plans. An attempt to acquire rival fleet vehicle leasing company Eclipx Group was abandoned in April 2019. However, McMillan Shakespeare continues to seek out further acquisition opportunities.

Year to 30 June	2018	2019
Revenues ($mn)	543.8	547.9
Asset management (%)	45	45
Group remuneration services (%)	38	40
Retail financial services (%)	17	15
EBIT ($mn)	140.7	135.5
EBIT margin (%)	25.9	24.7
Profit before tax ($mn)	132.6	126.8
Profit after tax ($mn)	93.5	88.7
Earnings per share (c)	113.20	107.29
Cash flow per share (c)	217.34	205.41
Dividend (c)	73	74
Percentage franked	100	100
Net tangible assets per share ($)	2.00	2.16
Interest cover (times)	17.5	15.5
Return on equity (%)	25.2	23.9
Debt-to-equity ratio (%)	64.1	51.3
Current ratio	2.1	2.5

McPherson's Limited

ASX code: MCP   www.mcphersons.com.au

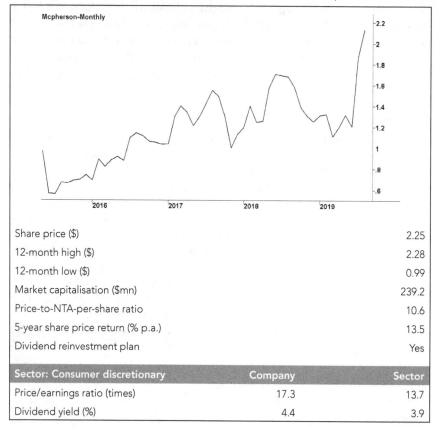

Share price ($)	2.25
12-month high ($)	2.28
12-month low ($)	0.99
Market capitalisation ($mn)	239.2
Price-to-NTA-per-share ratio	10.6
5-year share price return (% p.a.)	13.5
Dividend reinvestment plan	Yes

Sector: Consumer discretionary	Company	Sector
Price/earnings ratio (times)	17.3	13.7
Dividend yield (%)	4.4	3.9

Melbourne-based McPherson's, established in 1860, is a supplier of health, wellness and beauty products. Its brands include Manicare, Lady Jayne, Dr. LeWinn's, A'kin, Glam by Manicare, Swisspers, Moosehead, Maseur and Multix. The company also distributes the products of some external manufacturers. It sells to major retail chains, independent stores and pharmacies, with extensive operations in both Australia and New Zealand. It also has a small business in Singapore, focused on personal care products and household consumables. A branch in Hong Kong manages contract manufacturing.

Latest business results (June 2019, full year)

Revenues and profits were up, in a year of restructuring and consolidation. The figures used in this book are underlying results from continuing operations. Virtually all the growth came from the skin, hair and body category, with the Dr. LeWinn's brand more than doubling its sales revenues and good growth for the A'kin brand. Increased supply to grocery customers boosted private label sales. The company's largest category, household essentials, achieved growth for the Multix range of products, but this was more than offset by declines in other brands. The essential beauty category saw sales edge down for the year, with growth in the Manicare brand offset by a decline for Lady Jayne products. Sales to New Zealand, representing less than 5 per cent of total revenues, made a very small profit.

Outlook

McPherson's has launched a major restructuring of its operations, with a focus on three broad segments, health, wellness and beauty. It sees particular potential for its Dr. LeWinn's and A'kin brands, and is working to promote these. It is also placing a new emphasis on its own brands, which now represent 76 per cent of total sales, up from 69 per cent in June 2018. It has introduced measures aimed at boosting New Zealand profits, and it also hopes to increase exports to other countries, with a focus on Asian markets. It has established a New Business Development team, which has already evaluated more than 100 potential opportunities. New products include the Kotia range of deer milk cosmetics from New Zealand, Sugarbaby tanning and skincare products, and the Soulful range of dried fruit snacks, infused honey and student, pregnancy and adult milk powders. However, with much of its product range imported, McPherson's is hurt by weakness in the dollar. It is also vulnerable to changes in consumer sentiment. Its early forecast is that pre-tax profit will grow by about 10 per cent in the June 2020 year.

Year to 30 June	2018	2019
Revenues ($mn)	196.2	210.3
Household essentials & others (%)	33	30
Essential beauty (%)	29	27
Skin, hair & body (%)	12	19
Private label (%)	13	13
Agency brands (%)	13	11
EBIT ($mn)	20.3	19.9
EBIT margin (%)	10.3	9.4
Profit before tax ($mn)	16.3	19.0
Profit after tax ($mn)	10.2	13.7
Earnings per share (c)	9.78	13.02
Cash flow per share (c)	11.90	15.04
Dividend (c)	8.5	10
Percentage franked	100	100
Net tangible assets per share ($)	0.15	0.21
Interest cover (times)	5.1	22.4
Return on equity (%)	11.4	14.7
Debt-to-equity ratio (%)	10.9	7.7
Current ratio	1.4	1.9

Medibank Private Limited

ASX code: MPL www.medibank.com.au

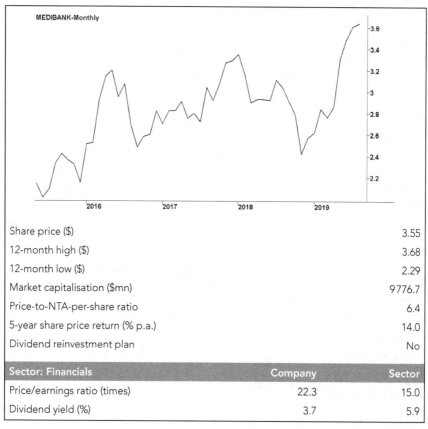

Share price ($)	3.55
12-month high ($)	3.68
12-month low ($)	2.29
Market capitalisation ($mn)	9776.7
Price-to-NTA-per-share ratio	6.4
5-year share price return (% p.a.)	14.0
Dividend reinvestment plan	No

Sector: Financials	Company	Sector
Price/earnings ratio (times)	22.3	15.0
Dividend yield (%)	3.7	5.9

Melbourne-based Medibank Private was established by the Australian government in 1976 as a not-for-profit private health insurer under the Health Insurance Commission. It was privatised and listed on the ASX in 2014. Today it is Australia's largest private health insurer, with a market share of 27 per cent, operating under the Medibank and ahm brands. It has also branched into other areas, including travel insurance, pet insurance, life insurance, income protection and funeral insurance. Its Medibank Health Solutions division specialises in the provision of healthcare services over the phone, online or face-to-face.

Latest business results (June 2019, full year)

Revenues and profits rose in a pleasing result, and the company claimed it had gained some market share. During the year the customer base grew from 3.74 million to 3.77 million, and the company also raised premiums. Consequently, total premium revenues rose 2.3 per cent to $6.46 billion, with health insurance profits up 1.3 per cent. The very small Medibank Health division enjoyed double-digit increases in sales and profits, although this largely reflected the acquisition in August 2018 of Home Support Services. In June 2019 the company's services to the Australian Defence Force ceased, and this business has been reported as a discontinued operation. The company's $2.7 billion investment portfolio generated net investment income of $7.2 million, up 7.5 per cent from the previous year.

Outlook

Medibank occupies a central role in the national health sector. Nevertheless, its business is heavily regulated, and it is difficult to achieve significant growth. In addition, as the population ages it is possible that customer claim volumes will grow. The company is also subject to political pressures that can hurt profits. Maintaining a tight control on expenses is important for the company, and it generated $40.4 million in annual cost savings over the two years to June 2019, with a target of an additional $50 million in annual savings over the ensuing three years. It is adopting a variety of strategies aimed at reducing costs and boosting membership numbers. It has introduced a new dental network, with reduced rates for members, and plans a new optical network. It has finalised its Medibank Priority program, rewarding long-term members. It has initiated an innovative trial with Nexus Hospitals to send patients home early after joint replacement surgery, which is expected to lead to better outcomes for the patients. Its acquisition of Home Support Services and the growth of its Medibank at Home service are allowing it to offer home treatment to certain patients.

Year to 30 June	2018	2019
Revenues ($mn)	6468.8	6655.8
EBIT ($mn)	558.3	573.4
EBIT margin (%)	8.6	8.6
Profit before tax ($mn)	598.4	616.3
Profit after tax ($mn)	424.2	437.7
Earnings per share (c)	15.40	15.89
Cash flow per share (c)	18.54	19.32
Dividend (c)	12.7	13.1
Percentage franked	100	100
Net tangible assets per share ($)	0.54	0.56
Interest cover (times)	~	~
Return on equity (%)	23.9	23.3
Debt-to-equity ratio (%)	~	~
Current ratio	2.0	2.1

Mineral Resources Limited

ASX code: MIN   www.mineralresources.com.au

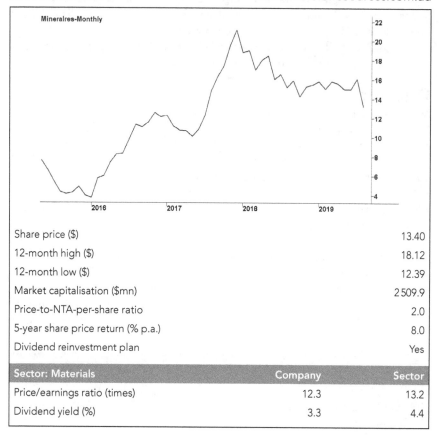

Share price ($)	13.40
12-month high ($)	18.12
12-month low ($)	12.39
Market capitalisation ($mn)	2509.9
Price-to-NTA-per-share ratio	2.0
5-year share price return (% p.a.)	8.0
Dividend reinvestment plan	Yes

Sector: Materials	Company	Sector
Price/earnings ratio (times)	12.3	13.2
Dividend yield (%)	3.3	4.4

Mineral Resources, based in Perth, was founded in 1993, and is a mining and mining services company. Its mining services side operates through a group of three subsidiaries. They are PIHA, a leader in specialist pipeline engineering and construction; Crushing Services International, which provides contract crushing, screening and processing services to the resources sector; and Process Minerals International, a minerals processor and exporter, with a specialty in bringing new mines into production on behalf of owners. The company's mining side comprises iron ore production assets and holdings in the Wodgina lithium mine and the Mount Marion lithium project.

Latest business results (June 2019, full year)

Weakness in mining services operations drove revenues and profits lower. During the year the company suspended operations at its Wodgina lithium mine, which led to a substantial reduction in demand for mining services. There were also delays in the Mount Marion upgrade project and a reduction in crushing volumes at its Iron Valley iron ore mine. This was all partially offset by benefits from the commencement of operations at the Koolyanobbing iron ore mine. The company's mining operations saw profits rise for the year. Lithium production fell sharply, but iron ore production rose 13 per cent to 10.6 million tonnes, with a 35 per cent increase in average prices.

Outlook

Mineral Resources is strongly geared to the resources industry. Though this sector is volatile, the company is confident that it can generate significant and sustainable long-term growth through the expansion of existing operations and moves into new businesses. It sees particularly strong potential for its Wodgina lithium mine, the world's largest known hard-rock lithium deposit, with a mine life of as much as 50 years and with a worth that might exceed $3 billion. The company is in the process of selling for US$820 million a 60 per cent stake in the Wodgina project to Albermarle Corporation of the US. It will also take a stake in a lithium hydroxide plant that Albermarle is building in Western Australia, and it is spending heavily on mining and processing capacity at the two lithium mines. In addition, it is ramping up production at its Koolyanobbing iron ore mine to an expected 7.5 million tonnes per year and is also investing in further iron ore assets in the Pilbara region. It has signed a joint venture agreement with Hong Kong–based Brockman Mining to develop the Marillana iron ore mine in the Pilbara, with expected eventual production of 20 million tonnes per year.

Year to 30 June	2018	2019
Revenues ($mn)	1624.4	1512.0
EBIT ($mn)	396.9	324.4
EBIT margin (%)	24.4	21.5
Profit before tax ($mn)	390.2	293.0
Profit after tax ($mn)	272.5	205.0
Earnings per share (c)	145.30	109.08
Cash flow per share (c)	205.49	166.89
Dividend (c)	65	44
Percentage franked	100	100
Net tangible assets per share ($)	6.50	6.81
Interest cover (times)	59.2	10.3
Return on equity (%)	22.7	15.5
Debt-to-equity ratio (%)	~	63.1
Current ratio	1.4	2.8

MNF Group Limited

ASX code: MNF

mnfgroup.limited

Share price ($)	5.08
12-month high ($)	5.21
12-month low ($)	3.25
Market capitalisation ($mn)	372.9
Price-to-NTA-per-share ratio	~
5-year share price return (% p.a.)	13.1
Dividend reinvestment plan	Yes

Sector: Communication services	Company	Sector
Price/earnings ratio (times)	32.7	17.2
Dividend yield (%)	1.2	3.8

Sydney telecommunications services provider MNF Group, formerly known as MyNetFone, dates back to 2004. Its largest business, Global Wholesale, comprises the TNZI international voice traffic operation and the Tollshield and OpenCA toll fraud prevention brands. The Australia/New Zealand Wholesale division includes the core Symbio and iBoss brands, providing retail service providers with a range of telecommunications products and services. The Australia Retail division incorporates many brands, including MyNetFone, Conference Call International, Connexus, Callstream, PennyTel and The Buzz, and provides telecommunications services to residential, business and government customers.

Latest business results (June 2019, full year)

Revenues and profits edged down in a mixed year. At the EBITDA level profits actually rose, but a big increase in borrowings led to higher interest payments and depreciation charges were also up. The company is working to boost its recurring revenue streams, as these generally provide higher margins than usage-based sales. During the year the company was able to boost recurring revenues 86 per cent to

$74 million, with a notable increase in its gross margin. The best divisional result came from the Australia/New Zealand Wholesale division, with a near-doubling of revenues and profits. A large part of this was due to the acquisition in December 2018 of much of the business of wholesale telecommunications services provider Inabox Group. However, the division's underlying business was also strong. The Australia Retail division saw sales up a little, but profits fell in a competitive environment. However, some slowing business hurt the Global Wholesale division, with a double-digit decline in sales and profits also weak.

Outlook

MNF has adopted a multi-pronged strategy for expansion. It believes the Global Wholesale division offers the best potential for long-term growth, through building a strong business in the Asia-Pacific region. Its 2018 acquisition of the niche Singapore telecommunications company SuperInternet Group was part of this strategy, and it plans a steady expansion of its infrastructure to neighbouring countries. A second growth strategy is an expansion of the company's portfolio of communications software products and services. Thirdly, MNF plans a vigorous marketing effort to acquire new customers, with targeted brands and tailored products. A fourth strategy is building long-term relationships with wholesale customers, leading to steady margin growth. It is the only communications platform provider with its own Australia–New Zealand voice network, with Singapore about to be added, and sees this as offering a great competitive advantage. Its early forecast is for a June 2020 after-tax profit of between $13.5 million and $15.5 million.

Year to 30 June	2018	2019
Revenues ($mn)	220.7	215.6
Global wholesale (%)	69	52
ANZ wholesale (%)	15	31
Australia retail (%)	16	17
EBIT ($mn)	17.4	16.1
EBIT margin (%)	7.9	7.5
Gross margin (%)	31.3	38.3
Profit before tax ($mn)	16.8	14.4
Profit after tax ($mn)	11.9	11.4
Earnings per share (c)	16.25	15.55
Cash flow per share (c)	24.90	27.79
Dividend (c)	8.35	6.1
Percentage franked	100	100
Net tangible assets per share ($)	0.38	~
Interest cover (times)	25.1	9.3
Return on equity (%)	16.4	14.2
Debt-to-equity ratio (%)	~	47.5
Current ratio	1.4	1.6

Monadelphous Group Limited

ASX code: MND   www.monadelphous.com.au

Share price ($)	15.69
12-month high ($)	20.07
12-month low ($)	12.51
Market capitalisation ($mn)	1 479.5
Price-to-NTA-per-share ratio	3.8
5-year share price return (% p.a.)	3.7
Dividend reinvestment plan	Yes

Sector: Industrials	Company	Sector
Price/earnings ratio (times)	25.7	18.3
Dividend yield (%)	3.1	4.1

Perth-based Monadelphous, established in the early 1970s, is an engineering company that provides a wide range of construction, maintenance, project management and support services to the minerals, energy and infrastructure industries. It operates from branches throughout Australia, with a client base that includes most of the country's resource majors. It has also established a presence in some overseas markets.

Latest business results (June 2019, full year)

A 46 per cent slump in business for the Engineering Construction division sent revenues and profits down. In the previous year this division had seen its revenues jump by 54 per cent, with a particular benefit from its completion of the Ichthys LNG Project in Darwin. Some good growth in the renewable energy sector was insufficient to offset the subdued activity in the resources construction market. The Maintenance and Industrial Services division enjoyed another good year, with revenues up 19 per cent, following a 29 per cent gain in the previous year. This reflected increased demand from the oil and gas market and continuing work for the resources sector. Important maintenance services contracts included the Prelude floating liquefied natural gas (LNG) facility and the North West Shelf offshore gas production facilities, both in Western Australia. During the year the company received $1.35 billion worth of new contracts or contract extensions, up from $600 million in the previous year.

Outlook

Monadelphous believes that market conditions are becoming increasingly favourable, and it expects this to generate a solid pipeline of opportunities. Nevertheless, much depends on the timing of work, and the company is also affected by high levels of competition and customer price sensitivity. In addition, it has been experiencing pressure in the labour market. Within the resources sector it notes an upsurge in iron ore and lithium projects. It also expects continuing solid demand for its services from the LNG sector. Maintenance work continues to grow, including a three-year $240 million contract from BHP for general maintenance services at its Pilbara iron ore mine sites. The Zenviron renewable energy joint venture has secured additional contracts in the wind energy sector, and the water and irrigation business has also been enjoying growing demand, in Australia and New Zealand. Its Chinese subsidiary SinoStruct has been generating high levels of repeat business for fabricated products, and has successfully won contracts in Mongolia for the massive Oyu Tolgoi project, as well as in Australia and North America. At June 2019 Monadelphous had net cash holdings of more than $125 million.

Year to 30 June	2018	2019
Revenues ($mn)	1734.9	1477.3
Maintenance & industrial services (%)	47	68
Engineering construction (%)	53	32
EBIT ($mn)	100.7	82.5
EBIT margin (%)	5.8	5.6
Gross margin (%)	8.3	8.5
Profit before tax ($mn)	102.8	83.4
Profit after tax ($mn)	71.5	57.4
Earnings per share (c)	76.11	61.03
Cash flow per share (c)	95.11	83.13
Dividend (c)	62	48
Percentage franked	100	100
Net tangible assets per share ($)	4.16	4.14
Interest cover (times)	~	~
Return on equity (%)	18.5	14.6
Debt-to-equity ratio (%)	~	~
Current ratio	2.0	2.0

Money3 Corporation Limited

ASX code: MNY

investors.money3.com.au

Share price ($)	2.29
12-month high ($)	2.38
12-month low ($)	1.50
Market capitalisation ($mn)	417.1
Price-to-NTA-per-share ratio	1.9
5-year share price return (% p.a.)	18.3
Dividend reinvestment plan	Yes

Sector: Financials	Company	Sector
Price/earnings ratio (times)	17.0	15.0
Dividend yield (%)	4.4	5.9

Melbourne-based moneylender Money3 was formally established in 2005 through the consolidation of nine separate loans businesses operating in Melbourne and Geelong. In 2019 it sold its online and branch-based small-loans business, and it now specialises in car loans of up to $35 000 and personal loans up to $12 000. It has entered the New Zealand car loans business with the acquisition of Go Car Finance.

Latest business results (June 2019, full year)

Money3 has reported success in its moves to become a specialist auto finance business, with revenues and profits up on a continuing business basis. It now segments its operations into two divisions, Broker (Australia) and International (New Zealand). The Broker division saw revenues up 15 per cent to $84.9 million, with profits at the EBITDA level rising 9 per cent to $49.9 million. The year-end loan book of

$310 million was up 23 per cent from a year earlier. Go Car Finance, acquired in March 2019, contributed $6.8 million in revenues and $2.8 million in EBITDA, and boosted the year-end loan book by $63 million. In addition to these figures, the company reported sales and profits from its discontinued businesses.

Outlook

With its origins as a provider of short-term unsecured loans, also known as payday lending, Money3 had come under some government and social pressures, with questions raised about the ethics of its activities. Consequently, it has been working to transform itself into a diversified financial services company. In February 2019 it announced the $46 million sale, effective from May, of its short-term lending business, through a management buyout. This has transformed the company into a specialist provider of mainly car finance. The Australian market for consumer vehicle financing is estimated at around $20 billion annually, with $6.3 billion for used vehicles, and Money3 sees substantial scope for growth. It is investing in new digital systems to lower operating costs, and is introducing new products. It has established a new team that aims at lifting the number of returning customers. With the exit from the short-term loans business, the company's quality of earnings has been enhanced, and it expects that this will reduce its costs of funding. Nevertheless, it is vulnerable to any downturn in the economy, or to a rise in interest rates, which could lead to an increase in loan defaults. With the acquisition of Go Car Finance, for a price of up to NZ$24 million, it sees significant scope for growth in the buoyant New Zealand used car sector.

Year to 30 June	2018	2019
Revenues ($mn)	73.6	91.7
EBIT ($mn)	40.2	46.9
EBIT margin (%)	54.7	51.1
Profit before tax ($mn)	31.2	35.3
Profit after tax ($mn)	21.2	24.2
Earnings per share (c)	13.17	13.48
Cash flow per share (c)	13.33	13.82
Dividend (c)	9.5	10
Percentage franked	100	100
Net tangible assets per share ($)	1.14	1.19
Interest cover (times)	4.4	4.1
Return on equity (%)	10.6	10.5
Debt-to-equity ratio (%)	23.5	41.4
Current ratio	19.4	12.8

Mortgage Choice Limited

ASX code: MOC www.mortgagechoice.com.au

Mortchoice-Monthly

Share price ($)	1.14
12-month high ($)	1.64
12-month low ($)	0.69
Market capitalisation ($mn)	141.5
Price-to-NTA-per-share ratio	1.9
5-year share price return (% p.a.)	−8.9
Dividend reinvestment plan	No

Sector: Financials	Company	Sector
Price/earnings ratio (times)	10.2	15.0
Dividend yield (%)	5.3	5.9

Sydney company Mortgage Choice, established in 1992, is today one of the country's largest mortgage brokers. It works through a national network of hundreds of franchises and loan consultants, supported by its own offices and providing advice on mortgages, personal loans, commercial loans, equipment finance and insurance products. The company also operates the Mortgage Choice Financial Planning business.

Latest business results (June 2019, full year)

A weak housing market sent revenues and profits lower. During the year the company settled home loans worth $11.5 billion, down 18 per cent from the previous year, and below expectations, as demand fell and banks tightened their lending processes. At June 2019 the loan book totalled $54.3 billion, down from $54.6 billion. Its share of the national home loans market held steady at 3.4 per cent. The results were also affected by a new remuneration structure introduced by the company. Mortgage Choice Financial Planning — representing 6 per cent of total company income — also saw revenues and profits down, affected by the new remuneration structure. However, its underlying business continued to grow, with funds under advice at June 2019 of $952.2 million, up 30 per cent from the previous year. At June 2019 Mortgage Choice managed a mortgage broking network of 391 franchisees, down from 449 a year earlier.

Outlook

Mortgage Choice is well established throughout Australia, at a time when the use of mortgage brokers has grown to nearly 60 per cent of the housing market. It was a beneficiary of a buoyant housing environment lasting many years, thanks especially to low interest rates and a firm economy. It came under fire in 2018 with reports that some franchisees were considering legal action, alleging that high loan-writing targets were placing them in financial stress and in some cases leading them to cut corners in order to avoid being penalised with low commissions. This forced the company to introduce a new remuneration structure, which has raised costs. It has reported signs of a recovery in the housing market, and expects business to improve during the June 2020 year. It is looking to boost its business with the addition of new franchisees. It is also investing in new IT systems, in order to attract customers and lower operating costs. It believes it can achieve strong growth for its financial planning business. It sees the disruption to the industry caused by the Banking Royal Commission — with some banks closing down their financial advisory operations — as a chance to attract talented advisers.

Year to 30 June	2018	2019
Revenues ($mn)	214.2	174.4
EBIT ($mn)	32.7	19.3
EBIT margin (%)	15.3	11.1
Profit before tax ($mn)	33.3	19.9
Profit after tax ($mn)	23.4	14.0
Earnings per share (c)	18.72	11.20
Cash flow per share (c)	19.99	12.91
Dividend (c)	18	6
Percentage franked	100	100
Net tangible assets per share ($)	0.62	0.62
Interest cover (times)	~	~
Return on equity (%)	24.7	16.3
Debt-to-equity ratio (%)	~	0.7
Current ratio	1.4	1.3

National Australia Bank Limited

ASX code: NAB   www.nab.com.au

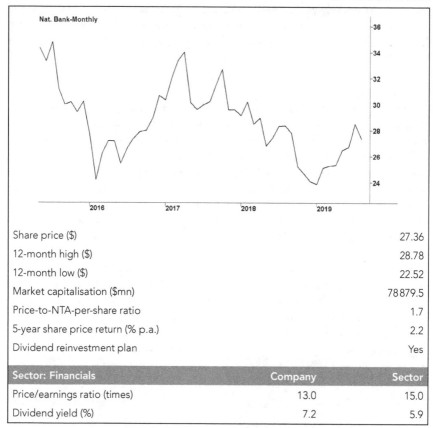

Share price ($)	27.36
12-month high ($)	28.78
12-month low ($)	22.52
Market capitalisation ($mn)	78 879.5
Price-to-NTA-per-share ratio	1.7
5-year share price return (% p.a.)	2.2
Dividend reinvestment plan	Yes

Sector: Financials	Company	Sector
Price/earnings ratio (times)	13.0	15.0
Dividend yield (%)	7.2	5.9

National Australia Bank, based in Melbourne, has a history dating back to the establishment of the National Bank of Australasia in 1858. It is one of Australia's largest banks, with a wide spread of financial activities and particular strength in business banking. It owns the Bank of New Zealand, and also operates offices in several countries in Asia. It has a big involvement in financial planning and wealth management, with businesses that include MLC Wealth and JBWere. Other activities include the nabtrade online broking service and the UBank online bank.

Latest business results (March 2019, half year)

A significant reduction in restructuring costs and some buoyant New Zealand business helped the bank to a rise in its cash earnings. This was despite the payment of $325 million in customer-related remediation costs, largely due to findings from the Banking Royal Commission. The result also came despite increased investment spending and higher credit impairment charges for much domestic business. New Zealand profits rose by nearly 8 per cent, thanks to higher margins and strong growth in both home mortgages and business lending. Australian corporate and institutional banking saw profits up a little, with some pleasing growth in non-markets revenue. But business and private banking, representing more than 40 per cent of bank profits, saw earnings edge down, despite the bank's traditional strength in business lending. Profits slumped more than 20 per cent for the consumer banking and wealth businesses, with weakness in the bank's wealth operations and lower lending margins offsetting continuing growth in home lending. The bank cut its dividend for the first time in five years, in a move intended to help strengthen its balance sheet.

Outlook

Facing the same headwinds as the other large banks — including higher regulatory costs, growing competition and the possibility of a slowing housing market and weaker Australian economy — NAB is working to restructure its operations. It launched a three-year transformation program in November 2017, with a target of $1 billion in cost savings by September 2020. It is also working to boost even further its strong position in business lending. New leadership at MLC Wealth has led to some attractive new products. However, the bank has expressed its desire to demerge or sell this business during 2020. NAB is also boosting its digital offerings, and its UBank digital bank has achieved some impressive results, including a 10 per cent rise in customer numbers in the March 2019 half and a 13 per cent increase in home loan business.

Year to 30 September	2017	2018
Operating income ($mn)	17 895.0	17 977.0
Net interest income ($mn)	13 166.0	13 467.0
Operating expenses ($mn)	7 635.0	8 126.0
Profit before tax ($mn)	9 450.0	8 206.0
Profit after tax ($mn)	6 642.0	5 702.0
Earnings per share (c)	249.28	210.45
Dividend (c)	198	198
Percentage franked	100	100
Non-interest income to total income (%)	26.4	25.1
Cost-to-income ratio (%)	42.6	45.2
Return on equity (%)	12.9	11.0
Return on assets (%)	0.8	0.7
Half year to 31 March	2018	2019
Operating income ($mn)	9 093.0	8 874.0
Profit before tax ($mn)	3 976.0	4 250.0
Profit after tax ($mn)	2 759.0	2 954.0
Earnings per share (c)	102.20	107.20
Dividend (c)	99	83
Percentage franked	100	100
Net tangible assets per share ($)	16.11	16.46

NIB Holdings Limited

ASX code: NHF   www.nib.com.au

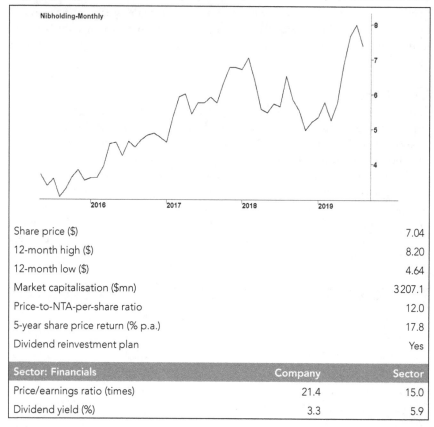

Share price ($)	7.04
12-month high ($)	8.20
12-month low ($)	4.64
Market capitalisation ($mn)	3207.1
Price-to-NTA-per-share ratio	12.0
5-year share price return (% p.a.)	17.8
Dividend reinvestment plan	Yes

Sector: Financials	Company	Sector
Price/earnings ratio (times)	21.4	15.0
Dividend yield (%)	3.3	5.9

Newcastle private health insurer NIB Holdings was established as the Newcastle Industrial Benefits Hospital Fund in 1952 by workers at the BHP steelworks. It subsequently demutualised and became the first private health insurer to list on the ASX. It is also active in New Zealand. Other businesses are travel insurance and the provision of specialist insurance services to international students and workers in Australia. In May 2019 it acquired QBE's travel insurance business.

Latest business results (June 2019, full year)

NIB enjoyed another good year, with a further increase in its revenues and profits. The company's flagship Australian Residents Health Insurance (ARHI) was again the key, with the policyholder base growing by 2.1 per cent for the year — down from 3 per cent in the previous year — compared with virtually no growth at all for the industry as a whole. With a 3.4 per cent premium increase during the year the company saw premium revenues for this business rise 7.6 per cent, with profits up by more than 14 per cent. ARHI represents about 85 per cent of company revenues and 75 per cent of company profit. New Zealand activities contribute 9 per cent of total turnover, and while premium revenues rose, thanks to 7.2 per cent growth in policyholder numbers, profits fell for the second successive year, as claims increased. Profits were also down for the company's travel insurance business, despite a 7.5 per cent increase in premium revenues. However, the company's high-margin health insurance program for international students and workers in Australia continued its impressive growth rate, with premium revenues and profits rising by around 19 per cent.

Outlook

NIB is adopting a variety of strategies for expansion. It benefits from an ageing population that needs more medical care and it is working to build a national profile for its domestic health insurance business. However, medical insurance is a highly regulated industry, and claim rates in recent years have been below long-term averages, which the company does not expect to continue. In addition, the growth in its policyholder base has been above the industry average, and this too may not endure. Its new partnership with Chinese pharmaceuticals company Tasly Holding to enter the Chinese health insurance market is awaiting Chinese government approval. It has launched nib International Student Services to provide health insurance services for international students on a global basis. The $24 million acquisition of QBE Travel is expected to bolster its travel insurance business.

Year to 30 June	2018	2019
Premium revenues ($mn)	2186.9	2372.6
EBIT ($mn)	190.9	211.5
EBIT margin (%)	8.7	8.9
Profit before tax ($mn)	192.3	213.0
Profit after tax ($mn)	132.4	149.8
Earnings per share (c)	29.38	32.89
Cash flow per share (c)	34.80	38.34
Dividend (c)	20	23
Percentage franked	100	100
Net tangible assets per share ($)	0.53	0.59
Interest cover (times)	~	~
Return on equity (%)	26.8	25.6
Debt-to-equity ratio (%)	6.9	15.7
Current ratio	1.8	1.9

Nick Scali Limited

ASX code: NCK   www.nickscali.com.au

Share price ($)	6.71
12-month high ($)	7.39
12-month low ($)	4.80
Market capitalisation ($mn)	543.5
Price-to-NTA-per-share ratio	6.6
5-year share price return (% p.a.)	22.0
Dividend reinvestment plan	No

Sector: Consumer discretionary	Company	Sector
Price/earnings ratio (times)	12.9	13.7
Dividend yield (%)	6.7	3.9

Sydney-based Nick Scali is one of Australia's largest furniture importers and retailers, with a history dating back more than 50 years. It specialises in leather and fabric lounge suites along with dining room and bedroom furniture. It has six distribution centres and at June 2019 operated 57 Nick Scali Furniture stores, including two in New Zealand, and five Nick Scali Clearance stores.

Latest business results (June 2019, full year)

Revenues and profits rose once again. However, this reflected the company's continuing expansion, with six new stores opened during the year, and a further six in the previous year. On a same-store basis sales actually fell by around 1 per cent, with notable weakness in the fourth quarter. The company was also adversely affected by an increase in operating expenses, with rising wages, marketing expenses and property costs outpacing the growth in revenues. Nevertheless, some new-product initiatives helped boost gross margins. Three of the new stores opened in the June 2019 year were in Queensland, at Morayfield, Mackay and the Skygate Centre at Brisbane Airport. One was at Prospect, New South Wales, one at Craigieburn, Victoria, and one at Hamilton, New Zealand.

Outlook

Nick Scali is directly affected by trends in consumer spending, interest rates, housing sales and renovation activity, and the general economy. It is also affected by the dollar's decline, which has boosted the cost of its furniture imports. It has expressed concern about a cooling of the housing market, and is wary about the near-term outlook for its business. For two years it has not achieved overall same-store growth, and it has noted a slowdown in sales at the end of the June 2019 year that continued into July 2019. Company management have also expressed uncertainty about whether the low interest rates and low unemployment prevailing in Australia will translate into a boost in consumer confidence. Nevertheless, it continues to expand, with four new stores planned to open during the June 2020 year. These include two new ones in Auckland, New Zealand, where the company believes its prospects for strong profit expansion are excellent, having already achieved robust same-store sales growth and a high level of product and brand acceptance. Its long-term target is for 80 to 85 stores throughout Australia and New Zealand. At June 2019 Nick Scali had net cash holdings of $2.6 million and it has said that it continues to review strategic growth opportunities, including possible bolt-on acquisitions.

Year to 30 June	2018	2019
Revenues ($mn)	250.8	268.0
EBIT ($mn)	59.0	59.9
EBIT margin (%)	23.5	22.3
Gross margin (%)	62.7	62.9
Profit before tax ($mn)	58.9	59.7
Profit after tax ($mn)	41.0	42.1
Earnings per share (c)	50.59	52.00
Cash flow per share (c)	55.26	57.25
Dividend (c)	40	45
Percentage franked	100	100
Net tangible assets per share ($)	1.00	1.02
Interest cover (times)	331.7	264.9
Return on equity (%)	53.2	49.9
Debt-to-equity ratio (%)	~	~
Current ratio	1.1	1.3

Northern Star Resources Limited

ASX code: NST　　　　　　　　　　　　　　　　www.nsrltd.com

Share price ($)	11.74
12-month high ($)	14.05
12-month low ($)	7.63
Market capitalisation ($mn)	7 508.8
Price-to-NTA-per-share ratio	6.8
5-year share price return (% p.a.)	48.2
Dividend reinvestment plan	No

Sector: Materials	Company	Sector
Price/earnings ratio (times)	48.2	13.2
Dividend yield (%)	1.1	4.4

Perth-based Northern Star Resources, Australia's third-largest gold producer, was founded in 2000. It mines gold deposits at its Jundee and Kalgoorlie sites in Western Australia. In 2018 it acquired the Pogo gold mine in Alaska — the eighth-largest gold mine in the US — and this too has become a producing asset. It has an active exploration program in Western Australia and the Northern Territory. It has made a takeover bid for gold explorer Echo Resources.

Latest business results (June 2019, full year)

Revenues rose, in a solid year for the company, and at the EBITDA level profits too were up. But acquisition activity during the year led to a steep increase in depreciation charges and interest payments, and pre-tax and after-tax profits fell. The newly acquired Pogo operation reported a loss. Gold sales of a total of 840 580 ounces — including 201 337 ounces from Pogo — were up from 575 110 ounces in the previous year, with a 4 per cent rise in the average realised gold sales price. Average costs rose from $1029 per ounce to $1296, in part because of Pogo, which recorded higher costs than the Australian mines.

Outlook

Northern Star is a low-cost producer by global standards and is actively working to boost its output. In August 2019 it said that its gold reserves had risen to 5.4 million ounces, with resources of 20.8 million ounces. It has already succeeded in cutting costs and boosting output at the Pogo mine, and it plans a $44 million investment during the June 2020 year to launch production at new mining areas at Pogo, as well as work at the site to streamline operations, reduce costs further and boost processing capacity. It will invest an additional $76 million in new exploration work at Pogo and at its Jundee and South Kalgoorlie operations in Western Australia. It sees great potential in its Tanami projects in Western Australia and the Northern Territory, and believes these have the potential to be producing 120 000 ounces to 150 000 ounces of gold annually. Its $0.33-per-share takeover bid for Echo Resources, announced in August 2019, values the company at $243 million. Echo directors have recommended that shareholders accept the offer. Echo is developing the Yandal gold project, near Northern Star's Jundee mine, and also owns the Bronzewing gold processing facility. Northern Star's forecast is for production during the June 2020 year of 800 000 ounces to 900 000 ounces of gold, at a cost of $1200 to $1300 per ounce.

Year to 30 June	2018	2019
Revenues ($mn)	964.0	1401.2
EBIT ($mn)	273.7	222.3
EBIT margin (%)	28.4	15.9
Gross margin (%)	35.3	21.4
Profit before tax ($mn)	277.8	214.8
Profit after tax ($mn)	194.1	154.7
Earnings per share (c)	32.11	24.38
Cash flow per share (c)	57.94	63.02
Dividend (c)	9.5	13.5
Percentage franked	100	100
Net tangible assets per share ($)	1.31	1.72
Interest cover (times)	~	29.5
Return on equity (%)	27.0	16.0
Debt-to-equity ratio (%)	~	~
Current ratio	2.8	2.1

Objective Corporation Limited

ASX code: OCL   www.objective.com

Share price ($)	3.99
12-month high ($)	3.99
12-month low ($)	2.50
Market capitalisation ($mn)	370.6
Price-to-NTA-per-share ratio	21.9
5-year share price return (% p.a.)	22.7
Dividend reinvestment plan	No

Sector: Information technology	Company	Sector
Price/earnings ratio (times)	40.9	29.4
Dividend yield (%)	1.3	1.6

Sydney-based Objective, founded in 1987, provides information technology software and services. Its particular specialty is working with federal, state and local governments, as well as government agencies and regulated industries, and it has operations in Australia, the Asia-Pacific and Europe. It operates under many product categories. Objective Enterprise Connect Management (ECM) allows a public or private body to manage all its physical and electronic records. Objective Connect allows organisations to exchange content securely and easily. Objective Keystone helps organisations create and publish new content, and manage the way documents are authorised and executed. Objective Trapeze assists the digitisation process for complex files and documents. Objective Redact removes sensitive information from a document.

Latest business results (June 2019, full year)

Revenues edged down, due to the completion in the previous year of a large consulting project. But increasing sales of high-margin software generated a double-digit increase in profits for the year. There was a small contribution from the New Zealand software developer Alpha Group, which was acquired in April 2019. For reporting purposes the company divides its businesses into four broad segments. The largest of these, Objective Content Solutions — essentially the Object ECM business — represents 78 per cent of company turnover, and actually saw revenues down, though with profits largely flat. Objective Keystone represents about 12 per cent of company income, and this segment moved from loss to profit. Two other very small divisions produced mixed results. Objective Planning Solutions — incorporating Objective Trapeze and Objective Redact products — also moved from loss to profit, but Objective Connect widened its loss.

Outlook

Objective is a small company working in niche businesses but with a solid reputation and a high level of profitability in its domestic operations. It is working to move its businesses, as much as possible, to a subscription model, which will make revenues and earnings more predictable each year. Recurring revenues rose by 13 per cent in the June 2019 year, to represent 70 per cent of total income. The company's particular goal is to help regulated businesses streamline the processes of compliance, accountability and governance. Its products share a common interface, and as the product range grows it is increasingly able to cross-sell to its existing customer base. The newly acquired Alpha Group — whose software allows local councils to process building development applications — is to be combined with Objective Trapeze into a new operation. At June 2019 Objective had net cash holdings of more than $21 million, and it continues to seek out complementary acquisitions.

Year to 30 June	2018	2019
Revenues ($mn)	63.1	62.1
EBIT ($mn)	9.0	10.8
EBIT margin (%)	14.3	17.3
Profit before tax ($mn)	9.4	10.8
Profit after tax ($mn)	7.4	9.1
Earnings per share (c)	8.02	9.77
Cash flow per share (c)	9.69	13.39
Dividend (c)	5	5
Percentage franked	100	100
Net tangible assets per share ($)	0.17	0.18
Interest cover (times)	~	~
Return on equity (%)	32.0	33.0
Debt-to-equity ratio (%)	~	~
Current ratio	1.4	1.3

OFX Group Limited

ASX code: OFX

www.ofx.com

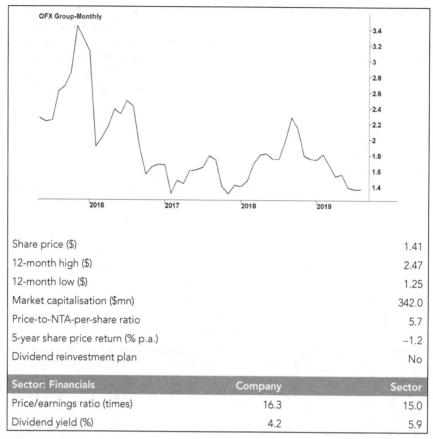

Share price ($)	1.41
12-month high ($)	2.47
12-month low ($)	1.25
Market capitalisation ($mn)	342.0
Price-to-NTA-per-share ratio	5.7
5-year share price return (% p.a.)	−1.2
Dividend reinvestment plan	No

Sector: Financials	Company	Sector
Price/earnings ratio (times)	16.3	15.0
Dividend yield (%)	4.2	5.9

Sydney-based foreign exchange specialist OFX Group, formerly known as OzForex, was launched in 1998 as a currency information website. It provides international payments services in 55 currencies to more than 190 countries, with offices in Sydney, London, Hong Kong, Singapore, Toronto, Auckland and San Francisco.

Latest business results (March 2019, full year)

OFX enjoyed a positive year, despite a subdued second half, with growth in revenues and profits. Australian and New Zealand business — which contributes about 50 per cent of company turnover and nearly two-thirds of profit — was especially strong. North America and Europe — together representing nearly 40 per cent of income — saw solid rises in revenues, and Europe enjoyed a 29 per cent rise in profits. However, North American earnings fell sharply. Asian profits also fell, despite higher income.

The total number of the company's active clients fell by 3 per cent to 156 500, but the number of transactions per active client rose by nearly 13 per cent to 6.7, with the average transaction value also higher. In addition to the figures in this book, the company incurred $4.3 million in non-operating expenses from discussions concerning a possible acquisition of British foreign exchange specialist Currencies Direct, and at the statutory level profits fell.

Outlook

OFX occupies a small position in the huge global foreign currency market. This is a highly competitive business, and much of the company's success derives from developing strong relationships with its clients and from offering them more attractive rates than competitors like the big banks. It is also highly dependent on new technologies in order to help it maintain a cost advantage. The foreign exchange business appears to offer low barriers to entry, and with interest rates low it has been attracting many new entrants. However, levels of profitability are low for many of these companies, and OFX expects market consolidation to increase. It has expressed an interest in expanding more strongly into Europe through an offshore acquisition, and this lay behind its ultimately unsuccessful acquisition talks with Currencies Direct. It is also working to boost its activities in North America and Asia. However, there has been speculation that Facebook's plans to launch its own global foreign exchange network, called Libra, will severely hurt OFX. For the time being OFX management states that it believes the advent of Libra will actually encourage more consumers to shop around for currency exchange deals, to the ultimate benefit of companies like OFX.

Year to 31 March	2018	2019
Revenues ($mn)	109.9	118.7
EBIT ($mn)	23.3	24.9
EBIT margin (%)	21.2	21.0
Profit before tax ($mn)	24.9	26.4
Profit after tax ($mn)	18.7	21.0
Earnings per share (c)	7.79	8.67
Cash flow per share (c)	9.84	11.08
Dividend (c)	5.4	5.92
Percentage franked	100	100
Net tangible assets per share ($)	0.23	0.25
Interest cover (times)	~	~
Return on equity (%)	31.0	31.2
Debt-to-equity ratio (%)	~	~

Orica Limited

ASX code: ORI

www.orica.com

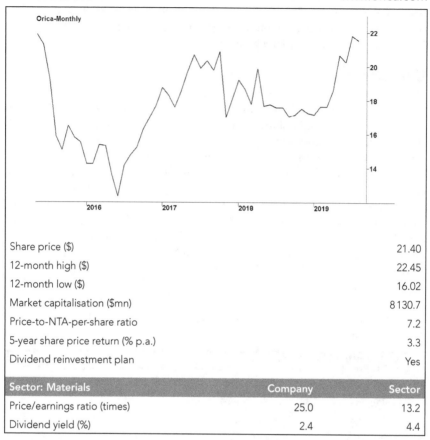

Share price ($)	21.40
12-month high ($)	22.45
12-month low ($)	16.02
Market capitalisation ($mn)	8 130.7
Price-to-NTA-per-share ratio	7.2
5-year share price return (% p.a.)	3.3
Dividend reinvestment plan	Yes

Sector: Materials	Company	Sector
Price/earnings ratio (times)	25.0	13.2
Dividend yield (%)	2.4	4.4

Melbourne-based Orica was founded in 1874 as a supplier of explosives to the Victorian gold mining industry, and for many years it was a subsidiary of Britain's Imperial Chemical Industries. It is today a global leader in commercial explosives for the mining, quarrying, oil and gas, infrastructure and construction sectors. It is also a leading supplier of sodium cyanide for gold extraction. Its Minova business provides support equipment for underground mining and tunnelling operations. It has customers in more than 100 countries, and overseas sales represent nearly three-quarters of total income.

Latest business results (March 2019, half year)

Rising demand, an improved manufacturing performance and favourable exchange rates combined to generate a strong result for Orica. Orica segments its operations on a regional basis. Rising demand from gold miners helped the North America segment to a solid increase in revenues and profits. Australia/Pacific/Asia reported moderate growth in revenues and profits, driven especially by the coal and iron ore markets. Continuing demand from the copper industry helped sales edge up in Latin America, with profits flat. The smallest regional segment, Europe/Middle East/Africa, enjoyed the best result, with double-digit increases in revenues and profits, thanks to strong sales to a new customer in the Middle East, along with gold-related demand from Russia and Africa. The Minova business, representing about 10 per cent of total turnover, saw sales rise by more than 20 per cent, and it moved from loss to a small profit. However, Orica continued to suffer production problems with its new $800 million joint venture Burrup ammonium nitrate unit in Western Australia, and it reported $134 million in after-tax significant items, much of it related to a write-down of Burrup assets.

Outlook

With most of its business geared towards the mining industry, Orica's fortunes will rise or fall accordingly. It is optimistic about the near-term outlook, expecting solid growth in demand for its products during the remainder of the September 2019 year, and extending into 2020. Demand from the gold industry represents 20 per cent of sales, and the company will benefit from any increase in gold activity. It is also a beneficiary of a weaker dollar. It continues to upgrade its production facilities, aiming to lower its cost base. Its Minova unit is seeing solid demand for its products and services, and it has been successful in rationalising operations. However, the Burrup plant is unlikely to be fully operational before at least April 2020. The company is also vulnerable to rising energy prices.

Year to 30 September	2017	2018
Revenues ($mn)	5039.2	5373.8
EBIT ($mn)	635.1	618.1
EBIT margin (%)	12.6	11.5
Profit before tax ($mn)	563.4	496.8
Profit after tax ($mn)	386.2	324.2
Earnings per share (c)	102.67	85.72
Cash flow per share (c)	172.11	156.29
Dividend (c)	51.5	51.5
Percentage franked	6	0
Interest cover (times)	8.9	5.1
Return on equity (%)	13.4	11.1
Half year to 31 March	2018	2019
Revenues ($mn)	2532.0	2828.9
Profit before tax ($mn)	197.4	244.9
Profit after tax ($mn)	123.6	166.7
Earnings per share (c)	32.72	43.91
Dividend (c)	20	22
Percentage franked	0	0
Net tangible assets per share ($)	3.08	2.97
Debt-to-equity ratio (%)	68.5	61.6
Current ratio	1.3	1.3

Orora Limited

ASX code: ORA

www.ororagroup.com

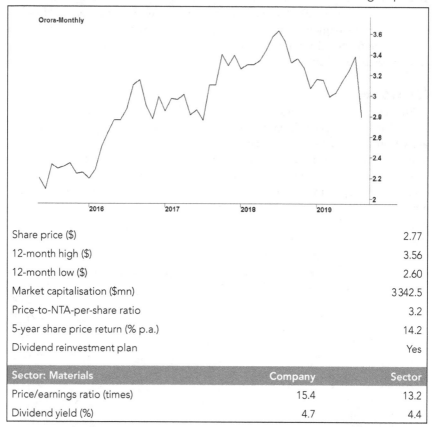

Share price ($)	2.77
12-month high ($)	3.56
12-month low ($)	2.60
Market capitalisation ($mn)	3342.5
Price-to-NTA-per-share ratio	3.2
5-year share price return (% p.a.)	14.2
Dividend reinvestment plan	Yes

Sector: Materials	Company	Sector
Price/earnings ratio (times)	15.4	13.2
Dividend yield (%)	4.7	4.4

Melbourne-based Orora was originally the Australasian and packaging distribution businesses of packaging giant Amcor. It was demerged from Amcor in 2013 and listed on the ASX. Today it is a prominent manufacturer of glass bottles, aluminium cans, closures and caps, boxes and cartons, fibre packaging, point of purchase displays, and packaging materials and supplies. It also provides a wide array of package-related services and has a particular specialty in cardboard recycling and the manufacture of recycled packaging paper. It has manufacturing facilities in Australia, New Zealand and the US.

Latest business results (June 2019, full year)

Strength in Australia and New Zealand offset weakness in North America, and profits edged up. Orora Australasia achieved a 6.2 per cent increase in EBIT on a sales rise of 2.1 per cent, thanks especially to strong sales of packaging products, growing demand for beverage cans and the company's cost-cutting initiatives. By contrast, Orora North America saw EBIT down 3.6 per cent, despite sales rising by 21.9 per cent, although this largely reflected the addition of two recent acquisitions.

The company benefited from the dollar's weakness, and in local currency terms the North American EBIT was actually down by 11.1 per cent. Though Orora North America was responsible for more than half of total income, it contributed only about a third of company profit.

Outlook

Orora occupies a strong position for many of its products, with high market shares in Australia. Nevertheless, demand is greatly dependent on economic trends, and the company is vulnerable to any economic slowdown. It has been undertaking a series of measures to reduce costs and stimulate growth, including upgrades for many of its manufacturing facilities. A substantial capital investment at its Botany mill in New South Wales has greatly boosted profit margins. It is introducing a new can production line in New Zealand and is building a major warehouse at its Gawler glass plant in South Australia. In North America it has initiated a big corporate restructuring program designed to drive growth and lower costs. A particular strategy has been a series of bolt-on acquisitions in an effort to build scale in its activities and improve operational efficiency. The latest of these are two Texas-based companies, acquired for $143 million. The first is Pollock, a leading provider of packaging and facility supplies, and the other is Bronco, a packaging distributor. Nevertheless, Orora has some large and well-established rivals in the North American market, and it faces many challenges as it works to boost profitability there.

Year to 30 June	2018	2019
Revenues ($mn)	4 248.0	4 761.5
EBIT ($mn)	323.4	335.2
EBIT margin (%)	7.6	7.0
Gross margin (%)	19.0	18.3
Profit before tax ($mn)	288.9	295.8
Profit after tax ($mn)	214.1	217.0
Earnings per share (c)	17.84	18.02
Cash flow per share (c)	28.00	29.05
Dividend (c)	12.5	13
Percentage franked	30	40
Net tangible assets per share ($)	0.94	0.85
Interest cover (times)	9.4	8.5
Return on equity (%)	13.5	13.3
Debt-to-equity ratio (%)	40.9	54.1
Current ratio	1.2	1.2

Pacific Energy Limited

ASX code: PEA　　　　　　　　　　　　www.pacificenergy.com.au

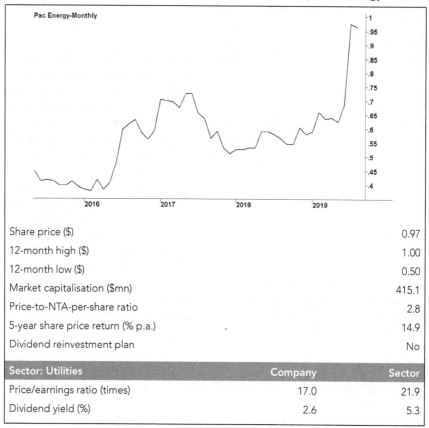

Share price ($)	0.97
12-month high ($)	1.00
12-month low ($)	0.50
Market capitalisation ($mn)	415.1
Price-to-NTA-per-share ratio	2.8
5-year share price return (% p.a.)	14.9
Dividend reinvestment plan	No

Sector: Utilities	Company	Sector
Price/earnings ratio (times)	17.0	21.9
Dividend yield (%)	2.6	5.3

Perth power generator and supplier Pacific Energy traces its origins to the establishment of Kalgoorlie Power Systems in 1981. Pacific acquired this business in 2009 and is now a leading supplier of off-grid electricity — powered by gas, diesel and solar — to mine sites in Western Australia, South Australia and the Northern Territory. It operates under the brands KPS Australia, Contract Power and NovaPower. Through its subsidiary Pacific Energy Victorian Hydro it also owns two small hydro-electric power stations, at Cardinia Reservoir and Blue Rock Dam, 70 kilometres east of Melbourne. NovaPower owns and operates a 10-megawatt gas-fired power plant in Traralgon, Victoria. In addition, the company maintains a small power supply business in South Africa. In July 2019 investment management company QGIF Swan Bidco made a takeover bid for Pacific Energy.

Latest business results (June 2019, full year)

A full year's contribution from NovaPower, acquired in 2017, and from Contract Power, acquired in 2018, delivered a substantial boost to revenues and profits, and comparisons with previous years' results have little relevance. The company reported that 65 per cent of the profit growth derived from Contract Energy. Around 85 per cent of revenues came from Western Australia, with about 65 per cent from the gold sector. Pacific Energy Victorian Hydro made a very small contribution to the result. No revenues were received from the company's South African operations. During the year the company made a substantial reduction in its debt levels. At June 2019 its total contracted generation capacity was around 345 megawatts, with operations that included seven remote township power stations and 29 remote mine power stations.

Outlook

In July 2019 Pacific Energy entered into a Scheme Implementation Deed with QGIF Swan Bidco to acquire Pacific Energy for 97.5 cents per share. The directors of Pacific Energy have all supported the proposal. Shareholders are expected to have the chance to vote on the matter in October 2019. QGIF Swan Bidco is part of the Global Infrastructure Fund of the Queensland Investment Corporation, which is owned by the Queensland government. However, in September 2019 a Canadian pension fund announced a $1.085 per-share counter-bid for the company. Meanwhile, Pacific Energy is optimistic about its future, with many companies in the resources sector now working to boost output, and it is actively tendering for more work. It is a leader in the supply of power generation for gold projects, and its Contract Power acquisition now makes it a leader in hard-rock lithium as well.

Year to 30 June	2018	2019
Revenues ($mn)	68.1	120.8
EBIT ($mn)	25.3	41.0
EBIT margin (%)	37.2	34.0
Profit before tax ($mn)	22.7	36.6
Profit after tax ($mn)	18.3	24.5
Earnings per share (c)	4.85	5.72
Cash flow per share (c)	9.83	11.49
Dividend (c)	1	2.5
Percentage franked	100	100
Net tangible assets per share ($)	0.30	0.35
Interest cover (times)	9.9	9.3
Return on equity (%)	11.6	13.5
Debt-to-equity ratio (%)	55.3	34.1
Current ratio	1.1	0.6

Pacific Smiles Group Limited

ASX code: PSQ   investors.pacificsmilesgroup.com.au

Share price ($)	1.68
12-month high ($)	1.80
12-month low ($)	1.05
Market capitalisation ($mn)	255.3
Price-to-NTA-per-share ratio	8.5
5-year share price return (% p.a.)	2.0
Dividend reinvestment plan	No

Sector: Health care	Company	Sector
Price/earnings ratio (times)	28.6	37.1
Dividend yield (%)	3.5	1.4

Based in Maitland, New South Wales, Pacific Smiles was formally established in 2003 from a group of dental partnerships. Today it provides its dental practices with a wide array of support staff and back-office services that allow the dentists to focus on their clinical services. It operates in New South Wales, Victoria, Queensland and Canberra under the Pacific Smiles Dental and the nib Dental Care brands.

Latest business results (June 2019, full year)

The steady growth of the company boosted revenues. Profits were up too at the EBITDA level, but rising depreciation charges pushed them down at the EBIT level. Total patient fees for the year of $187.4 million were up nearly 14 per cent from the June 2018 year. On a same-centre basis, fees rose 8.6 per cent. During the year the company added 10 new centres, bringing the total number of centres at June 2019 to 89, with 351 chairs, up from 308. However, the large number of new centres led to a rise in operating costs, and profit margins were down. In addition, the company was hit by higher-than-expected telecommunication infrastructure costs of $0.7 million and lower-than-expected fees per appointment totalling $0.4 million.

Outlook

Pacific Smiles is similar to ASX-listed 1300SMILES — which was established several years earlier — in its activities. The dental business in Australia is fragmented, with around 70 per cent of dentists working in their own private practices or in small partnerships, and some companies — both listed and unlisted — are now working to consolidate them. Pacific Smiles has a long-term target of 250 centres, 800 dental chairs and a dental industry market share of more than 5 per cent. It finds that as it grows it is able to introduce efficiencies to its practices, boosting business and reducing operating costs. However, the costs associated with its expansion, especially higher depreciation charges, are restricting short-term profit growth. In addition, the company has been borrowing more to finance its growth, and this is leading to higher interest payments. It is also subject to the risk of overpaying for new practices, especially when it has set itself a far more ambitious growth target than a rival like 1300SMILES. The company's early forecast for the June 2020 year is for same-centre patient fee percentage growth in the high single digits, the opening of 7 to 10 new dental centres and an EBITDA that is up 6 per cent to 12 per cent from June 2019.

Year to 30 June	2018	2019
Revenues ($mn)	104.5	122.2
EBIT ($mn)	13.3	12.9
EBIT margin (%)	12.7	10.6
Profit before tax ($mn)	12.9	12.2
Profit after tax ($mn)	9.3	8.9
Earnings per share (c)	6.09	5.87
Cash flow per share (c)	11.24	12.06
Dividend (c)	6.1	5.8
Percentage franked	100	100
Net tangible assets per share ($)	0.20	0.20
Interest cover (times)	33.8	19.5
Return on equity (%)	21.5	21.5
Debt-to-equity ratio (%)	12.7	24.5
Current ratio	0.8	0.7

Pendal Group Limited

ASX code: PDL   www.pendalgroup.com

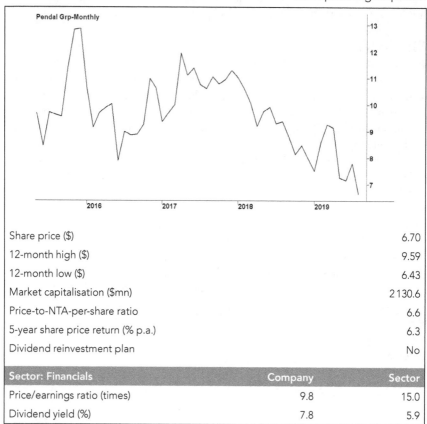

Share price ($)	6.70
12-month high ($)	9.59
12-month low ($)	6.43
Market capitalisation ($mn)	2130.6
Price-to-NTA-per-share ratio	6.6
5-year share price return (% p.a.)	6.3
Dividend reinvestment plan	No

Sector: Financials	Company	Sector
Price/earnings ratio (times)	9.8	15.0
Dividend yield (%)	7.8	5.9

Sydney-based funds management company Pendal Group started life as part of Ord-BT, an investment banking firm established in 1969. Ord-BT, later renamed as BT Financial Group, was subsequently acquired by Westpac Banking Corporation, which added to it some other funds management businesses, then created BT Investment Management as a new entity to be listed on the ASX. It was later renamed as Pendal Group. Today Pendal actively manages a wide range of investments in Australian equities, listed property and fixed interest, in international fixed interest, in multi-asset portfolios and in alternative investments. Its London-based subsidiary J O Hambro Capital Management, with offices in Singapore and the US, manages international funds. Other Pendal international funds are managed by external firms.

Latest business results (March 2019, half year)

Revenues and the cash profit fell, as volatile markets affected fund performance. Consequently the company saw a sharp decline in the performance fees it received, from $47.6 million in the March 2018 half to $4.4 million. Base management fees slipped 4 per cent to $237.6 million. Funds under management of $100.9 billion were down one per cent for the half, due to lower market levels, although partially offset by the weaker dollar and strong inflows to cash and fixed income funds. Operating expenses declined by 13 per cent as the company's wage bill fell. Note that the cash profit factors out certain non-cash items, including amortisation and unrealised losses. On a statutory basis the company's after-tax profit fell from $110.1 million to $69.6 million.

Outlook

Pendal is heavily dependent on market activity and investor sentiment. Its business can also be buffeted by its own performance, which helps determine levels of performance fees. It would suffer in any big market downturn. However, it benefits from moves by Australian investors into overseas equities. With 72 per cent of its equities funds under management held in foreign currencies, it is also a beneficiary of a weaker dollar. Its traditional ties with Westpac help deliver new investment monies although this relationship has been weakening. It has achieved success in diversifying its sources of fund inflows, with overseas clients now responsible for more than half the funds under management. It is working to boost this overseas business, with a particular focus on the huge US market, and has opened a new West Coast office. At March 2019 Pendal had no debt and $75 million in cash holdings.

Year to 30 September	2017	2018
Revenues ($mn)	490.9	558.5
EBIT ($mn)	193.6	248.8
EBIT margin (%)	39.4	44.6
Profit before tax ($mn)	193.6	249.1
Profit after tax ($mn)	147.5	191.0
Earnings per share (c)	54.80	68.26
Cash flow per share (c)	58.32	72.13
Dividend (c)	45	52
Percentage franked	27	15
Interest cover (times)	32 272.3	~
Return on equity (%)	19.2	22.6
Half year to 31 March	2018	2019
Revenues ($mn)	296.4	243.1
Profit before tax ($mn)	141.7	92.3
Profit after tax ($mn)	114.5	84.5
Earnings per share (c)	39.50	24.40
Dividend (c)	22	20
Percentage franked	15	10
Net tangible assets per share ($)	0.92	1.02
Debt-to-equity ratio (%)	~	~
Current ratio	1.7	1.5

Perpetual Limited

ASX code: PPT   www.perpetual.com.au

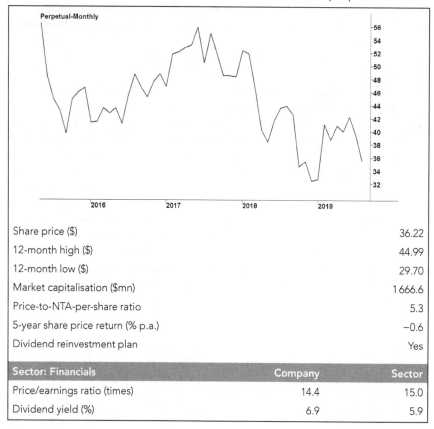

Share price ($)	36.22
12-month high ($)	44.99
12-month low ($)	29.70
Market capitalisation ($mn)	1 666.6
Price-to-NTA-per-share ratio	5.3
5-year share price return (% p.a.)	−0.6
Dividend reinvestment plan	Yes

Sector: Financials	Company	Sector
Price/earnings ratio (times)	14.4	15.0
Dividend yield (%)	6.9	5.9

Sydney-based financial services company Perpetual was established in 1886 as Perpetual Trustees. It divides its operations into three broad areas. Perpetual Investments is a funds management business offering a range of managed investment products to the retail, wholesale and institutional markets. Perpetual Private is a specialist boutique financial services business aimed at high-net-worth individuals, and providing its clients with access to tailored financial, tax, legal and estate planning advice. The Perpetual Corporate Trust division is a leading provider of corporate trustee and transaction support services to the financial services industry.

Latest business results (June 2019, full year)

Another poor performance from the Perpetual Investments division sent revenues and profits lower. This business saw revenues down 11 per cent and pre-tax profit tumbling 29 per cent, largely the result of some significant net outflows from its funds by institutional clients. At June 2019 the division had $27.1 billion in funds under management, down from $30.8 billion a year earlier, and $31.4 billion in the year before that. It was the fourth consecutive year of lower profits for this division. The Perpetual Private business reported revenues in line with the previous year, but profits fell 11 per cent as the company boosted investments in strategic initiatives aimed at future growth. Funds under advice for this division rose 5 per cent to $14.8 billion. The Perpetual Corporate Trust division saw revenues and profits up, thanks to strong performances from the debt market services and the managed fund services operations.

Outlook

Perpetual has built a strong long-term reputation for its equities funds, and they continue to generate solid profit margins. During the year it raised $440 million for its new Perpetual Credit Income Trust and an additional $101 million for its Perpetual Equity Investment Company. Nevertheless, poor performances in recent years have caused some institutional investors to withdraw money. Perpetual blames its underperformance on its style of investing, which favours value stocks, at a time when it is largely growth stocks that are leading markets higher. In addition, the company's fortunes remain heavily dependent on financial market movements, and it could be hit by any substantial market downturn. It is actively seeking acquisitions to bolster this business. It believes that its Perpetual Private division will benefit from disruption in the financial advisory business sparked by the Banking Royal Commission. Perpetual Corporate Trust continues to perform well, and the December 2018 acquisition of RFi Analytics has boosted its debt market services capabilities. This division has been undertaking a major technology modernisation program.

Year to 30 June	2018	2019
Revenues ($mn)	526.7	508.9
Perpetual investments (%)	45	41
Perpetual private (%)	35	37
Perpetual corporate trust (%)	20	22
EBIT ($mn)	193.5	164.5
EBIT margin (%)	36.7	32.3
Profit before tax ($mn)	191.3	162.2
Profit after tax ($mn)	139.0	115.9
Earnings per share (c)	302.32	250.89
Cash flow per share (c)	341.34	293.81
Dividend (c)	275	250
Percentage franked	100	100
Net tangible assets per share ($)	7.28	6.88
Interest cover (times)	88.3	70.3
Return on equity (%)	21.5	17.5
Debt-to-equity ratio (%)	7.5	6.0
Current ratio	1.7	1.9

Platinum Asset Management Limited

ASX code: PTM

www.platinum.com.au

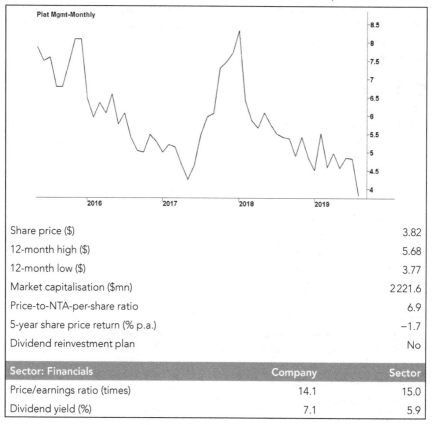

Share price ($)	3.82
12-month high ($)	5.68
12-month low ($)	3.77
Market capitalisation ($mn)	2 221.6
Price-to-NTA-per-share ratio	6.9
5-year share price return (% p.a.)	−1.7
Dividend reinvestment plan	No

Sector: Financials	Company	Sector
Price/earnings ratio (times)	14.1	15.0
Dividend yield (%)	7.1	5.9

Sydney funds management company Platinum Asset Management was established in 1994 by former chief executive Kerr Neilson. It has developed a specialty in managing portfolios of international equities. Its primary product is the $10.1 billion Platinum International Fund. Other funds specialise in Europe, Asia, Japan, health care, technology and international brands. Much of the company equity is held by Platinum directors and staff members and by Kerr Neilson and his former wife.

Latest business results (June 2019, full year)

A relatively poor investment performance led to a slump in fee income, and revenues and profits fell. Average funds under management for the year fell 4 per cent to $25.3 billion, due to net fund outflows in the second half of the year. In the previous year funds under management had risen 13 per cent. Consequently, management fees dropped 4 per cent to $295 million and performance fees were reported as just $30 000, down from $21.9 million in the previous year. There was a loss of nearly $1 million from the company's seed investments to nurture new funds. The weak investment performance meant that staff bonuses were slashed, leading to a sharp 21 per cent reduction in employee costs, with total company expenses down for the year. At June 2019 the company held funds under management of $24.8 billion, down from $25.7 billion a year earlier.

Outlook

Platinum has gained a degree of renown among Australian investors for an impressive long-term period of outperformance for its international equity funds, thanks to its stock-picking skills, and this has sparked some solid growth in funds under management. However, during the June 2019 year only one of its eight leading funds outperformed its benchmark, with five of them underperforming by more than 10 per cent. The company has attributed this to its preference for value stocks, at a time when growth stocks were leading global markets higher. Platinum's managing director has stated that global tensions, coupled with low interest rates, have upset investors and led them into defensive and growth stocks. He also noted that the last period of significant outperformance by growth stocks was in the late 1990s, and ended with the crash of technology stocks in 2001. Nevertheless, he cautioned that if the company's underperformance continues it can expect further fund outflows. Platinum is working to boost its business with international clients, and late in 2018 it opened an office in London. At June 2019 Platinum had no debt and cash holdings of nearly $113 million.

Year to 30 June	2018	2019
Revenues ($mn)	328.7	295.2
EBIT ($mn)	264.6	219.4
EBIT margin (%)	80.5	74.3
Profit before tax ($mn)	268.3	222.9
Profit after tax ($mn)	189.2	157.7
Earnings per share (c)	32.36	27.03
Cash flow per share (c)	32.48	27.16
Dividend (c)	32	27
Percentage franked	100	100
Net tangible assets per share ($)	0.57	0.55
Interest cover (times)	~	~
Return on equity (%)	56.5	48.0
Debt-to-equity ratio (%)	~	~
Current ratio	9.2	13.1

Pro Medicus Limited

ASX code: PME

www.promed.com.au

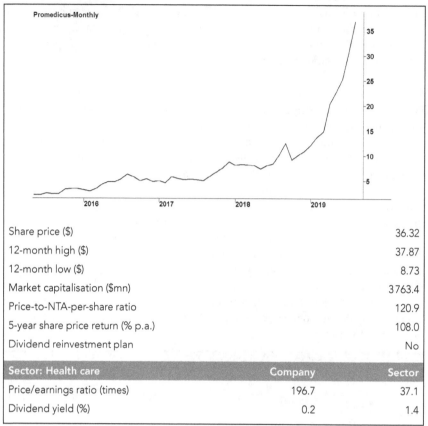

Share price ($)	36.32
12-month high ($)	37.87
12-month low ($)	8.73
Market capitalisation ($mn)	3 763.4
Price-to-NTA-per-share ratio	120.9
5-year share price return (% p.a.)	108.0
Dividend reinvestment plan	No

Sector: Health care	Company	Sector
Price/earnings ratio (times)	196.7	37.1
Dividend yield (%)	0.2	1.4

Melbourne-based Pro Medicus, established in 1983, provides software and internet products and services to the medical profession. Its Visage 7.0 medical imaging software provides radiologists and clinicians with advanced visualisation capability for the rapid viewing of medical images. Its Radiology Information Systems (RIS) product provides proprietary medical software for practice management. In Australia it operates the Promedicus.net online network for doctors. It has extensive business operations throughout Australia, Europe and North America, and overseas sales represent more than 80 per cent of total turnover.

Latest business results (June 2019, full year)

Strong overseas sales generated yet another stellar result, with the weak dollar enhancing the performance. North America represents nearly 70 per cent of total income, and sales rose 42 per cent, following the signing of two significant new contracts, with Partners Healthcare in Massachusetts — a seven-year, $27 million deal, the largest contract in the company's history — and with Duke Health in North Carolina. The best result came from Europe, with revenues more than doubling, thanks to an extension of the company's contract with the German government. Europe now contributes 13 per cent of total company income. Australian operations were also strong, with revenues up 30 per cent, largely due to RIS contracts with Healius and I-MED Radiology Network. The Promedicus.net online network held its market position in the face of increasing competition.

Outlook

Pro Medicus has been enjoying some outstanding success in America for its Visage 7 software, which has the speed and functionality to meet the requirements of many different kinds of users. Thanks to new development work, the product also has the ability to handle very large amounts of data, making it suitable for large health systems and hospitals. The company is now one of the market leaders in this business, and it is making a substantial investment in research and development activities aimed at new products and enhancements to existing products, including artificial intelligence–based products and cloud-based systems. As more contracts are signed, generally for periods of from five to seven years, the company generates an increasing amount of annuity-style recurring revenue, depending on how much the products are used. Also, as the company expands, its profit margins rise. Thanks to recent contract signings, the company says it is now the imaging provider at five of the top 20 hospitals in the US, including what it describes as the top two, Mayo Clinic and Massachusetts General Hospital. It also has a growing pipeline of new business opportunities.

Year to 30 June	2018	2019
Revenues ($mn)	33.9	50.1
EBIT ($mn)	15.2	25.9
EBIT margin (%)	45.0	51.6
Profit before tax ($mn)	15.3	26.1
Profit after tax ($mn)	10.0	19.1
Earnings per share (c)	9.66	18.46
Cash flow per share (c)	14.44	24.34
Dividend (c)	6	8
Percentage franked	100	100
Net tangible assets per share ($)	0.18	0.30
Interest cover (times)	~	~
Return on equity (%)	28.5	45.3
Debt-to-equity ratio (%)	~	~
Current ratio	3.5	3.8

REA Group Limited

ASX code: REA

www.rea-group.com

Share price ($)	105.52
12-month high ($)	108.00
12-month low ($)	69.23
Market capitalisation ($mn)	13 898.5
Price-to-NTA-per-share ratio	114.0
5-year share price return (% p.a.)	18.4
Dividend reinvestment plan	No

Sector: Communication services	Company	Sector
Price/earnings ratio (times)	47.0	17.2
Dividend yield (%)	1.1	3.8

Melbourne-based REA was founded in 1995 and was formerly known as Realestate.com.au Limited. Through its websites realestate.com.au and realcommercial.com.au it is a leader in the provision of online real estate advertising services in Australia, with roughly a 60 per cent market share. It also owns Flatmates.com.au and the residential property data company Hometrack Australia. It operates property websites throughout Asia, and has a 20 per cent shareholding in the Move online property marketing company in the US. It has also entered the mortgage business, and owns the mortgage broking franchise group Smartline Home Loans. News Corp owns more than 60 per cent of REA's equity.

Latest business results (June 2019, full year)

Revenues and underlying profits rose in a challenging real estate environment. Despite a nationwide decline in residential listings and in new development project commencements, the company's Australian revenues rose 8 per cent, thanks to higher rates for residential listings, an improved product mix, the acquisition of new commercial customers and the inclusion of the newly acquired Hometrack business. However, its small mortgage business saw revenues and profits fall. Asian operations contributed revenues of $48.6 million, up 10 per cent from a year earlier, but profits were down. American losses deepened, in spite of higher income. Some substantial non-cash, one-off impairment charges for its Asian operations meant that on a statutory basis the company's after-tax profit slumped 58 per cent to $105.3 million.

Outlook

REA is heavily geared to trends in the domestic housing market, and it is wary about the near-term outlook, despite some early signs of a pick-up in growth. However, the company is able to benefit from a weaker market, as sellers are forced to advertise for longer periods and may choose to take out multiple listings in order to sell their properties. In addition, REA believes that price increases implemented in July 2019 and continuing moves by customers to premium products will help boost revenues. It is optimistic about the outlook for its home loans business, and has moved from 80 per cent to 100 per cent ownership of Smartline Home Loans. It also sees great potential in its Asian strategy, with the continuing introduction of new products. It is the market leader for residential listings in both Malaysia and Indonesia, with Hong Kong also showing notable strength. REA's 20 per cent holding of Move, one of the largest real estate websites in the US, has given the company a foothold in the vast American property market.

Year to 30 June	2018	2019
Revenues ($mn)	807.7	874.9
EBIT ($mn)	415.0	443.8
EBIT margin (%)	51.4	50.7
Profit before tax ($mn)	406.9	435.1
Profit after tax ($mn)	279.9	295.5
Earnings per share (c)	212.54	224.34
Cash flow per share (c)	249.52	269.57
Dividend (c)	109	118
Percentage franked	100	100
Net tangible assets per share ($)	~	0.93
Interest cover (times)	51.3	50.9
Return on equity (%)	32.1	32.0
Debt-to-equity ratio (%)	33.6	19.0
Current ratio	0.9	0.7

Regis Resources Limited

ASX code: RRL   www.regisresources.com.au

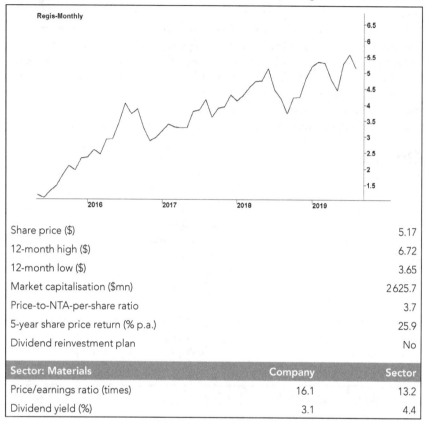

Share price ($)	5.17
12-month high ($)	6.72
12-month low ($)	3.65
Market capitalisation ($mn)	2625.7
Price-to-NTA-per-share ratio	3.7
5-year share price return (% p.a.)	25.9
Dividend reinvestment plan	No

Sector: Materials	Company	Sector
Price/earnings ratio (times)	16.1	13.2
Dividend yield (%)	3.1	4.4

Perth-based Regis Resources is a gold exploration and production company. Its core business is the Duketon Gold Project in the north-eastern goldfields region of Western Australia. Since operations started at Duketon in 2010 the company has been steadily expanding the size of the project and extending mine life. In 2012 Regis acquired the McPhillamys Gold Project in western New South Wales, and it is currently determining whether to proceed with development.

Latest business results (June 2019, full year)

Increased production and a rising gold price pushed revenues higher, but an increase in costs forced a decline in profits. During the year the company produced 363 418 ounces of gold, up from 361 373 ounces in the previous year, and sold 369 721 ounces, up from 359 750 ounces. The average sales price of $1765 per ounce was up from $1680. The average production all-in sustaining cost of $1029 per ounce rose

14.2 per cent from $901 in the previous year, following higher contractor expenses and harder ore encountered at Duketon North. For reporting purposes the company groups its various mines into two groupings. Duketon South comprises the Garden Well, Rosemont, Erlistoun and Tooheys Well mines. Revenues for this segment rose 14.6 per cent, with the pre-tax profit up 8.5 per cent. Duketon North comprises the Moolart Well, Gloster, Anchor and Dogbolter mines, with revenues down 8.3 per cent and the pre-tax profit slumping by 31.4 per cent.

Outlook

Regis has an estimated seven to 10 years of reserves at its mines, although the company's costs could begin to rise as it works to exploit this resource base. In February 2019 it initiated the development of an underground mining operation at its Rosemont open pit mine, with the first ore expected later in the year. This followed a mining study estimating the potential for 314 000 ounces of gold. It has been engaged in extensive test drilling at its Garden Well mine, and has identified a possible new underground resource. It has also carried out tests at the Moolart Well mine, identifying a further 89 000 ounces of gold, which will extend the life of the mine for at least a further 12 months. Its McPhillamys Gold Project in New South Wales contains an estimated 2.02 million ounces of gold, sufficient for a 10-year life. The company is developing a feasibility study that will determine the viability of proceeding with this project. At June 2019 Regis had net cash holdings of more than $186 million.

Year to 30 June	2018	2019
Revenues ($mn)	604.4	652.5
Duketon South operations (%)	71	75
Duketon North operations (%)	29	25
EBIT ($mn)	248.1	232.6
EBIT margin (%)	41.1	35.6
Gross margin (%)	43.2	38.4
Profit before tax ($mn)	248.9	233.5
Profit after tax ($mn)	174.2	163.2
Earnings per share (c)	34.60	32.18
Cash flow per share (c)	47.42	46.86
Dividend (c)	16	16
Percentage franked	100	100
Net tangible assets per share ($)	1.26	1.41
Interest cover (times)	~	~
Return on equity (%)	29.7	24.1
Debt-to-equity ratio (%)	~	~
Current ratio	3.8	3.0

Rio Tinto Limited

ASX code: RIO www.riotinto.com

Rio Tinto-Monthly

Share price ($)	87.76
12-month high ($)	107.99
12-month low ($)	69.41
Market capitalisation ($mn)	143 540.3
Price-to-NTA-per-share ratio	2.8
5-year share price return (% p.a.)	11.5
Dividend reinvestment plan	Yes

Sector: Materials	Company	Sector
Price/earnings ratio (times)	12.8	13.2
Dividend yield (%)	4.8	4.4

British-based Rio Tinto, one of the world's largest mining companies, was founded by European investors in 1873 in order to reopen some ancient copper mines at the Tinto River in Spain. It now maintains an ASX presence in a dual-listing structure and continues to pay franked dividends to Australian shareholders. Its products include iron ore, copper, gold, industrial minerals, diamonds and aluminium. Subsidiaries include uranium miner Energy Resources of Australia.

Latest business results (June 2019, half year)

A recovery in iron ore prices helped generate a rise in revenues and underlying earnings, more than offsetting declines in most other areas of business. The iron ore production and sales volume actually fell by 8 per cent, constrained by adverse weather, a fire at one of the company's ports and disruptions at some Western Australian mining operations. However, a 36 per cent jump in the average sales price boosted revenues and profits. Iron ore generates about half the company's revenues, but in June 2019 was responsible for more than 75 per cent of profit. Price declines hit the Aluminium division, which represents nearly a quarter of company turnover. The sales volume was little changed from the June 2018 half, but revenues and profits fell. The Copper and Diamonds division also suffered from lower prices. The Energy and Minerals division enjoyed a good period, with increased volumes and higher prices, although profits were down, reflecting the contribution in the June 2018 half from coking coal assets that have since been sold. Note that Rio Tinto reports its results in US dollars. The tables in this book are based on Australian dollar figures and exchange rates supplied by the company.

Outlook

Rio Tinto maintains a substantial portfolio of well-run assets across many countries, and with generally low operating costs. However, having disposed of most of its coal operations, the company's fortunes are markedly dependent on trends in the global iron ore market, which in turn is strongly influenced by Chinese economic developments. It maintains a high level of capital spending, with US$6 billion expected in 2019, rising to around US$6.5 billion in 2020 and 2021. Its major growth project is the Oyu Tolgoi copper mine development in Mongolia, which is destined eventually to become the world's largest copper mine, though has been hit by delays and cost blow-outs. Other significant projects include the Zulti South industrial minerals mine in South Africa, the Amrun bauxite project in Queensland and the Koodaideri iron ore mine in Western Australia.

Year to 31 December	2017	2018
Revenues ($mn)	51 987.0	54 029.0
EBIT ($mn)	17 562.2	17 108.0
EBIT margin (%)	33.8	31.7
Profit before tax ($mn)	16 644.0	16 704.0
Profit after tax ($mn)	11 204.0	11 744.0
Earnings per share (c)	627.08	683.07
Cash flow per share (c)	945.08	992.03
Dividend (c)	366.25	421.73
Percentage franked	100	100
Interest cover (times)	19.1	42.3
Return on equity (%)	20.0	19.6
Half year to 30 June	2018	2019
Revenues ($mn)	25 805.0	29 341.0
Profit before tax ($mn)	8 724.0	7 343.0
Profit after tax ($mn)	5 722.0	6 983.0
Earnings per share (c)	328.70	427.00
Dividend (c)	170.84	219.08
Percentage franked	100	100
Net tangible assets per share ($)	29.79	31.44
Debt-to-equity ratio (%)	15.9	19.1
Current ratio	1.8	1.5

Ruralco Holdings Limited

ASX code: RHL　　　　　　　　　　　www.ruralco.com.au

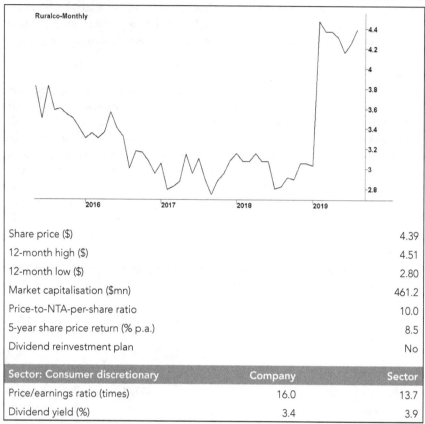

Share price ($)	4.39
12-month high ($)	4.51
12-month low ($)	2.80
Market capitalisation ($mn)	461.2
Price-to-NTA-per-share ratio	10.0
5-year share price return (% p.a.)	8.5
Dividend reinvestment plan	No

Sector: Consumer discretionary	Company	Sector
Price/earnings ratio (times)	16.0	13.7
Dividend yield (%)	3.4	3.9

Sydney-based farm supplies company Ruralco has grown out of a long series of mergers and acquisitions, most notably the 2006 merger with Tasmanian company Roberts, which itself was established in 1865. Today it operates through dozens of brands with businesses that include rural merchandise, wool and livestock agency, real estate agency, fertiliser manufacture, stock feed and grain storage, handling and distribution, water products and financial services. In February 2019 the Canadian fertiliser company Nutrien made a $469 million takeover bid for Ruralco.

Latest business results (March 2019, half year)

Revenues edged up and profits marked time. The core Rural Services division, responsible for more than 60 per cent of company turnover, saw profits flat, with good rains in northern Queensland and a strong season in Tasmania offset by inconsistent rainfall in South Australia and Victoria and reduced cotton and rice plantings. Profits declined slightly for the Water Services division, following a slowdown in water project activity along the Murray Darling basin and northern New South Wales. The Live Export division moved from loss to profit, thanks to an increase in volumes, especially to Indonesia. The very small Financial Services division enjoyed a big jump in profits.

Outlook

Nutrien has offered to acquire Ruralco for a price of $4.40 per share, and Ruralco directors have recommended that shareholders accept this offer. A vote on the matter was due for September 2019, and it is possible that Ruralco will have ceased to exist as an independent company by the time this book is published. However, the Australian Competition and Consumer Commission has expressed some concerns over the proposal and may delay matters. Nutrien is already the largest participant in the Australian farm services sector, through its subsidiary Landmark, with Ruralco also prominent in the industry. The Commission is concerned that the proposed takeover would lead to market dominance for some products and services. In response, Nutrien has said that the combination of Landmark and Ruralco would allow it to offer a much improved service to farmers across Australia. Meanwhile Ruralco is proceeding with plans to expand its range of private label products aimed at farmers. It is also working to boost its water business and its financial services operations. It sees scope for growth in Vietnam for its live export business, although this business is being hurt by higher feed costs. Overall, the company's activities remain heavily affected by the weather and other factors that influence the rural economy.

Year to 30 September	2017	2018
Revenues ($mn)	1826.1	1913.5
EBIT ($mn)	49.5	53.0
EBIT margin (%)	2.7	2.8
Gross margin (%)	18.3	17.9
Profit before tax ($mn)	49.4	51.5
Profit after tax ($mn)	26.2	28.8
Earnings per share (c)	27.47	27.49
Cash flow per share (c)	38.47	39.63
Dividend (c)	15	15
Percentage franked	100	100
Interest cover (times)	454.2	34.7
Return on equity (%)	10.9	10.2
Half year to 31 March	2018	2019
Revenues ($mn)	667.3	685.2
Profit before tax ($mn)	28.2	27.7
Profit after tax ($mn)	16.7	16.6
Earnings per share (c)	15.96	15.77
Dividend (c)	9	10
Percentage franked	100	100
Net tangible assets per share ($)	0.60	0.44
Debt-to-equity ratio (%)	46.8	52.9
Current ratio	1.3	1.3

Sandfire Resources NL

ASX code: SFR www.sandfire.com.au

Share price ($)	5.98
12-month high ($)	8.34
12-month low ($)	5.51
Market capitalisation ($mn)	954.2
Price-to-NTA-per-share ratio	1.6
5-year share price return (% p.a.)	2.3
Dividend reinvestment plan	No

Sector: Materials	Company	Sector
Price/earnings ratio (times)	9.0	13.2
Dividend yield (%)	3.8	4.4

Perth-based Sandfire Resources dates back to 2004 when geologist Graeme Hutton listed the company on the ASX, with a portfolio of exploration projects. In 2009 the company discovered a significant copper and gold resource, and today it is a major copper and gold producer at its DeGrussa mine in Western Australia. It also maintains an active exploration program in Australia and the US. It has made a takeover bid for copper exploration company MOD Resources.

Latest business results (June 2019, full year)

Higher production at its DeGrussa mine boosted revenues, but a lower copper price pushed down profits. During the year the company produced 69 394 tonnes of copper, up from 64 918 tonnes in the previous year, and 44 455 ounces of gold, up from 39 273 ounces. The average operating cost of US$0.83 per pound was substantially down from US$0.93 per pound in the previous year. The impact of the fall in global copper prices was partly mitigated by the weakness of the dollar. The figures also include production from the newly acquired Monty copper–gold mine, which is near DeGrussa.

Outlook

Despite some copper price weakness, the company is optimistic about long-term trends, particularly given the tight balance between supply and demand as well as the underlying strength of demand from China. The company also believes that the metal will remain firmly in demand as long as the global economy stays strong, and it will be a beneficiary of major new infrastructure initiatives throughout Asia and the rapid rise of new sources of demand from the electric vehicle and energy storage industries. Its forecast for the June 2020 year is for production of between 70 000 tonnes and 75 000 tonnes of copper and between 38 000 ounces and 40 000 ounces of gold, at an average cost of between US$0.90 and US$0.95 per pound. The DeGrussa mine has an estimated life of only several more years, and the company is looking elsewhere for growth. It is ramping up production at the Monty mine, and expects it to make an increasingly significant contribution in coming years. Sandfire owns an 85 per cent stake in the Black Butte Copper Project in Montana, USA, and is completing a feasibility study with a view to starting construction of an underground mine. In June 2019 it initiated a friendly takeover of MOD Resources, which owns assets in Botswana that offer the potential to become a high-margin, low-cost copper mine. At June 2019 Sandfire had net cash holdings of $247 million.

Year to 30 June	2018	2019
Revenues ($mn)	570.0	592.2
EBIT ($mn)	173.8	153.1
EBIT margin (%)	30.5	25.8
Profit before tax ($mn)	175.5	158.6
Profit after tax ($mn)	123.0	106.5
Earnings per share (c)	77.85	66.76
Cash flow per share (c)	160.31	155.06
Dividend (c)	27	23
Percentage franked	100	100
Net tangible assets per share ($)	3.34	3.77
Interest cover (times)	~	~
Return on equity (%)	25.5	18.8
Debt-to-equity ratio (%)	~	~
Current ratio	3.8	5.0

Schaffer Corporation Limited

ASX code: SFC www.schaffer.com.au

Schaffer-Monthly

Share price ($)	14.81
12-month high ($)	17.05
12-month low ($)	12.80
Market capitalisation ($mn)	204.6
Price-to-NTA-per-share ratio	2.0
5-year share price return (% p.a.)	22.3
Dividend reinvestment plan	No

Sector: Consumer discretionary	Company	Sector
Price/earnings ratio (times)	8.9	13.7
Dividend yield (%)	4.7	3.9

Perth company Schaffer was founded in 1955 to manufacture sand-lime bricks for the construction industry. Today its Delta Corporation subsidiary produces precast and prestressed concrete floors, beams and wall products, aimed mainly at the Western Australian construction market. However, its primary business now is the manufacture of leather goods, with a particular emphasis on products for the automotive industry, through its 83-per-cent-owned subsidiary Automotive Leather. This business operates from facilities in Australia, China and Slovakia, and supplies leading auto makers around the world. A third business for Schaffer is investments and property development, and it owns a portfolio of rental and development sites, mainly in Western Australia.

Latest business results (June 2019, full year)

Revenues and the after-tax profit fell, as the company was hit by weakness in the global automobile industry. Revenues for this business fell 13 per cent to $176 million, although profits held steady, thanks to operational efficiencies at the company's plants, along with a favourable impact from the weak dollar. Despite challenging conditions in the West Australian construction industry, revenues for building materials rose 15 per cent to $19.5 million. This mainly reflected the completion in the first half of a large civil infrastructure project, with the second half hurt by project schedule delays. This business managed to break even for the year, having previously been in the red. The company's investment portfolio — comprising SFC Investments and an 83 per cent holding in Gosh Capital — rose in value from $110.6 million in June 2018 to $134.4 million.

Outlook

The bulk of the company's profits derive from its automotive leather business, and this is highly dependent on trends in the global car-making sector. This industry is currently suffering weakness, due to concerns over Brexit, the possibility of a US–China trade war and tightening emission regulations in Europe. The company is also affected by the delay of a new production program at its plants, and it expects sales to continue to decline in the June 2020 first half. However, an expanded investment in computer numerical controlled cutting machines at its plants is cutting costs, and it will also benefit from any continued dollar weakness. A firm order book for building materials suggests that revenues and profits for this business are set to improve. The company sees significant long-term potential from the development of its 29-hectare site at Jandakot in Western Australia. Its SFC Investments business has established a base in the US, and has invested $4.1 million in four property syndicates.

Year to 30 June	2018	2019
Revenues ($mn)	226.8	202.9
EBIT ($mn)	36.1	40.3
EBIT margin (%)	15.9	19.9
Gross margin (%)	27.5	29.2
Profit before tax ($mn)	34.3	38.6
Profit after tax ($mn)	23.3	22.9
Earnings per share (c)	166.72	165.61
Cash flow per share (c)	201.14	199.39
Dividend (c)	45	70
Percentage franked	100	100
Net tangible assets per share ($)	6.47	7.55
Interest cover (times)	19.6	23.0
Return on equity (%)	28.2	23.3
Debt-to-equity ratio (%)	7.1	18.0
Current ratio	2.3	1.9

SeaLink Travel Group Limited

ASX code: SLK www.sealinktravelgroup.com.au

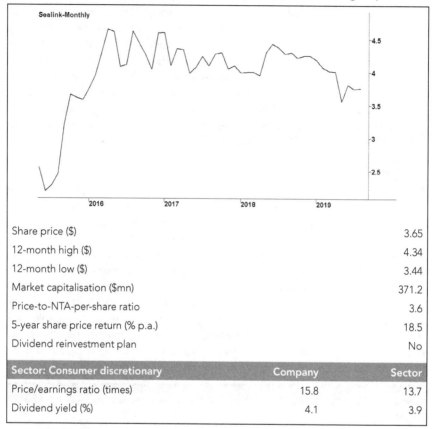

Share price ($)	3.65
12-month high ($)	4.34
12-month low ($)	3.44
Market capitalisation ($mn)	371.2
Price-to-NTA-per-share ratio	3.6
5-year share price return (% p.a.)	18.5
Dividend reinvestment plan	No

Sector: Consumer discretionary	Company	Sector
Price/earnings ratio (times)	15.8	13.7
Dividend yield (%)	4.1	3.9

Adelaide tourism and transport company SeaLink has its roots in the launch of a Kangaroo Island ferry service, Philanderer Ferries, in the 1970s. It has since expanded considerably through organic growth and acquisition, and today provides a wide range of ferry, resort and tourism services under more than 20 brands. It divides its operations into four key segments. SeaLink Queensland provides ferry and barging operations, as well as packaged holidays, throughout Queensland and the Northern Territory. SeaLink South Australia manages a wide range of travel services throughout South Australia and on the Murray River. Captain Cook Cruises offers water-based services in Sydney and Perth. In 2018 SeaLink acquired the Kingfisher Bay Resort Group on Fraser Island in Queensland, and this business has become a fourth division.

Latest business results (June 2019, full year)

A full year's contribution from Fraser Island operations boosted revenues. But higher costs hurt profits, although a substantially reduced tax rate meant a rise in the after-tax profit. The best result came from the new Fraser Island business, which contributed sales of $54 million, ahead of expectations, and moved from loss to profit. But the two core divisions, SeaLink Queensland and SeaLink South Australia, both saw profits down. In Queensland the company was affected by the ending of leases on some vessels at its Gladstone operations. South Australian business was hurt by a decline in bookings for the company's Murray Princess paddle steamer, which sails on the Murray River. The Captain Cook Cruises business was also weak, affected by a softening in international tourism demand, and it recorded a loss for the year.

Outlook

SeaLink Travel benefits from a firm economy and a buoyant tourism industry. Its strategy is to leverage its many assets into generating multiple streams of revenue, and it also expects to continue to grow by acquisition. It has experienced a decline in Chinese tourist numbers for its services, but believes that the dollar's weakness may help revive business. A strategic review of its Sydney Harbour operations will mean the termination of the loss-making Manly-to-Barangaroo ferry service, and the company expects a recovery in its Captain Cook Cruises division. It is working to upgrade facilities at its new $43 million Fraser Island acquisition, and is seeing growing numbers of bookings from the wedding market. The company regards the Fraser Island operation as one of the drivers of its future growth, and it has benefited from publicity surrounding the October 2018 visit by the Duke and Duchess of Sussex.

Year to 30 June	2018	2019
Revenues ($mn)	208.2	248.8
SeaLink Queensland (%)	37	31
SeaLink South Australia (%)	31	26
Fraser Island (%)	6	22
Captain Cook Cruises (%)	26	21
EBIT ($mn)	33.5	31.4
EBIT margin (%)	16.1	12.6
Profit before tax ($mn)	30.5	26.9
Profit after tax ($mn)	22.1	23.4
Earnings per share (c)	21.85	23.07
Cash flow per share (c)	34.60	39.25
Dividend (c)	14.5	15
Percentage franked	100	100
Net tangible assets per share ($)	0.96	1.03
Interest cover (times)	11.0	6.9
Return on equity (%)	14.7	15.1
Debt-to-equity ratio (%)	69.2	53.1
Current ratio	1.0	1.1

Servcorp Limited

ASX code: SRV

www.servcorp.com.au

Share price ($)	4.84
12-month high ($)	5.00
12-month low ($)	2.55
Market capitalisation ($mn)	468.6
Price-to-NTA-per-share ratio	2.1
5-year share price return (% p.a.)	1.2
Dividend reinvestment plan	No

Sector: Financials	Company	Sector
Price/earnings ratio (times)	16.0	15.0
Dividend yield (%)	4.8	5.9

Sydney-based Servcorp was founded in 1978 to provide serviced office space to small businesses. It has expanded to provide advanced corporate infrastructure, including IT and telecommunications services, and office support services. It also offers what it terms virtual offices, providing a prestigious address and a range of services for businesses that do not need a physical office. A third of the company's business is in northern Asia, with a quarter in Europe and the Middle East and 12 per cent in the US. In June 2019 it was operating 154 floors of offices in 54 cities across 24 countries.

Latest business results (June 2019, full year)

Revenues rose, as the company continued to expand, but underlying profits were hit by weakness in Hong Kong and Europe. However, a significantly lower tax rate led to a rise in the after-tax profit. On a like-for-like basis, the total occupancy rate was 73 per cent at June 2019, up from 72 per cent a year earlier. The big North Asian market has been one of the company's drivers of growth and it continued to do well, apart from Hong Kong, which produced a poor result. The Australia/New Zealand/Southeast Asia segment was generally flat for the year. The Europe/Middle East segment produced a decline in profits due to poor performances in France and Belgium and costs associated with new floor openings in Germany and Saudi Arabia. The US market continued to grow, with a reduced loss from the previous year. During the year Servcorp opened new floors in Berlin, Osaka, Riyadh and Tokyo. It closed locations in Abu Dhabi, Auckland, Perth, Melbourne, Singapore and Shanghai.

Outlook

Servcorp is a world leader in its business, with good market shares and a reputation for quality. Until the June 2017 year it had been growing strongly and generating large, regular increases in revenues and profits. Its forecast is that shared office space will grow over time from 5 per cent of all commercial real estate to around 20 per cent. But such growth prospects have drawn in many new participants and high levels of competition. These include a sharp increase in demand for casual and flexible co-working hubs that do not require the extra services that Servcorp's offices often provide. To meet this challenge the company has launched a series of restructuring initiatives and is also upgrading many of its properties to enhance their appeal. Its early forecast is for a June 2020 pre-tax profit of $36 million to $40 million.

Year to 30 June	2018	2019
Revenues ($mn)	310.1	334.9
EBIT ($mn)	35.2	29.9
EBIT margin (%)	11.4	8.9
Profit before tax ($mn)	37.9	32.0
Profit after tax ($mn)	28.9	29.2
Earnings per share (c)	29.42	30.16
Cash flow per share (c)	54.75	58.65
Dividend (c)	26	23
Percentage franked	16	49
Net tangible assets per share ($)	2.43	2.32
Interest cover (times)	~	~
Return on equity (%)	11.2	11.9
Debt-to-equity ratio (%)	~	~
Current ratio	1.7	1.3

Service Stream Limited

ASX code: SSM   www.servicestream.com

Share price ($)	2.74
12-month high ($)	3.06
12-month low ($)	1.47
Market capitalisation ($mn)	1 100.4
Price-to-NTA-per-share ratio	~
5-year share price return (% p.a.)	65.6
Dividend reinvestment plan	Yes

Sector: Industrials	Company	Sector
Price/earnings ratio (times)	20.9	18.3
Dividend yield (%)	3.3	4.1

Melbourne-based contractor Service Stream provides a variety of engineering services to the telecommunications, electricity, gas, water and new energy industries. It segments its operations into four divisions. The Fixed Communications division offers construction and maintenance services for fixed-line communications networks, with Telstra and the National Broadband Network (NBN) among its major customers. The Network Construction division is engaged in the design, construction and engineering of infrastructure projects, mainly in the telecommunications sector. The Energy and Water division is involved in a range of specialist metering and other services to the electricity, gas and water sectors. A fourth division is based on the $162 million acquisition in January 2019 of Comdain Infrastructure, and provides engineering and asset management services to owners and operators of gas and water networks.

Latest business results (June 2019, full year)

The Comdain acquisition led to a big jump in revenues and profits. However, even excluding this the company reported some pleasing growth. The telecommunications segment — incorporating the Fixed Communications and the Network Construction divisions — achieved sales growth of nearly 10 per cent, with profits up 22 per cent, thanks especially to increasing amounts of work for the NBN. The utilities segment — comprising the Energy and Water division and Comdain Infrastructure — saw sales jump by 156 per cent, with profits up 127 per cent, although this mainly reflected the addition of Comdain. However, this segment also achieved growth for metering services, new energy and inspection services.

Outlook

Service Stream has been transformed by the Comdain acquisition. It was previously heavily dependent on the telecommunications sector, which contributed more than 80 per cent of its revenues. This ratio will now fall to around 55 per cent. Comdain's engineering and asset management services, mainly in east coast markets, combine well with Service Stream's own core capabilities of design, construction, operations and maintenance. The company believes it is now able to offer a greatly enhanced service to clients, and with the potential for expansion to new markets. It also expects significant synergy benefits. On the telecommunications side, it expects continuing strong demand for NBN work, with a growing amount of annuity-style revenue. It has also secured contracts relating to the roll-out of 5G telecommunications networks in Australia, and this business has the potential for significant growth. Despite borrowing to fund the Comdain acquisition, Service Stream at June 2019 had net cash holdings of $10.5 million, and it continues to seek further complementary acquisitions.

Year to 30 June	2018	2019
Revenues ($mn)	629.6	851.0
Telecommunications (%)	83	68
Utilities (%)	17	32
EBIT ($mn)	57.9	73.3
EBIT margin (%)	9.2	8.6
Profit before tax ($mn)	58.3	72.1
Profit after tax ($mn)	41.1	49.9
Earnings per share (c)	11.29	13.09
Cash flow per share (c)	13.89	17.35
Dividend (c)	7.5	9
Percentage franked	100	100
Net tangible assets per share ($)	0.16	~
Interest cover (times)	~	61.0
Return on equity (%)	19.9	19.4
Debt-to-equity ratio (%)	~	~
Current ratio	1.5	1.2

SG Fleet Group Limited

ASX code: SGF

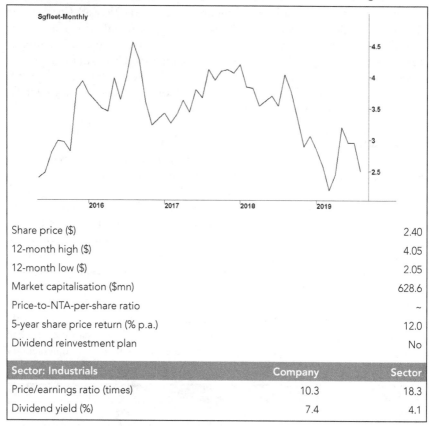

Share price ($)	2.40
12-month high ($)	4.05
12-month low ($)	2.05
Market capitalisation ($mn)	628.6
Price-to-NTA-per-share ratio	~
5-year share price return (% p.a.)	12.0
Dividend reinvestment plan	No

Sector: Industrials	Company	Sector
Price/earnings ratio (times)	10.3	18.3
Dividend yield (%)	7.4	4.1

SG Fleet, based in Sydney, has its roots in the formation in 1986 of Leaseway Transportation, a specialist fleet management company. Leaseway was later sold to the Commonwealth Bank, which in turn sold it in 2004 to a South African company, Super Group, who renamed it FleetAustralia. In 2014 it was listed on the ASX as SG Fleet Group. Today it offers a range of fleet management services, in Australia, New Zealand and the United Kingdom. It also provides salary packaging services. It operates under the brands SG Fleet and, in the UK, Fleet Hire. South Africa's Super Group continues to hold a 59 per cent equity stake in the company.

Latest business results (June 2019, full year)

A decline in new car sales hit the company, and revenues and profits were down, with some second-half strength — following the federal election and an interest rate cut —insufficient to offset the declines of the first half. Despite a 10 per cent decline in new car sales during the year, the company saw novated sales down only 3 per cent. The company's corporate business remained steady, with some new contracts and growth in accessory sales. British business represents around 20 per cent of total company turnover, and sales and profits were up, thanks to some new contract wins. These came despite poor business confidence and continuing Brexit uncertainty. New Zealand operations enjoyed an excellent year, with a double-digit rise in sales and profits, though this business is responsible for only about 3 per cent of company income. The company's total fleet size fell from 147 703 vehicles in June 2018 to 139 945 vehicles in June 2019.

Outlook

SG Fleet occupies a solid position in a competitive industry. It generates good profit margins, and as it grows it achieves significant economies of scale that boost margins higher. However, its business is influenced to a degree by the state of the economy, and in particular the level of new car sales. Nevertheless, it enjoys a large amount of annuity-style income, with many long-term clients, as it is costly for a car fleet customer to switch providers. It expects a series of new products to solidify relationships with existing customers and attract new ones. Its new Inspect365 vehicle inspection system has generated a pleasing response and its eStart electric vehicle transition planning service has helped deliver new customers. The company expects continuing solid growth from British operations, although Brexit issues may dampen short-term results.

Year to 30 June	2018	2019
Revenues ($mn)	513.9	508.1
EBIT ($mn)	104.2	93.7
EBIT margin (%)	20.3	18.4
Profit before tax ($mn)	96.0	85.8
Profit after tax ($mn)	67.5	60.5
Earnings per share (c)	26.30	23.20
Cash flow per share (c)	37.46	35.33
Dividend (c)	18.74	17.69
Percentage franked	100	100
Net tangible assets per share ($)	~	~
Interest cover (times)	12.7	11.8
Return on equity (%)	28.3	22.8
Debt-to-equity ratio (%)	12.4	8.9

Smartgroup Corporation Limited

ASX code: SIQ   www.smartgroup.com.au

Share price ($)	11.66
12-month high ($)	12.99
12-month low ($)	7.26
Market capitalisation ($mn)	1 473.1
Price-to-NTA-per-share ratio	~
5-year share price return (% p.a.)	52.7
Dividend reinvestment plan	No

Sector: Industrials	Company	Sector
Price/earnings ratio (times)	25.0	18.3
Dividend yield (%)	3.6	4.1

Sydney-based Smartgroup got its start in 1999 as Smartsalary, a salary packaging specialist. It later branched into other businesses, and has grown significantly, both organically and through acquisition. It is now engaged in salary packaging services, as well as vehicle novated leasing, fleet management, payroll administration, share plan administration and workforce optimisation consulting services.

Latest business results (June 2019, half year)

Revenues and profits rose modestly, as core businesses continued to grow and the company achieved success in constraining costs. Nearly 80 per cent of its income derives from what the company calls outsourced administration—essentially outsourced salary packaging services, novated leasing, share plan administration and outsourced payroll services—and this business saw a solid rise in revenues and profits. There was 4 per cent growth in numbers of both salary package arrangements and novated leases. The company's smaller businesses are software services and fleet management, and these too saw modest growth. During the year the company acquired a pair of Perth-based companies, Pay-Plan and Set Leasing. It also acquired the novated leasing assets of Melbourne-based Mylease.

Outlook

Smartgroup is one of Australia's two largest companies involved in the salary packaging and novated leasing businesses. The other is McMillan Shakespeare. Essentially this business involves taking advantage of complex legislation to provide tax deductions for employees, mainly those working in charities or in the public sector. Smartgroup has grown considerably through a series of acquisitions in recent years, and at June 2019 it had more than 4000 clients. As it grows it achieves economies of scale, and profit margins increase. The April 2019 acquisition for $6.9 million of the novated leasing assets of Mylease delivered the company some 1000 novated leases with around 500 employer clients. The $2.2 million acquisition in June 2019 of Pay-Plan and Set Leasing gave the company about 1500 salary packaging arrangements and about 500 novated leases from around 30 clients. The company is also working to boost cross-selling of its various products among existing clients, and at June 2019 there were 180 clients using two or more of its products, up from 149 clients a year earlier. Nevertheless, Smartgroup is vulnerable to weakness in the economy and in employment trends. Its business is also affected by trends in new car sales, and these have recently been weak in Australia, as some companies choose to cut costs by retaining and refinancing existing staff cars, rather than buying new ones.

Year to 31 December	2017	2018
Revenues ($mn)	205.4	242.3
EBIT ($mn)	65.6	86.9
EBIT margin (%)	31.9	35.9
Profit before tax ($mn)	61.9	84.3
Profit after tax ($mn)	41.2	59.3
Earnings per share (c)	34.45	46.65
Cash flow per share (c)	50.84	66.33
Dividend (c)	35	41.5
Percentage franked	100	100
Interest cover (times)	17.7	32.9
Return on equity (%)	20.7	23.9
Half year to 30 June	2018	2019
Revenues ($mn)	122.8	126.0
Profit before tax ($mn)	41.1	44.2
Profit after tax ($mn)	29.0	30.9
Earnings per share (c)	23.10	23.90
Dividend (c)	20.5	21.5
Percentage franked	100	100
Net tangible assets per share ($)	~	~
Debt-to-equity ratio (%)	9.4	11.8
Current ratio	1.2	1.1

Sonic Healthcare Limited

ASX code: SHL
www.sonichealthcare.com

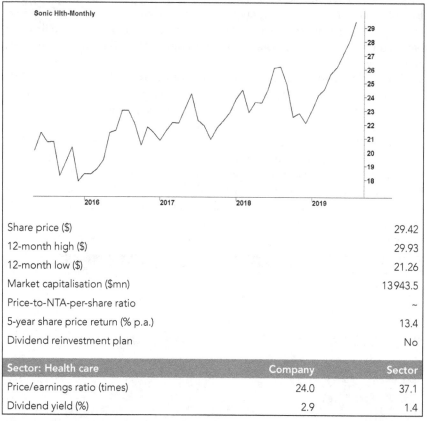

Share price ($)	29.42
12-month high ($)	29.93
12-month low ($)	21.26
Market capitalisation ($mn)	13943.5
Price-to-NTA-per-share ratio	~
5-year share price return (% p.a.)	13.4
Dividend reinvestment plan	No

Sector: Health care	Company	Sector
Price/earnings ratio (times)	24.0	37.1
Dividend yield (%)	2.9	1.4

Sydney-based Sonic Healthcare has its roots in the pathology practice of Douglass Laboratories, which it acquired in 1987. It has since expanded dramatically through acquisition and organic growth, and now operates through numerous separate companies. It has become Australia's largest private provider of pathology services and second-largest provider of radiology services. It is also now the world's third-largest pathology services provider, with services to medical practitioners, hospitals, community medical services and their patients in the United States, Germany, Switzerland, Belgium, the United Kingdom, Ireland and New Zealand. Its Sonic Clinical Services division operates 233 medical centres in Australia, including the Independent Practitioner Network group of medical practices and Sonic HealthPlus occupational health clinics.

Latest business results (June 2019, full year)

Acquisitions and the weak dollar generated an excellent result for Sonic, although even excluding these benefits it achieved 4 per cent growth in revenues. The Australian pathology business represents 24 per cent of turnover, and it enjoyed a year of revenue and profit growth, with a gain in market share. American pathology also now represents 24 per cent of revenues, thanks to the $750 million acquisition of anatomical pathology specialist Aurora Diagnostics in January 2019. However, US profits were hurt by some Medicare fee cuts. German pathology is a further 20 per cent of revenues, with income up. The company's smaller pathology businesses, in the UK, Ireland and Switzerland, reported good results, but with Belgium flat for the year.

Outlook

Sonic has achieved sustained success through its drive to consolidate the once-fragmented Australian pathology industry. It is now doing the same abroad, and has become the market leader in Germany, Switzerland and Britain, and one of the leaders in Belgium and the United States. However, most of its businesses are subject to heavy government regulation, which can impede or enhance profit growth, and the company is also affected by currency movements. Its acquisition of Florida-based Aurora Diagnostics, following the acquisition in 2018 of German company Pathologie Trier, has extended the company's coverage in the field of anatomical pathology. Sonic is now seeking further acquisitions in the fragmented US pathology sector. In the UK the company has won a cervical screening contract from the National Health Service to provide HPV (human papillomavirus) testing for the population of London, and it is bidding for further contracts. Its early forecast is for profit growth of 6 per cent to 8 per cent on a constant currency basis in the June 2020 year.

Year to 30 June	2018	2019
Revenues ($mn)	5538.2	6177.4
EBIT ($mn)	692.3	801.7
EBIT margin (%)	12.5	13.0
Profit before tax ($mn)	617.0	722.3
Profit after tax ($mn)	475.6	549.7
Earnings per share (c)	112.65	122.49
Cash flow per share (c)	158.08	169.25
Dividend (c)	81	84
Percentage franked	26	26
Net tangible assets per share ($)	~	~
Interest cover (times)	9.2	10.1
Return on equity (%)	11.9	11.5
Debt-to-equity ratio (%)	58.0	41.9
Current ratio	1.4	0.9

Southern Cross Media Group Limited

ASX code: SXL   www.southerncrossaustereo.com.au

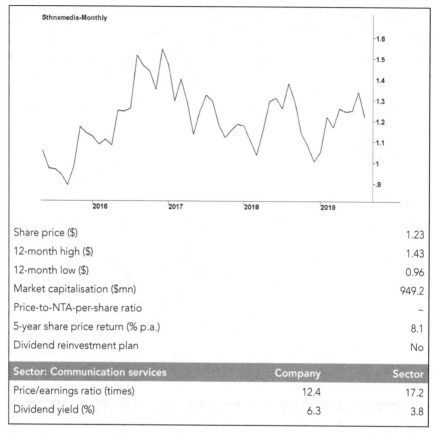

Share price ($)	1.23
12-month high ($)	1.43
12-month low ($)	0.96
Market capitalisation ($mn)	949.2
Price-to-NTA-per-share ratio	~
5-year share price return (% p.a.)	8.1
Dividend reinvestment plan	No

Sector: Communication services	Company	Sector
Price/earnings ratio (times)	12.4	17.2
Dividend yield (%)	6.3	3.8

Melbourne-based Southern Cross Media is one of Australia's leading radio and television broadcasters, with a growing online presence. It runs the Hit network of FM radio stations, which broadcast to the metropolitan markets of Sydney, Melbourne, Brisbane, Adelaide and Perth, as well as to regional stations. These stations are targeted towards women in the 18 to 49 age bracket. It also operates the Triple M radio network, aimed at men aged 25 to 54. Its TV stations cover wide areas of regional Victoria, New South Wales, Queensland, Northern Territory and South Australia.

Latest business results (June 2019, full year)

Revenues and profits edged up in a mixed year for the company. The Audio division experienced some modest growth, thanks especially to growing demand from national advertisers, attracted by the company's FM and regional radio strength and its new digital radio audiences. But local advertising was relatively weak, with federal and state elections and falling housing and auto markets all hurting business. Broadcast and production expenses rose, but the company achieved success in cutting staffing costs, and profits were up, with slightly expanded margins. Television revenues fell, with national advertising generally flat from the previous year and local advertising down. However, the company benefited from a reduction in the division's expenses, and profits were up a little. Nevertheless, the television business, though 31 per cent of turnover, generated only about 15 per cent of company profit. The company actually booked a statutory after-tax loss of $91.4 million, mainly due to a $227 million non-cash impairment charge against the value of its television assets.

Outlook

The media business is volatile and is changing rapidly. It can be dependent on hit productions and fashionable personalities, with new technologies also important. In addition, it is a heavily regulated industry. Southern Cross has achieved success with its switch in July 2016 to a five-year affiliation agreement with Channel Nine, which led to growth in its television audience. Nevertheless, it operates in an environment of continuing declines in viewer numbers nationwide for free-to-air television. Its radio stations enjoy solid shares of their respective markets, and Southern Cross is developing new revenue streams through moves into digital broadcasting. Its PodcastOne Australia business provides premium digital audio on demand and is now producing 2500 episodes per year, with audiences and revenues up 260 per cent in the June 2019 year. The company is achieving success with its initiative, dubbed Boomtown, to promote the regional radio market to national advertisers.

Year to 30 June	2018	2019
Revenues ($mn)	656.8	660.1
Audio (%)	67	68
Television (%)	32	31
EBIT ($mn)	127.7	129.3
EBIT margin (%)	19.4	19.6
Profit before tax ($mn)	107.2	110.0
Profit after tax ($mn)	73.9	76.2
Earnings per share (c)	9.61	9.91
Cash flow per share (c)	13.60	13.89
Dividend (c)	7.75	7.75
Percentage franked	100	100
Net tangible assets per share ($)	~	~
Interest cover (times)	6.2	6.7
Return on equity (%)	11.9	14.9
Debt-to-equity ratio (%)	50.7	67.0
Current ratio	2.0	2.1

Super Retail Group Limited

ASX code: SUL　　　　　　　　　　　www.superretailgroup.com.au

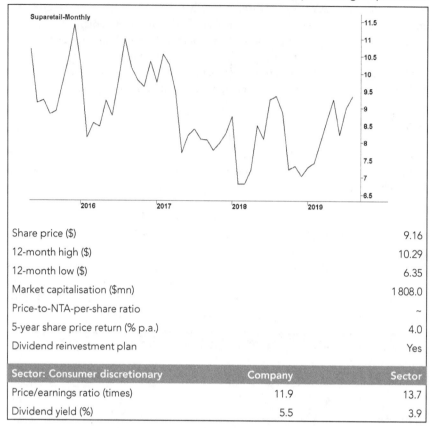

Share price ($)	9.16
12-month high ($)	10.29
12-month low ($)	6.35
Market capitalisation ($mn)	1 808.0
Price-to-NTA-per-share ratio	~
5-year share price return (% p.a.)	4.0
Dividend reinvestment plan	Yes

Sector: Consumer discretionary	Company	Sector
Price/earnings ratio (times)	11.9	13.7
Dividend yield (%)	5.5	3.9

Specialist retail chain Super Retail Group was established as a mail-order business in 1972 and has its headquarters in Lawnton, north of Brisbane. It now comprises a number of key retail brands, with around 690 stores throughout Australia and New Zealand. Supercheap Auto is a retailer of automotive spare parts and related products. Rebel is a prominent sporting goods chain. BCF is a retailer of boating, camping and fishing products. Macpac, acquired in March 2018, is an outdoor adventure and activity specialist retailer.

Latest business results (June 2019, full year)

Revenues and underlying profits rose, with 2.9 per cent same-store sales growth and strength in all divisions. Supercheap Auto achieved growth in all states and in New Zealand, with particular strength in auto maintenance and auto accessories, which represent three-quarters of business. Rebel enjoyed solid demand for apparel and footwear, with accessory sales also strong. The camping and apparel categories boosted business for BCF, more than offsetting a decline in fishing equipment. However, a competitive sales environment dented profit margins. The new Macpac business made a full-year contribution. Total online sales of $201 million represented a 25 per cent jump from the previous year. The company also reported several one-off items not included in the underlying profit figure. These included $8.9 million in wage and remediation expenses, to compensate for underpayments to store staff in previous years.

Outlook

Having restructured its operations, including the acquisition of Macpac and the termination of the Rays and Amart Sports brands, Super Retail now controls four prominent brands with strong positions in their respective markets. It is working to build these businesses with a variety of strategies. It plans a steady roll-out of new stores. It is also boosting its digital capacity, and expects online sales to continue their strong growth. It is increasing its range of higher-margin own-brand and exclusive products at its stores, and is harnessing customer loyalty through the promotion of members' clubs. It sees its Macpac acquisition as offering some strong growth potential. The adventure outdoors retail market in Australia is estimated to be worth about $2.2 billion annually, and Super Retail now seeks to be the leader in this sector, with new large-format stores and a compelling online strategy. Nevertheless, despite Super Retail's strengths it operates in a challenging retail environment, with online businesses like Amazon a competitor for many of its products. It is also hurt by the dollar's weakness and is vulnerable to any downturn in consumer sentiment.

Year to 29 June*	2018	2019
Revenues ($mn)	2570.4	2710.4
Supercheap Auto (%)	39	38
Rebel (%)	38	38
BCF (%)	19	19
Macpac** (%)	3	5
EBIT ($mn)	219.6	228.0
EBIT margin (%)	8.5	8.4
Gross margin (%)	44.9	45.1
Profit before tax ($mn)	201.9	206.7
Profit after tax ($mn)	145.3	152.5
Earnings per share (c)	73.67	77.28
Cash flow per share (c)	111.44	121.16
Dividend (c)	49	50
Percentage franked	100	100
Net tangible assets per share ($)	~	~
Interest cover (times)	12.4	10.7
Return on equity (%)	19.3	19.2
Debt-to-equity ratio (%)	54.6	47.4
Current ratio	1.4	1.3

* 30 June 2018
** includes the Rays business, now discontinued

Supply Network Limited

ASX code: SNL   www.supplynetwork.com.au

Share price ($)	3.99
12-month high ($)	5.13
12-month low ($)	3.41
Market capitalisation ($mn)	162.6
Price-to-NTA-per-share ratio	4.3
5-year share price return (% p.a.)	13.2
Dividend reinvestment plan	No

Sector: Consumer discretionary	Company	Sector
Price/earnings ratio (times)	18.7	13.7
Dividend yield (%)	3.6	3.9

Sydney-based Supply Network is a supplier of bus and truck parts in the commercial vehicle aftermarket, operating under the brand name Multispares, which was established in 1976. It manages offices, distribution centres and workshops at 16 locations throughout Australia and five in New Zealand.

Latest business results (June 2019, full year)

Sales and profits rose in a solid result for the company. Australian business comprises more than 80 per cent of total company turnover, and sales were up 10 per cent, with the pre-tax profit rising by 17 per cent. The result included the first full year of operations at the new Port Hedland facility. New Zealand operations achieved a 12 per cent increase in sales. But the pre-tax profit there fell by 11 per cent, hurt by rising costs associated with the opening of the company's new branch and distribution centre in Hamilton. During the year the company also relocated its Christchurch operations to a new facility.

Outlook

Supply Network is one of the leaders in the competitive Australian market for the supply of truck and bus parts. With a great diversity of vehicle makes and models, and with a considerable difference in requirements between various regions of the country, the company has established a decentralised management structure with a strong regional focus. Its core activity in recent years has become the supply of truck components, with this business growing at a faster pace than the supply of bus components. In part, this results from large numbers of newer bus fleets around the country, reducing demand for replacement parts. Consequently, nearly 80 per cent of company sales now are to the trucking sector. Company fleets are the largest customer group, and these are sophisticated buyers of parts with a focus on costs, making this business highly competitive. Independent repair workshops are the next-largest customer group. The company has reported that the new Port Hedland branch is performing well in a challenging environment with unique work conditions. The new Hamilton branch and distribution centre is also performing to expectations, and has relieved pressure on Auckland operations. A second branch in Brisbane is opening in October 2019 and this is expected to streamline Queensland operations significantly. As Supply Network's business expands the company needs to boost its inventory, and it is coming up against capacity constraints at its warehouses. It is now investigating ways to add a series of smaller distribution centres to its network, in order best to manage future growth.

Year to 30 June	2018	2019
Revenues ($mn)	112.1	123.9
EBIT ($mn)	12.0	12.8
EBIT margin (%)	10.7	10.3
Profit before tax ($mn)	11.7	12.3
Profit after tax ($mn)	8.2	8.7
Earnings per share (c)	20.06	21.32
Cash flow per share (c)	22.73	24.61
Dividend (c)	13.5	14.5
Percentage franked	100	100
Net tangible assets per share ($)	0.85	0.94
Interest cover (times)	46.1	28.8
Return on equity (%)	24.7	23.8
Debt-to-equity ratio (%)	4.7	20.4
Current ratio	2.4	2.6

Technology One Limited

ASX code: TNE   www.technologyonecorp.com

Share price ($)	7.47
12-month high ($)	9.39
12-month low ($)	5.05
Market capitalisation ($mn)	2369.1
Price-to-NTA-per-share ratio	149.4
5-year share price return (% p.a.)	19.0
Dividend reinvestment plan	No

Sector: Information Technology	Company	Sector
Price/earnings ratio (times)	46.3	29.4
Dividend yield (%)	1.2	1.6

Brisbane-based TechnologyOne, founded in 1987, designs, develops, implements and supports a wide range of financial management, accounting and business software. It has gained success with its TechnologyOne Financials software product, and enjoys particular strength in local government. Its software is also used by educational institutions, including many Australian universities. Other key markets are financial services, central government, and health and community services. It derives revenues not only from the supply of its products but also from annual licence fees. It operates from offices in Australia, New Zealand, Papua New Guinea, Malaysia and the UK. It has opened research and development centres in Indonesia and Vietnam.

Latest business results (March 2019, half year)

TechnologyOne enjoyed a big surge in profits as increasingly it succeeded in moving its customers onto its Software as a Service (SaaS) cloud platforms. The number of large-scale enterprise SaaS customers rose from 280 at March 2018 to 389 a year later, with fees up 42 per cent to $37.5 million. The company also benefited from a turnaround in its consulting services — essentially the implementation of its software — with this business moving from loss to profit, despite a slight dip in revenues.

The company's British operation saw its loss falling from $3.2 million to $0.9 million. In addition, company operating expenses fell 7 per cent to $104.8 million. However, the company conceded that new accounting standards have magnified the extent of its profit growth. It maintained its high level of research and development spending, up nearly 9 per cent to $27.8 million.

Outlook

TechnologyOne has become a star among Australian high-tech companies, with growing profits and regular dividend increases. In large part this reflects a strong product line, a solid flow of recurring income and a heavy investment in new products and services. It is now achieving great success with its SaaS offerings, which put software in the cloud, rather than on the customers' own computers, meaning that the customers always have the latest software versions, and giving them greater flexibility than previously. TechnologyOne has achieved an SaaS annual contract value of $85.8 million, and believes this could rise to $107 million by September 2019. The company forecasts a September 2019 pre-tax profit of $71.6 million to $76.3 million, and predicts that it will double in size over the coming five years, with new machine learning and artificial intelligence products, a significant contribution from British operations and the possibility of an entry to the US market.

Year to 30 September	2017	2018
Revenues ($mn)	271.6	297.1
EBIT ($mn)	57.3	66.2
EBIT margin (%)	21.1	22.3
Profit before tax ($mn)	58.0	66.5
Profit after tax ($mn)	44.5	51.0
Earnings per share (c)	14.18	16.14
Cash flow per share (c)	15.53	17.50
Dividend (c)	8.2	9.02
Percentage franked	75	80
Interest cover (times)	~	~
Return on equity (%)	30.1	30.3
Half year to 31 March	2018	2019
Revenues ($mn)	123.6	129.3
Profit before tax ($mn)	10.6	24.5
Profit after tax ($mn)	8.2	17.9
Earnings per share (c)	2.59	5.65
Dividend (c)	2.86	3.15
Percentage franked	75	75
Net tangible assets per share ($)	0.10	0.05
Debt-to-equity ratio (%)	~	~
Current ratio	1.8	0.8

TPG Telecom Limited

ASX code: TPM

www.tpg.com.au

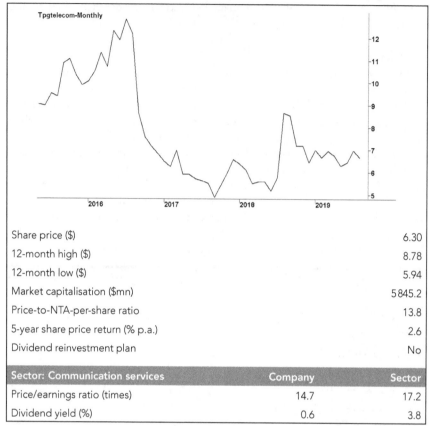

Share price ($)	6.30
12-month high ($)	8.78
12-month low ($)	5.94
Market capitalisation ($mn)	5 845.2
Price-to-NTA-per-share ratio	13.8
5-year share price return (% p.a.)	2.6
Dividend reinvestment plan	No

Sector: Communication services	Company	Sector
Price/earnings ratio (times)	14.7	17.2
Dividend yield (%)	0.6	3.8

Sydney company TPG Telecom was founded in 1986 as Total Peripherals Group, a supplier of computers and electronic equipment. It later moved into telecommunications services, and has grown through merger and acquisition to become a major internet service provider, particularly since the 2015 acquisition of iiNet. It also offers a full range of communications services to residential users, small and medium enterprises, government, large corporations and wholesale customers. It operates telephone exchanges across Australia, and owns the international PPC-1 submarine cable connecting Australia and Guam, with onward connectivity to Asia and the US. It has launched a mobile phone service in Singapore. Washington H. Soul Pattinson holds 25 per cent of the equity. TPG has announced plans to merge with Vodaphone Hutchison Australia.

Latest business results (January 2019, half year)

Strong corporate business helped TPG to a modest rise in profits. In particular, the company benefited from a significant increase in the contribution from its contract to provide fibre services to Vodaphone. Increasingly, this business is shifting to TPG's own fibre infrastructure, which has led to a substantial boost to margins.

By contrast, consumer business was hurt by the continuing National Broadband Network rollout, which has led to declining home phone voice revenue and to broadband gross margin erosion. The company has announced that it will cease the rollout of its mobile network in Australia, due to government restrictions — on national security grounds — on the use of equipment from Chinese company Huawei.

Outlook

In August 2018 TPG announced that it has reached agreement on a $15 billion merger with rival telecommunications giant Vodaphone Hutchison Australia. This will create a third major telecommunications company in Australia, after Telstra and Optus, with annual revenues of more than $6 billion and a base of more than eight million customers. TPG shareholders will own 49.9 per cent of the new merged company, with Vodaphone Hutchison Australia shareholders owning the remaining 50.1 per cent. The new company will continue to operate under the name TPG Telecom, and is expected to hold a national market share of around 20 per cent for mobile phones and 22 per cent for fixed line phones. Before the merger TPG will divest itself of its Singapore mobile network. However, in May 2019 the Australian Competition and Consumer Commission (ACCC) announced that it opposes the merger. Consequently, TPG and Vodaphone Hutchison have initiated proceedings in the Federal Court of Australia, seeking to overturn the ACCC decision.

Year to 31 July	2017	2018
Revenues ($mn)	2490.7	2495.2
EBIT ($mn)	646.4	598.2
EBIT margin (%)	26.0	24.0
Profit before tax ($mn)	595.5	563.8
Profit after tax ($mn)	413.8	396.9
Earnings per share (c)	47.88	42.85
Cash flow per share (c)	76.15	69.08
Dividend (c)	10	4
Percentage franked	100	100
Interest cover (times)	12.7	17.4
Return on equity (%)	19.9	15.3
Half year to 31 January	2018	2019
Revenues ($mn)	1254.6	1235.8
Profit before tax ($mn)	279.5	297.7
Profit after tax ($mn)	217.7	225.2
Earnings per share (c)	23.52	24.27
Dividend (c)	2	2
Percentage franked	100	100
Net tangible assets per share ($)	~	0.46
Debt-to-equity ratio (%)	53.1	55.0
Current ratio	0.3	0.2

Treasury Wine Estates Limited

ASX code: TWE   www.tweglobal.com

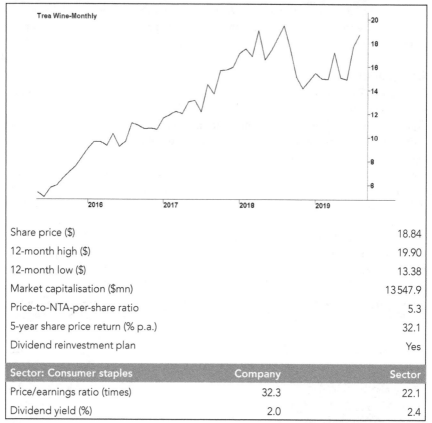

Share price ($)	18.84
12-month high ($)	19.90
12-month low ($)	13.38
Market capitalisation ($mn)	13 547.9
Price-to-NTA-per-share ratio	5.3
5-year share price return (% p.a.)	32.1
Dividend reinvestment plan	Yes

Sector: Consumer staples	Company	Sector
Price/earnings ratio (times)	32.3	22.1
Dividend yield (%)	2.0	2.4

Melbourne-based Treasury Wine can trace its origins to the establishment in the 19th century of iconic wineries such as Lindeman's and Penfolds. These and many others were progressively absorbed into the wine division of Foster's Group, then in 2011 separated into a new company. Today Treasury Wine is one of the world's largest wine companies, with sales to more than 100 countries. Its numerous brands include Beringer, Lindeman's, Penfolds, Stag's Leap, Pepperjack, Rawson's Retreat, Rosemount Estate, Wolf Blass, Wynns Coonawarra Estate and Yellowglen.

Latest business results (June 2019, full year)

Surging Asian demand for its premium wines once again helped generate a significant boost to revenues and profits for Treasury, with all other regions also strong. The company's preferred measure of profitability is a ratio it calls EBITS – earnings before interest, taxation and SGARA (self-generating and regenerating assets, an agribusiness measure). On this basis, Asian profits jumped 43 per cent, on sales growth of 37 per cent. Though representing little more than a quarter of company income, Asia now delivers around 40 per cent of total profit. Cost reductions and higher demand for premium wines boosted Australia/New Zealand profits by 15 per cent. New distribution channels and growing demand in Canada and Latin America helped the Americas segment to a 13 per cent rise in profits. The highly competitive European market recorded 4 per cent profit growth.

Outlook

Treasury Wine Estates has placed a focus on the high-margin premium wine market, and this has driven its recent strong growth. In particular, it has made a large investment in the huge Chinese market, and this has generated some fast-increasing sales. However, the company has faced accusations that it has antagonised Chinese wholesalers by forcing them to purchase large quantities of low-end wines if they also want access to the very desirable premium wines. In addition, with so much of its recent strong growth coming from China, the company is vulnerable to slackening demand that could be sparked by trade wars or a slowing global economy. It continues to invest in new distribution channels in North America, aimed at boosting margins there. In Europe its focus is on a limited portfolio of brands aimed at three key markets, the United Kingdom, Sweden and the Netherlands. It views its investments in French production and vineyard assets as supporting its next stage of global growth. The company's early forecast is for 15 per cent to 20 per cent EBITS growth in the June 2020 year.

Year to 30 June	2018	2019
Revenues ($mn)	2429.0	2831.6
Americas (%)	40	40
Asia (%)	23	27
Australia & New Zealand (%)	25	21
Europe (%)	12	12
EBIT ($mn)	508.9	643.0
EBIT margin (%)	21.0	22.7
Gross margin (%)	40.9	41.3
Profit before tax ($mn)	475.5	591.0
Profit after tax ($mn)	360.3	419.5
Earnings per share (c)	49.65	58.39
Cash flow per share (c)	63.09	72.73
Dividend (c)	32	38
Percentage franked	88	100
Net tangible assets per share ($)	3.29	3.53
Interest cover (times)	15.2	12.4
Return on equity (%)	10.2	11.7
Debt-to-equity ratio (%)	22.5	20.1
Current ratio	2.2	2.5

Virtus Health Limited

ASX code: VRT   www.virtushealth.com.au

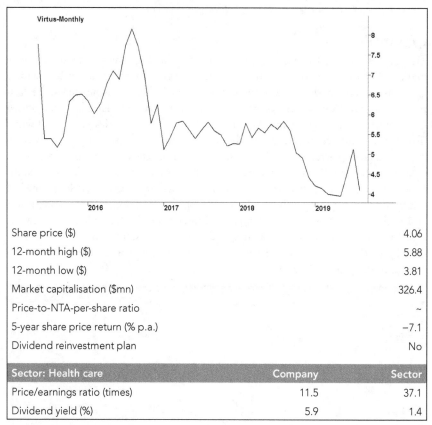

Share price ($)	4.06
12-month high ($)	5.88
12-month low ($)	3.81
Market capitalisation ($mn)	326.4
Price-to-NTA-per-share ratio	~
5-year share price return (% p.a.)	−7.1
Dividend reinvestment plan	No

Sector: Health care	Company	Sector
Price/earnings ratio (times)	11.5	37.1
Dividend yield (%)	5.9	1.4

Fertility clinic specialist Virtus Health, based in Sydney, was founded in 2002 from the amalgamation of four Sydney IVF (in-vitro fertilisation) practices. It has since joined in partnership with more clinics, and today operates a network in New South Wales, Victoria, Queensland and Tasmania, and has also expanded abroad, to the United Kingdom, Ireland, Denmark and Singapore. In addition, it has moved into other medical sectors, including the provision of a range of patient diagnostic services and day hospital procedures.

Latest business results (June 2019, full year)

Revenues were up but profits fell, as a competitive IVF market in Australia hit the company's operations, and it lost market share. Australia represents nearly 80 per cent of total income, and revenues were generally flat from the previous year, with profits down. The company achieved 1.5 per cent growth in IVF treatment volume sales —

against overall market growth of 4.9 per cent — but with demand for its low-cost services rising while demand for premium services fell. The company's other domestic businesses, diagnostics and day hospitals, were also weak. By contrast, international operations were strong, with a first-year contribution from the new Danish clinic Trianglen and continued growth in Singapore. This was partially offset by reduced business at the other Danish clinic, Aagaard, and restructuring initiatives in Ireland. Profits were boosted by $4.1 million from the commercialisation of the company's Ivy artificial intelligence system — developed with two other companies — which predicts the likelihood of an individual IVF embryo leading to a viable pregnancy.

Outlook

Virtus is well regarded for its fertility services in Australia, with high market shares. However, the entry to this market of more low-cost service providers has intensified competition. The company has also been hit by rising compliance costs. In response to the competition it is placing more emphasis at its 36 domestic clinics on its low-cost services. It is also working to build its international network through organic growth and further acquisitions. This business now represents around 21 per cent of total turnover, and the company aims to raise it to 30 per cent. The relocation of its main pathology laboratory is enabling the company's diagnostics business to offer enhanced testing services. The day hospital business has been hit by relocation and renovation costs. However, these are now complete, and with the addition of the Hobart Specialist Day Hospital — bringing the total to seven hospitals — the company believes this business is set for renewed growth.

Year to 30 June	2018	2019
Revenues ($mn)	260.2	280.1
EBIT ($mn)	52.5	49.9
EBIT margin (%)	20.2	17.8
Profit before tax ($mn)	44.9	40.2
Profit after tax ($mn)	30.8	28.4
Earnings per share (c)	38.26	35.37
Cash flow per share (c)	53.80	52.32
Dividend (c)	26	24
Percentage franked	100	100
Net tangible assets per share ($)	~	~
Interest cover (times)	6.9	5.1
Return on equity (%)	11.8	10.2
Debt-to-equity ratio (%)	56.1	52.6
Current ratio	0.8	0.7

Vita Group Limited

ASX code: VTG

www.vitagroup.com.au

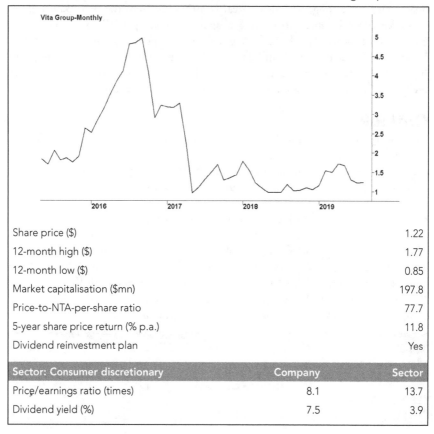

Share price ($)	1.22
12-month high ($)	1.77
12-month low ($)	0.85
Market capitalisation ($mn)	197.8
Price-to-NTA-per-share ratio	77.7
5-year share price return (% p.a.)	11.8
Dividend reinvestment plan	Yes

Sector: Consumer discretionary	Company	Sector
Price/earnings ratio (times)	8.1	13.7
Dividend yield (%)	7.5	3.9

Brisbane-based Vita, founded in 1995 as a single store, is a specialist retailer of technology and communication products and services, such as mobile phones and related products and services, along with third-party voice and data services. It also manages service and rental contracts, as well as selling voice and data services. In the business field it operates under the Telstra Business Centre and Vita Enterprise Solutions brands. It sells mobile accessories under its own Sprout brand. Since 2016 it has been moving into the health and wellness sector, with the Artisan Aesthetics chain of skincare clinics and the SQDAthletica brand of men's lifestyle products.

Latest business results (June 2019, full year)

Profits bounced back, after falling in the previous year when the company was hit by reduced payments from Telstra. Telecommunications-related sales provide the bulk of the company's business, and revenues rose 9 per cent to $739 million, with EBITDA up 13 per cent. Retail sales make up around 80 per cent of this business, with some excellent growth. By contrast, commercial sales fell sharply, in part from the transition of small business customers into the retail segment. Vita's own Sprout brand of mobile accessories continued to grow, especially in premium categories. The company's new Skin Health and Wellness division saw revenues more than double to nearly $14 million, although it reported a higher loss as Vita invested heavily for future growth. At June 2019 Vita Group operated 102 Telstra stores, four Telstra Business Centres, one Fone Zone store, 13 Artisan Aesthetics skincare clinics (under various brand names) and three SQDAthletica stores.

Outlook

Vita Group has grown to occupy a prominent position in the sale of telecommunications products to retail consumers and is a significant beneficiary of the continuing strong demand in Australia for the latest devices. However, it is highly dependent on Telstra, at a time when Telstra is working to cut costs. Under a planned new remuneration structure, Vita expects to receive higher payments for sales of devices, but lower payments from sales of connections to the Telstra network. The company has said it is too early to determine the financial impact of this on its business. Meanwhile, it is working to reduce its dependence on Telstra with moves into health and wellness. It has acquired a training organisation and specialist software for this business, and plans to add at least 12 more stores to the Artisan Aesthetics network during the June 2020 year, with an eventual target of 70 to 90 stores nationwide.

Year to 30 June	2018	2019
Revenues ($mn)	684.5	753.7
EBIT ($mn)	30.9	34.7
EBIT margin (%)	4.5	4.6
Profit before tax ($mn)	29.9	34.1
Profit after tax ($mn)	22.0	24.3
Earnings per share (c)	14.13	15.04
Cash flow per share (c)	20.60	21.86
Dividend (c)	9.1	9.2
Percentage franked	100	100
Net tangible assets per share ($)	~	0.02
Interest cover (times)	31.2	52.7
Return on equity (%)	24.1	23.5
Debt-to-equity ratio (%)	~	~
Current ratio	0.9	0.8

Webjet Limited

ASX code: WEB   www.webjetlimited.com

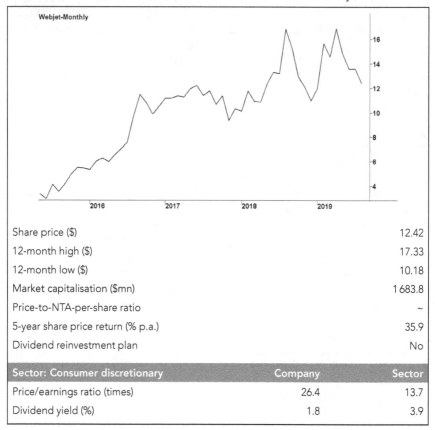

Share price ($)	12.42
12-month high ($)	17.33
12-month low ($)	10.18
Market capitalisation ($mn)	1 683.8
Price-to-NTA-per-share ratio	~
5-year share price return (% p.a.)	35.9
Dividend reinvestment plan	No

Sector: Consumer discretionary	Company	Sector
Price/earnings ratio (times)	26.4	13.7
Dividend yield (%)	1.8	3.9

Melbourne-based Webjet, established in 1998, is a leading travel business. It divides its operations into two broad segments. The B2B Travel segment (business to business), also known as WebBeds, provides the travel industry with hotel inventory. It operates under various regional brands, including Lots of Hotels, Sunhotels, Fit Ruums, JacTravel and — its new acquisition — Dubai-based Destinations of the World. The B2C Travel segment (business to consumer) operates the webjet.com.au business, the largest online travel agency in Australia and New Zealand, specialising in airline bookings, hotel reservations, travel insurance and rental cars. This segment also includes Online Republic, a cruise, rental car and rental motorhome booking agency.

Latest business results (June 2019, full year)

Webjet reported another excellent result, with profits rising strongly for the second straight year. The key was a sharp increase in the WebBeds business, with revenues up 62 per cent and profits more than doubling. In large part this reflected the

US$173 million acquisition, completed in November 2018, of Destinations of the World. However, even excluding the acquisition, profits rose 30 per cent at the EBITDA level, with scale efficiencies coming through in each region as the company expanded. Hotel bookings of 3.4 million were up 51 per cent from the previous year, with a total transaction value of $2.15 billion, up 59 per cent. The B2C Travel segment saw just modest gains, with profits up 4 per cent for the webjet.com.au online travel booking business, but falling for the second straight year for the small Online Republic operation.

Outlook

Webjet has been transformed by a series of acquisitions, and now claims to be the second-largest participant in the global hotel bed intermediary sector, with a market share approaching 4 per cent. This industry is highly fragmented, with the majority of companies having specialised, local offerings and very small market shares. Webjet sees the opportunity to become a major global force, and is now able to offer rooms at some 250 000 hotels, including approximately 30 000 with which it has direct contracts. As it grows it achieves significant economies of scale that boost profit margins. It also continues to invest in new technology platforms, including its innovative Rezchain blockchain initiative, that enable it to lower operating costs. It has launched a new business, Umrah Holidays International, which it says is the first truly online B2B provider of travel services for religious pilgrims to Mecca. At June 2019 Webjet had no net debt, and it continues to seek out new acquisitions.

Year to 30 June	2018	2019
Revenues ($mn)	291.0	366.4
B2B travel (%)	39	50
B2C travel (%)	61	50
EBIT ($mn)	64.3	87.1
EBIT margin (%)	22.1	23.8
Profit before tax ($mn)	58.6	74.7
Profit after tax ($mn)	43.2	60.3
Earnings per share (c)	37.53	47.00
Cash flow per share (c)	56.65	75.06
Dividend (c)	20	22
Percentage franked	100	100
Net tangible assets per share ($)	~	~
Interest cover (times)	11.3	7.0
Return on equity (%)	13.1	11.1
Debt-to-equity ratio (%)	~	~
Current ratio	0.9	0.9

Wellcom Group Limited

ASX code: WLL

www.wellcomww.com

Share price ($)	6.83
12-month high ($)	6.85
12-month low ($)	4.75
Market capitalisation ($mn)	268.7
Price-to-NTA-per-share ratio	17.6
5-year share price return (% p.a.)	19.1
Dividend reinvestment plan	No

Sector: Industrials	Company	Sector
Price/earnings ratio (times)	17.2	18.3
Dividend yield (%)	3.2	4.1

Founded in 2000, Melbourne-based Wellcom is a corporate design specialist. It specialises in creating, managing and delivering content in a variety of formats to corporate clients. This can range from brochures, catalogues, social media content and advertising material to outdoor billboards, radio content, online material and 3D animation. Its Knowledgewell software platform allows a company's marketing department to plan and manage a major promotional campaign. Much of Wellcom's work is complementary to the work of advertising agencies, and the company has numerous blue-chip customers. It operates from offices in Australia, New Zealand, Singapore, Malaysia, the US and the UK. It has announced that Korean advertising agency Innocean Worldwide had made a takeover bid for Wellcom.

Latest business results (June 2019, full year)

Revenues and profits rose for the second straight year. The result was influenced by a buyout agreement concerning the company's commercial property lease in the US. The surrender of this lease handed Wellcom additional revenues of $8.4 million. Excluding this, the after-tax profit for the year was $13.3 million. Australasian activities represent 63 per cent of total turnover, and revenues edged down, with profits flat. By contrast, both the UK and US segments achieved solid gains in sales and profits, with the result also helped by the weak dollar. The company reported pleasing contributions from new business wins, including David Jones in Australia, Countdown in New Zealand, Southeastern Grocers in the US, and HomeAway-Expedia, Body Shop International and Christie's, all in the UK.

Outlook

In July 2019 Wellcom announced that it had entered into a Scheme Implementation Deed with the giant South Korean advertising agency Innocean Worldwide for the latter to buy 85 per cent of Wellcom's shares, at a price of $6.70 per share. Wellcom directors have unanimously supported the proposal. A Scheme booklet is expected to be sent to shareholders in October, and at a later date shareholders will vote on the matter. If the takeover is approved, Wellcom will cease to exist as an independent, ASX-listed company. Consequently, when announcing its June 2019 financial results, the company did not make any comments on the outlook for its businesses. Wellcom occupies a small but prominent position in the world of corporate marketing in its countries of operation. It is seeing a structural change in its business as social media and new digital technologies force clients to change their media strategies, and it believes its experience in frequent delivery of large volumes of content make it well placed to benefit.

Year to 30 June	2018	2019
Revenues ($mn)	155.2	160.9
EBIT ($mn)	17.7	23.9
EBIT margin (%)	11.4	14.8
Profit before tax ($mn)	17.4	23.4
Profit after tax ($mn)	11.7	15.6
Earnings per share (c)	29.92	39.77
Cash flow per share (c)	37.09	49.83
Dividend (c)	21	22
Percentage franked	100	100
Net tangible assets per share ($)	0.28	0.39
Interest cover (times)	66.2	48.8
Return on equity (%)	18.6	24.0
Debt-to-equity ratio (%)	3.6	1.0
Current ratio	1.7	1.9

Wesfarmers Limited

ASX code: WES   www.wesfarmers.com.au

Wesfarmer-Monthly

Share price ($)	38.33
12-month high ($)	51.92
12-month low ($)	30.40
Market capitalisation ($mn)	43 460.1
Price-to-NTA-per-share ratio	7.4
5-year share price return (% p.a.)	8.3
Dividend reinvestment plan	Yes

Sector: Consumer discretionary	Company	Sector
Price/earnings ratio (times)	22.3	13.7
Dividend yield (%)	4.6	3.9

Perth-based Wesfarmers, founded in 1914 as a farmers' cooperative, is now a conglomerate with many areas of operation. Having divested itself of its Coles supermarket operations, its primary business now is the Bunnings network of hardware stores. Other retail businesses include the Officeworks, Kmart and Target chains. In addition, it produces fertilisers, chemicals and industrial safety products. It has retained a 15 per cent equity stake in Coles, holds 50 per cent of the Flybuys loyalty card business, owns a 25 per cent interest in the ASX-listed BWP property trust — which owns many Bunnings warehouses — and holds half the equity in the financial services business Gresham Partners and half the equity of timber business Wespine Industries. At June 2019 it operated 1061 Bunnings, Kmart, Target and Officeworks stores throughout Australia and New Zealand.

Latest business results (June 2019, full year)

Having spun off its Coles supermarkets business into a separate company, Wesfarmers now presented a slimmed-down result, with the June 2018 figures also revised to exclude Coles. It was a pleasing year, thanks especially to the Bunnings business, which reported an 8 per cent rise in EBIT on a 5 per cent increase in revenues. On a same-store basis, sales were up nearly 4 per cent, with growth in all regions and in all major product categories. Kmart sales were flat on a same-store basis, and Target sales were down, with combined EBIT for the two businesses down by 14 per cent. By contrast, Officeworks continued to report solid growth in sales and profits. Among the many industrial businesses, chemicals and fertilisers were strong but the low-margin Blackwoods safety products unit performed below expectations. The result was boosted by the company's share of the profits from its investments in Coles and other businesses.

Outlook

Wesfarmers expects continuing steady growth from Bunnings, driven by new stores, new sales categories, product innovation and the roll-out of a full online offering. It also remains optimistic about the prospects for Officeworks, enhanced by its newly acquired Geeks2U computer repair business. However, it has warned that profit growth at Officeworks could be hurt by increasing competition and by wage rises. It is working to cut costs and boost business at Kmart, and in August 2019 it acquired the online retailer Catch Group Holdings. It plans to merge this business into Kmart's operations in order to establish a strong presence in online marketing. However, the company's Target retail division and its Blackwoods safety products unit both continue to drag on business. In September 2019 Wesfarmers acquired lithium mining company Kidman Resources.

Year to 30 June	2018	2019
Revenues ($mn)	26 763.0	27 920.0
Bunnings (%)	47	47
Kmart group (%)	32	31
Industrials (%)	13	14
Officeworks (%)	8	8
EBIT ($mn)	2 337.0	2 948.0
EBIT margin (%)	8.7	10.6
Profit before tax ($mn)	2 134.0	2 799.0
Profit after tax ($mn)	1 409.0	1 940.0
Earnings per share (c)	124.58	171.68
Cash flow per share (c)	170.65	219.20
Dividend (c)	223	178
Percentage franked	100	100
Net tangible assets per share ($)	4.32	5.20
Interest cover (times)	11.5	19.8
Return on equity (%)	6.0	11.9
Debt-to-equity ratio (%)	15.1	22.4
Current ratio	0.9	1.2

Westpac Banking Corporation

ASX code: WBC

www.westpac.com.au

Share price ($)	28.34
12-month high ($)	29.11
12-month low ($)	23.30
Market capitalisation ($mn)	97 704.2
Price-to-NTA-per-share ratio	1.9
5-year share price return (% p.a.)	1.5
Dividend reinvestment plan	Yes

Sector: Financials	Company	Sector
Price/earnings ratio (times)	12.0	15.0
Dividend yield (%)	6.6	5.9

Sydney-based Westpac, which began trading in 1817 as the Bank of New South Wales, is one of Australia's big four banks, with interests in most areas of financial services. It is also one of New Zealand's leading banks and has some smaller businesses in the Pacific region. It owns St George Bank, BankSA and Bank of Melbourne. Its wealth management arm, BT Financial Group, incorporates brands that include Securitor, Asgard, Advance, Magnitude and Ascalon. It also owns XYLO Foreign Exchange and the RAMS home loans business.

Latest business results (March 2019, half year)

Cash earnings fell sharply in a disappointing result. A key element was remediation payments of $617 million after tax, to compensate customers who had been victims of aggressive sales techniques by bank representatives. Nevertheless, even excluding these payments, cash earnings were down 5 per cent in a weak banking environment. The Consumer Bank division reported an 11 per cent fall in profits, hit by a decline in the bank's net interest margin. The Business Bank division was down 6 per cent, due mainly to customer compensation payments. Westpac Institutional Bank earnings fell 2 per cent, following a reduction in financial markets revenue. Restructuring costs of $136 million sent the BT Financial Group into the red, though underlying profits were also sharply down as a result of higher weather-related insurance claims. However, solid growth in loans and deposits and a reduction in impairment charges helped Westpac New Zealand to a 15 per cent rise in profits. Staff cuts and other initiatives meant Westpac generated cost savings of $146 million during the period.

Outlook

Westpac has been hit hard by charges of aggressive sales tactics, and over three years has made $1.4 billion in pre-tax provisions for customer compensation work. It will close down much of its financial advisory business and is seeking ways to restore its tarnished public image, including a strengthening of governance procedures. It has a relatively high exposure to the mortgage market, and will be strongly influenced by trends in domestic housing. It continues to slash away at its cost base, with a target of $400 million in productivity savings over the September 2019 year. The first mortgages have been originated from a new Customer Service Hub, which is expected to deliver a reduction in lending costs. Over the longer term Westpac aims to become one of Australia's most efficient banks, with a cost-to-income ratio below 40 per cent.

Year to 30 September	2017	2018
Operating income ($mn)	21 556.0	21 951.0
Net interest income ($mn)	15 704.0	16 339.0
Operating expenses ($mn)	9 105.0	9 586.0
Profit before tax ($mn)	11 598.0	11 655.0
Profit after tax ($mn)	8 062.0	8 065.0
Earnings per share (c)	239.66	236.23
Dividend (c)	188	188
Percentage franked	100	100
Non-interest income to total income (%)	27.1	25.6
Cost-to-income ratio (%)	42.2	43.7
Return on equity (%)	13.5	12.8
Return on assets (%)	1.0	0.9
Half year to 31 March	2018	2019
Operating income ($mn)	11 239.0	10 103.0
Profit before tax ($mn)	6 104.0	4 729.0
Profit after tax ($mn)	4 251.0	3 293.0
Earnings per share (c)	123.97	95.67
Dividend (c)	94	94
Percentage franked	100	100
Net tangible assets per share ($)	15.00	15.09

Woolworths Group Limited

ASX code: WOW   www.woolworthsgroup.com.au

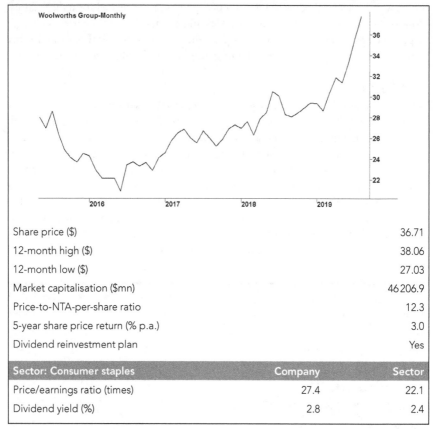

Share price ($)	36.71
12-month high ($)	38.06
12-month low ($)	27.03
Market capitalisation ($mn)	46 206.9
Price-to-NTA-per-share ratio	12.3
5-year share price return (% p.a.)	3.0
Dividend reinvestment plan	Yes

Sector: Consumer staples	Company	Sector
Price/earnings ratio (times)	27.4	22.1
Dividend yield (%)	2.8	2.4

Woolworths, founded in Sydney in 1924, is one of Australia's retail giants. Its 3300 outlets across Australia and New Zealand include Woolworths, Metro, Countdown, SuperValue and FreshChoice supermarkets, Big W mixed goods stores and Endeavour Drinks, which incorporates Dan Murphy's, BWS and Cellarmasters. It operates clubs and hotels through its 75-per-cent-owned subsidiary ALH Group. It plans to separate its liquor and hotels operations into a new business.

Latest business results (June 2019, full year)

Revenues and underlying profits rose in another good year for Woolworths. Note that the June 2019 financial year contained 53 weeks, compared with 52 weeks for June 2018. The Australian Food division reported a 5.3 per cent increase in sales, or 3.1 per cent on a same-store basis. There was particular momentum in the second half as the company benefited from a Disney 'Lion King' promotion. Online sales grew 31 per cent to $1.4 billion. New Zealand sales and profits rose modestly. The Endeavour Drinks business saw sales up, with a contribution from new store openings, strong online growth and moves to on-demand delivery services, but rising costs pushed profits down. Sales and profits edged up for the Hotels division. Big W sales rose again, but this operation remained in the red, as the company struggled to turn business around. During the year Woolworths sold its petrol business, and this is not included in the results on these pages.

Outlook

Woolworths has reported that solid sales growth in the June 2019 second half was continuing in the early part of the June 2020 financial year. Despite this, company management were wary about the outlook, noting that many of the company's customers were experiencing cost-of-living pressures. Its medium-term target is to open between 10 and 20 new supermarkets in Australia each year, and three to four in New Zealand, as well as 15 to 30 new Metro convenience stores. It is working to boost its successful WooliesX online business, and has expanded it to New Zealand, with the launch of CountdownX. It has been reducing the deficit at Big W, and it hopes to engineer a turnaround by closing approximately 30 of this business's 183 stores over three years, along with the introduction of new product ranges and an enhanced online offering. It plans to merge its Endeavour Drinks operation with its majority-owned ALH Group pubs and hotels subsidiary into a new company, Endeavour Group. It is then expected to consider options for divesting itself of this business.

Year to 30 June*	2018	2019
Revenues ($mn)	56 944.0	59 984.0
Australian food (%)	66	66
Endeavour drinks (%)	15	15
New Zealand food (%)	10	10
Big W (%)	6	6
Hotels (%)	3	3
EBIT ($mn)	2 548.0	2 724.0
EBIT margin (%)	4.5	4.5
Gross margin (%)	29.3	29.1
Profit before tax ($mn)	2 394.0	2 598.0
Profit after tax ($mn)	1 605.0	1 752.0
Earnings per share (c)	123.41	134.18
Cash flow per share (c)	208.23	227.77
Dividend (c)	93	102
Percentage franked	100	100
Net tangible assets per share ($)	3.06	2.99
Interest cover (times)	16.5	21.6
Return on equity (%)	16.0	16.9
Debt-to-equity ratio (%)	14.1	19.3
Current ratio	0.8	0.7

* 24 June 2018

PART II
THE TABLES

Table A
Market capitalisation

A company's market capitalisation is determined by multiplying the share price by the number of shares. To be included in this book, a company must be in the All Ordinaries Index, which comprises the 500 largest companies by market capitalisation.

	$mn
BHP Group	184 479.4
Rio Tinto	143 540.3
Commonwealth Bank of Australia	139 792.2
Westpac Banking	97 704.2
National Australia Bank	78 879.5
ANZ	75 597.5
Woolworths Group	46 206.9
Wesfarmers	43 460.1
Macquarie Group	42 095.1
Fortescue Metals	24 231.5
Insurance Australia	18 580.4
Brambles	17 937.1
ASX	16 602.7
Sonic Healthcare	13 943.5
REA Group	13 898.5
Treasury Wine Estates	13 547.9
AGL Energy	12 513.1
Cochlear	12 510.5
CIMIC Group	10 052.6
Medibank Private	9 776.7
Magellan Financial Group	9 015.5
Orica	8 130.7
Northern Star Resources	7 508.8
Bluescope Steel	6 435.1
Alumina	6 364.5
Caltex Australia	6 121.0
TPG Telecom	5 845.2
Beach Energy	5 627.3
Harvey Norman Holdings	5 226.2
Flight Centre Travel	4 860.3
Altium	4 804.1
ALS	3 767.6
Pro Medicus	3 763.4
JB Hi-Fi	3 707.3
Ansell	3 623.8
Orora	3 342.5
NIB Holdings	3 207.1
Regis Resources	2 625.7
Mineral Resources	2 509.9
Brickworks	2 397.8
Technology One	2 369.1
Platinum Asset Management	2 221.6
Pendal Group	2 130.6
IRESS	2 125.4
Breville Group	2 114.0
Adelaide Brighton	2 014.8
CSR	2 003.2
Corporate Travel Management	1 939.8
Bapcor	1 902.2
Super Retail Group	1 808.0
IPH	1 805.7
Webjet	1 683.8

Perpetual	1 666.6
Credit Corp Group	1 608.5
ARB Corporation	1 493.3
Monadelphous Group	1 479.5
Smartgroup Corporation	1 473.1
Jumbo Interactive	1 391.0
McMillan Shakespeare	1 308.8
Blackmores	1 234.9
Service Stream	1 100.4
Collins Foods	1 007.8
Sandfire Resources	954.2
Southern Cross Media	949.2
Accent Group	877.7
GWA Group	873.7
Codan	835.2
AUB Group	826.9
Lifestyle Communities	766.3
GUD Holdings	758.5
AMA Group	738.7
Infomedia	703.2
Hansen Technologies	665.2
Australian Pharmaceutical	645.2
SG Fleet Group	628.6
Nick Scali	543.5
Cedar Woods Properties	514.4
Integrated Research	508.7
Servcorp	468.6
Ruralco Holdings	461.2
Money3 Corporation	417.1
Pacific Energy	415.1
Data#3	391.1
MNF Group	372.9
SeaLink Travel Group	371.2
Objective Corporation	370.6
Clover Corporation	366.9
OFX Group	342.0
Virtus Health	326.4
Bell Financial Group	291.9
Wellcom Group	268.7
Pacific Smiles Group	255.3
Australian Ethical Investment	244.4
McPherson's	239.2
Beacon Lighting Group	225.8
Schaffer Corporation	204.6
Vita Group	197.8
Citadel Group	192.6
APN Property Group	172.6
Supply Network	162.6
Fiducian Group	150.9
1300SMILES	144.4
DWS	143.7
GR Engineering Services	142.9
Mortgage Choice	141.5

Table B
Revenues

This list ranks the companies in the book according to their most recent full-year revenues figures. The figures include revenues from sales and services, but other revenues — such as interest receipts and investment income — are not generally included.

	$mn
BHP Group	61 511.1
Woolworths Group	59 984.0
Rio Tinto	54 029.0
Wesfarmers	27 920.0
Commonwealth Bank of Australia	24 407.0
Westpac Banking	21 951.0
Caltex Australia	21 731.3
ANZ	19 214.0
National Australia Bank	17 977.0
CIMIC Group	14 670.2
Fortescue Metals	13 840.3
AGL Energy	13 246.0
Macquarie Group	12 754.0
Bluescope Steel	12 532.8
Insurance Australia	11 942.0
JB Hi-Fi	7 095.3
Medibank Private	6 655.8
Brambles	6 382.4
Sonic Healthcare	6 177.4
Orica	5 373.8
Orora	4 761.5
Australian Pharmaceutical	4 026.3
Harvey Norman Holdings	3 404.9
Flight Centre Travel	3 055.3
Treasury Wine Estates	2 831.6
Super Retail Group	2 710.4
TPG Telecom	2 495.2
NIB Holdings	2 372.6
CSR	2 322.8
Ansell	2 081.9
Beach Energy	2 077.7
Ruralco Holdings	1 913.5
ALS	1 664.8
Adelaide Brighton	1 630.6
Mineral Resources	1 512.0
Monadelphous Group	1 477.3
Cochlear	1 426.7
Data#3	1 414.4
Northern Star Resources	1 401.2
Bapcor	1 296.6
Collins Foods	901.2
Alumina	892.7
REA Group	874.9
ASX	863.8
Service Stream	851.0
Brickworks	818.9
Accent Group	796.3
Breville Group	760.0
Vita Group	753.7
Southern Cross Media	660.1
Regis Resources	652.5
Blackmores	609.5

AMA Group	602.1
Sandfire Resources	592.2
Magellan Financial Group	559.1
Pendal Group	558.5
McMillan Shakespeare	547.9
Perpetual	508.9
SG Fleet Group	508.1
IRESS	464.6
Corporate Travel Management	446.7
ARB Corporation	443.9
GUD Holdings	434.1
GWA Group	381.7
Cedar Woods Properties	375.1
Webjet	366.4
Servcorp	334.9
Credit Corp Group	313.8
Technology One	297.1
Platinum Asset Management	295.2
Virtus Health	280.1
AUB Group	276.4
Codan	270.8
Nick Scali	268.0
IPH	252.5
SeaLink Travel Group	248.8
Beacon Lighting Group	247.6
Smartgroup Corporation	242.3
Altium	239.9
Hansen Technologies	231.3
MNF Group	215.6
McPherson's	210.3
Schaffer Corporation	202.9
Bell Financial Group	202.2
GR Engineering Services	182.3
Mortgage Choice	174.4
DWS	163.5
Wellcom Group	160.9
Lifestyle Communities	144.0
Supply Network	123.9
Pacific Smiles Group	122.2
Pacific Energy	120.8
OFX Group	118.7
Integrated Research	100.8
Citadel Group	98.2
Money3 Corporation	91.7
Infomedia	84.6
Jumbo Interactive	65.2
Clover Corporation	63.0
Objective Corporation	62.1
Pro Medicus	50.1
Fiducian Group	48.9
Australian Ethical Investment	41.0
1300SMILES	40.3
APN Property Group	26.7

Table C

Year-on-year revenues growth

Companies generally strive for growth, though profit growth is usually of far more significance than a boost in revenues. In fact, it is possible for a company to increase its revenues by all kinds of means—including cutting profit margins or acquiring other companies—and year-on-year revenues growth is of little relevance if other ratios are not also improving. The figures used for this calculation are the latest full-year figures.

	%
Alumina	90.4
Pacific Energy	77.5
Jumbo Interactive	64.0
Beach Energy	63.9
Cedar Woods Properties	56.4
Fortescue Metals	52.7
Pro Medicus	47.9
Northern Star Resources	45.3
Service Stream	35.2
Caltex Australia	33.4
Clover Corporation	31.5
Magellan Financial Group	31.0
Altium	29.9
DWS	29.7
Webjet	25.9
Money3 Corporation	24.6
AMA Group	21.1
Corporate Travel Management	20.4
Data#3	19.8
SeaLink Travel Group	19.5
Lifestyle Communities	18.5
Smartgroup Corporation	17.9
Codan	17.8
Breville Group	17.5
Collins Foods	16.9
Pacific Smiles Group	16.9
Macquarie Group	16.8
Treasury Wine Estates	16.6
Infomedia	16.0
ALS	15.1
Australian Ethical Investment	13.9
IPH	13.8
Pendal Group	13.8
Accent Group	13.4
AUB Group	12.3
Orora	12.1
Sonic Healthcare	11.5
Integrated Research	10.6
Supply Network	10.5
Vita Group	10.1
GUD Holdings	9.4
Credit Corp Group	9.4
Technology One	9.4
CIMIC Group	9.2
Bluescope Steel	9.0
Brambles	8.5
NIB Holdings	8.5
BHP Group	8.4
REA Group	8.3
IRESS	8.1
OFX Group	8.0
Servcorp	8.0
Regis Resources	7.9
Harvey Norman Holdings	7.9
Fiducian Group	7.7
Virtus Health	7.6
McPherson's	7.2
Bell Financial Group	7.1
Bapcor	7.0
Nick Scali	6.9
Orica	6.6
GWA Group	6.4
Ansell	6.2
Super Retail Group	5.4
Woolworths Group	5.3
ARB Corporation	5.0
ASX	5.0
Ruralco Holdings	4.8
Cochlear	4.6
Adelaide Brighton	4.6
Flight Centre Travel	4.5
Wesfarmers	4.3
Beacon Lighting Group	4.2
Rio Tinto	3.9
Sandfire Resources	3.9
CSR	3.8
Wellcom Group	3.7
Insurance Australia	3.6
JB Hi-Fi	3.5
AGL Energy	3.4
APN Property Group	3.2
1300SMILES	3.1
Medibank Private	2.9
Westpac Banking	1.8
Blackmores	1.4
McMillan Shakespeare	0.8
Southern Cross Media	0.5
National Australia Bank	0.5
Hansen Technologies	0.2
TPG Telecom	0.2
Australian Pharmaceutical	−0.9
SG Fleet Group	−1.1
Objective Corporation	−1.7
Commonwealth Bank of Australia	−2.0
MNF Group	−2.3
Brickworks	−2.5
ANZ	−3.0
Perpetual	−3.4
Citadel Group	−6.8
Mineral Resources	−6.9
Platinum Asset Management	−10.2
Schaffer Corporation	−10.5
Monadelphous Group	−14.8
Mortgage Choice	−18.6
GR Engineering Services	−35.7

Table D
EBIT margin

A company's earnings before interest and taxation (EBIT) is sometimes regarded as a better measure of its profitability than the straight pre-tax or post-tax profit figure. EBIT is derived by adding net interest payments (that is, interest payments minus interest receipts) to the pre-tax profit. Different companies choose different methods of financing their operations; by adding back interest payments to their profits we can help minimise these differences and make comparisons between companies more valid.

The EBIT margin is the EBIT figure as a percentage of annual sales. Clearly a high figure is to be desired, though of course this can be achieved artificially by inflating borrowings (and hence interest payments). And it is noteworthy that efficient companies like some of the retailers can operate most satisfactorily on low margins. Woolworths, for example, has one of the lowest EBIT margins of all the companies in this book.

The EBIT margin figure has little relevance for banks, and they have been excluded.

	%
Alumina	95.1
Magellan Financial Group	91.4
APN Property Group	75.5
Platinum Asset Management	74.3
ASX	70.2
Jumbo Interactive	56.4
Lifestyle Communities	56.3
Pro Medicus	51.6
Money3 Corporation	51.1
REA Group	50.7
Fortescue Metals	48.4
Pendal Group	44.6
Beach Energy	40.8
BHP Group	38.5
Smartgroup Corporation	35.9
Credit Corp Group	35.8
Regis Resources	35.6
Brickworks	34.1
Pacific Energy	34.0
Altium	32.9
Perpetual	32.3
Rio Tinto	31.7
IPH	29.0
Integrated Research	28.7
Fiducian Group	28.2
Corporate Travel Management	27.6
1300SMILES	26.4
Infomedia	26.2
Cochlear	25.9
Sandfire Resources	25.8
AUB Group	25.3
McMillan Shakespeare	24.7
TPG Telecom	24.0
Webjet	23.8
Codan	23.4
Treasury Wine Estates	22.7
Nick Scali	22.3
Technology One	22.3
Australian Ethical Investment	21.5
Mineral Resources	21.5
OFX Group	21.0
GUD Holdings	20.6
GWA Group	20.3
Schaffer Corporation	19.9
IRESS	19.6
Southern Cross Media	19.6
Cedar Woods Properties	19.0
SG Fleet Group	18.4
Virtus Health	17.8

Harvey Norman Holdings	17.6
ARB Corporation	17.6
Objective Corporation	17.3
Clover Corporation	17.2
ALS	16.9
Adelaide Brighton	16.8
Brambles	16.1
Northern Star Resources	15.9
DWS	15.8
Citadel Group	15.5
Wellcom Group	14.8
Hansen Technologies	14.1
Ansell	13.4
Blackmores	13.2
Sonic Healthcare	13.0
Breville Group	12.8
SeaLink Travel Group	12.6
AGL Energy	12.5
Orica	11.5
CSR	11.4
Flight Centre Travel	11.3
Bell Financial Group	11.3
Bapcor	11.3
Mortgage Choice	11.1
Bluescope Steel	10.8
Pacific Smiles Group	10.6
Wesfarmers	10.6
Supply Network	10.3
Beacon Lighting Group	10.1
Accent Group	10.1
McPherson's	9.4
Servcorp	8.9
NIB Holdings	8.9
Service Stream	8.6
Medibank Private	8.6
Super Retail Group	8.4
CIMIC Group	7.8
Collins Foods	7.8
MNF Group	7.5
Orora	7.0
AMA Group	7.0
Monadelphous Group	5.6
JB Hi-Fi	5.3
GR Engineering Services	4.6
Vita Group	4.6
Woolworths Group	4.5
Caltex Australia	3.8
Ruralco Holdings	2.8
Australian Pharmaceutical	2.2
Data#3	1.8

Table E

Year-on-year EBIT margin growth

The EBIT (earnings before interest and taxation) margin is one of the measures of a company's efficiency. So a rising margin is much to be desired, as it suggests that a company is achieving success in cutting its costs. This table does not include banks.

	%
Fortescue Metals	77.9
Clover Corporation	65.4
Jumbo Interactive	38.0
Wellcom Group	30.2
Schaffer Corporation	24.8
Objective Corporation	21.5
Wesfarmers	20.9
Infomedia	17.7
IPH	17.3
Altium	16.8
Brickworks	16.5
Pro Medicus	14.8
Beach Energy	14.3
Pendal Group	13.0
Smartgroup Corporation	12.3
Magellan Financial Group	11.7
ALS	10.4
Data#3	10.1
Accent Group	9.9
Bell Financial Group	8.8
Treasury Wine Estates	8.4
Australian Ethical Investment	8.0
Webjet	7.7
Technology One	5.5
Ansell	5.3
CIMIC Group	4.3
Sonic Healthcare	3.8
Bapcor	3.7
JB Hi-Fi	2.7
IRESS	2.5
Ruralco Holdings	2.2
NIB Holdings	2.1
Vita Group	2.0
Collins Foods	1.6
Credit Corp Group	1.5
Cochlear	1.5
Woolworths Group	1.5
APN Property Group	1.1
Integrated Research	1.1
Harvey Norman Holdings	0.9
Southern Cross Media	0.8
Alumina	0.5
Australian Pharmaceutical	0.4
ASX	0.4
Codan	0.2
Medibank Private	−0.2
1300SMILES	−0.6
ARB Corporation	−0.6
OFX Group	−1.2
REA Group	−1.3

Fiducian Group	−1.4
Super Retail Group	−1.5
GUD Holdings	−2.5
AGL Energy	−3.5
Supply Network	−3.6
Monadelphous Group	−3.8
AMA Group	−3.8
Corporate Travel Management	−4.0
BHP Group	−4.3
McMillan Shakespeare	−4.3
GWA Group	−4.7
Breville Group	−4.7
Bluescope Steel	−4.9
Nick Scali	−5.1
MNF Group	−5.3
Service Stream	−6.2
Rio Tinto	−6.3
Money3 Corporation	−6.5
AUB Group	−7.4
Brambles	−7.4
Orora	−7.5
TPG Telecom	−7.6
Platinum Asset Management	−7.7
McPherson's	−8.5
Pacific Energy	−8.6
Orica	−8.7
SG Fleet Group	−9.0
Adelaide Brighton	−9.8
Lifestyle Communities	−9.8
DWS	−11.3
Virtus Health	−11.8
Perpetual	−12.0
Mineral Resources	−12.2
Regis Resources	−13.2
Flight Centre Travel	−14.4
Sandfire Resources	−15.2
GR Engineering Services	−16.5
Pacific Smiles Group	−17.0
Beacon Lighting Group	−17.7
Hansen Technologies	−18.0
CSR	−18.0
Servcorp	−21.3
SeaLink Travel Group	−21.5
Blackmores	−21.8
Mortgage Choice	−27.4
Cedar Woods Properties	−29.3
Caltex Australia	−33.1
Citadel Group	−38.7
Northern Star Resources	−44.1

Table F
After-tax profit

This table ranks all the companies according to their most recent full-year after-tax profit.

	$mn
BHP Group	13 147.2
Rio Tinto	11 744.0
Commonwealth Bank of Australia	8 492.0
Westpac Banking	8 065.0
ANZ	6 487.0
National Australia Bank	5 702.0
Fortescue Metals	4 426.4
Macquarie Group	2 982.0
Wesfarmers	1 940.0
Woolworths Group	1 752.0
AGL Energy	1 040.0
Bluescope Steel	966.3
Insurance Australia	871.0
Alumina	847.2
CIMIC Group	780.6
Brambles	630.7
Caltex Australia	560.4
Beach Energy	560.0
Sonic Healthcare	549.7
ASX	492.0
Medibank Private	437.7
Treasury Wine Estates	419.5
Harvey Norman Holdings	402.3
TPG Telecom	396.9
Magellan Financial Group	364.2
Orica	324.2
REA Group	295.5
Cochlear	276.7
Flight Centre Travel	266.6
JB Hi-Fi	249.8
Brickworks	223.7
Orora	217.0
Ansell	209.6
Mineral Resources	205.0
Adelaide Brighton	191.0
Pendal Group	191.0
CSR	181.7
ALS	181.0
Regis Resources	163.2
Platinum Asset Management	157.7
Northern Star Resources	154.7
Super Retail Group	152.5
NIB Holdings	149.8
Perpetual	115.9
Sandfire Resources	106.5
Bapcor	94.3
McMillan Shakespeare	88.7
Corporate Travel Management	86.2
Southern Cross Media	76.2
Altium	73.5
Credit Corp Group	70.3
Breville Group	67.4

IRESS	64.1
GUD Holdings	60.9
SG Fleet Group	60.5
Webjet	60.3
Smartgroup Corporation	59.3
Monadelphous Group	57.4
ARB Corporation	57.1
Lifestyle Communities	55.1
Australian Pharmaceutical	54.7
Accent Group	53.9
Blackmores	53.5
IPH	53.1
GWA Group	51.8
Technology One	51.0
Service Stream	49.9
Cedar Woods Properties	48.6
AUB Group	46.4
Codan	45.7
Nick Scali	42.1
Collins Foods	39.1
Servcorp	29.2
Ruralco Holdings	28.8
Virtus Health	28.4
AMA Group	28.1
Jumbo Interactive	26.4
Bell Financial Group	24.7
Pacific Energy	24.5
Vita Group	24.3
Money3 Corporation	24.2
Hansen Technologies	24.0
SeaLink Travel Group	23.4
Schaffer Corporation	22.9
Integrated Research	21.9
OFX Group	21.0
Pro Medicus	19.1
Data#3	18.1
DWS	16.8
Infomedia	16.1
Beacon Lighting Group	16.0
Wellcom Group	15.6
APN Property Group	14.5
Mortgage Choice	14.0
McPherson's	13.7
MNF Group	11.4
Citadel Group	10.9
Fiducian Group	10.4
Objective Corporation	9.1
Pacific Smiles Group	8.9
Supply Network	8.7
1300SMILES	7.8
Clover Corporation	7.6
Australian Ethical Investment	6.5
GR Engineering Services	6.5

Table G

Year-on-year earnings per share growth

The earnings per share (EPS) figure is a crucial one. It tells you—the shareholder—what your part is of the company's profits, for each of your shares. So investors invariably look for EPS growth in a stock. The year-on-year EPS growth figure is often one of the first ratios that investors look to when evaluating a stock. The figures used for this calculation are the latest full-year figures.

	%
Fortescue Metals	285.8
Clover Corporation	108.5
Jumbo Interactive	93.5
Alumina	92.0
Pro Medicus	91.2
Beach Energy	77.0
Altium	48.4
Wesfarmers	37.8
Smartgroup Corporation	35.4
McPherson's	33.1
Wellcom Group	32.9
Magellan Financial Group	32.9
ALS	30.9
Australian Ethical Investment	30.5
IPH	29.5
Data#3	28.7
Webjet	25.2
Infomedia	24.7
Pendal Group	24.6
Objective Corporation	21.8
Bluescope Steel	21.8
Accent Group	21.7
Collins Foods	18.7
Pacific Energy	17.9
Treasury Wine Estates	17.6
Macquarie Group	16.1
Service Stream	15.9
Ansell	15.4
Breville Group	15.2
Technology One	13.9
Integrated Research	13.7
Brickworks	13.7
AMA Group	13.0
Cedar Woods Properties	12.9
Cochlear	12.5
Fiducian Group	12.3
NIB Holdings	11.9
ARB Corporation	11.7
OFX Group	11.3
CIMIC Group	11.2
ASX	10.5
Bapcor	10.2
Corporate Travel Management	10.0
GUD Holdings	9.8
Codan	9.2
Rio Tinto	8.9
Sonic Healthcare	8.7
Woolworths Group	8.7
Bell Financial Group	8.4
APN Property Group	7.1
JB Hi-Fi	7.0
BHP Group	6.7

Vita Group	6.4
Supply Network	6.3
IRESS	6.2
SeaLink Travel Group	5.6
REA Group	5.6
DWS	5.5
Credit Corp Group	5.0
Super Retail Group	4.9
Lifestyle Communities	4.5
Harvey Norman Holdings	4.5
Australian Pharmaceutical	3.9
GWA Group	3.2
Medibank Private	3.2
Southern Cross Media	3.1
Nick Scali	2.8
Servcorp	2.5
Money3 Corporation	2.4
AGL Energy	2.2
1300SMILES	1.8
Orora	1.0
Ruralco Holdings	0.1
Schaffer Corporation	−0.7
Westpac Banking	−1.4
Pacific Smiles Group	−3.5
Adelaide Brighton	−3.8
ANZ	−4.0
MNF Group	−4.3
AUB Group	−4.5
McMillan Shakespeare	−5.2
Flight Centre Travel	−5.7
Commonwealth Bank of Australia	−5.8
Insurance Australia	−6.6
Regis Resources	−7.0
Virtus Health	−7.5
Caltex Australia	−9.5
TPG Telecom	−10.5
SG Fleet Group	−11.8
Brambles	−13.5
CSR	−13.7
Sandfire Resources	−14.2
National Australia Bank	−15.6
Platinum Asset Management	−16.5
Orica	−16.5
Perpetual	−17.0
Beacon Lighting Group	−19.0
Hansen Technologies	−19.3
Monadelphous Group	−19.8
Blackmores	−23.9
Northern Star Resources	−24.1
Mineral Resources	−24.9
Citadel Group	−24.9
Mortgage Choice	−40.2
GR Engineering Services	−44.0

Table H
Return on equity

Shareholders' equity is the company's assets minus its liabilities. It is, in theory, the amount owned by the shareholders of the company. Return on equity is the after-tax profit expressed as a percentage of that equity. Thus, it is the amount of profit that the company managers made for you—the shareholder—from your assets. For many investors it is one of the most important gauges of how well a company is doing. It is one of the requirements for inclusion in this book that all companies have a return on equity of at least 10 per cent in their latest financial year.

Company	%	Company	%	Company	%
Magellan Financial Group	53.8	SG Fleet Group	22.8	Bluescope Steel	14.6
Nick Scali	49.9	Breville Group	22.7	MNF Group	14.2
Platinum Asset Management	48.0	Pendal Group	22.6	Bapcor	13.9
Pro Medicus	45.3	GUD Holdings	22.4	Brambles	13.7
Jumbo Interactive	42.4	Pacific Smiles Group	21.5	Accent Group	13.6
Cochlear	41.4	Clover Corporation	21.5	Pacific Energy	13.5
Australian Ethical Investment	40.5	Beacon Lighting Group	20.1	Cedar Woods Properties	13.3
Data#3	39.6	1300SMILES	19.9	Insurance Australia	13.3
Integrated Research	34.2	Rio Tinto	19.6	Orora	13.3
Objective Corporation	33.0	Service Stream	19.4	Harvey Norman Holdings	13.2
REA Group	32.0	IPH	19.2	GR Engineering Services	13.2
Fiducian Group	31.4	Super Retail Group	19.2	AUB Group	13.1
Fortescue Metals	31.3	Sandfire Resources	18.8	Citadel Group	13.1
Altium	31.3	Credit Corp Group	18.7	Westpac Banking	12.8
OFX Group	31.2	BHP Group	18.4	ASX	12.5
Technology One	30.3	Flight Centre Travel	17.9	AGL Energy	12.4
Alumina	28.6	ARB Corporation	17.6	Commonwealth Bank of Australia	12.4
CIMIC Group	27.7	Perpetual	17.5	Bell Financial Group	12.4
Infomedia	27.3	Macquarie Group	17.5	Servcorp	11.9
Blackmores	26.7	Caltex Australia	17.3	Wesfarmers	11.9
Beach Energy	26.6	Woolworths Group	16.9	APN Property Group	11.7
NIB Holdings	25.6	Corporate Travel Management	16.9	Treasury Wine Estates	11.7
JB Hi-Fi	25.1	ALS	16.4	Sonic Healthcare	11.5
Regis Resources	24.1	Mortgage Choice	16.3	Collins Foods	11.4
Wellcom Group	24.0	Northern Star Resources	16.0	Webjet	11.1
Lifestyle Communities	24.0	IRESS	15.5	Brickworks	11.1
McMillan Shakespeare	23.9	AMA Group	15.5	Orica	11.1
Smartgroup Corporation	23.9	Mineral Resources	15.5	ANZ	11.0
Supply Network	23.8	Adelaide Brighton	15.4	National Australia Bank	11.0
DWS	23.5	TPG Telecom	15.3	Money3 Corporation	10.5
Vita Group	23.5	CSR	15.1	Ansell	10.3
Schaffer Corporation	23.3	SeaLink Travel Group	15.1	Australian Pharmaceutical	10.3
Medibank Private	23.3	Southern Cross Media	14.9	Virtus Health	10.2
Codan	22.9	McPherson's	14.7	Ruralco Holdings	10.2
		GWA Group	14.6	Hansen Technologies	10.0
		Monadelphous Group	14.6		

Table I

Year-on-year return on equity growth

Company managers have a variety of strategies they can use to boost profits. It is much harder to lift the return on equity (ROE). Find a company with a high ROE figure, and one that is growing year by year, and it is possible that you have found a real growth stock. This figure is simply the percentage change in the ROE figure from the previous year to the latest year.

	%
Fortescue Metals	249.3
Wesfarmers	96.5
Clover Corporation	85.1
Alumina	77.5
Jumbo Interactive	62.6
Pro Medicus	59.0
Beach Energy	42.9
ALS	32.0
CIMIC Group	30.7
Wellcom Group	29.5
McPherson's	28.7
Southern Cross Media	25.2
Altium	23.0
Data#3	21.0
IPH	19.9
Australian Ethical Investment	18.3
Pendal Group	18.0
Accent Group	17.2
Pacific Energy	17.0
Bell Financial Group	15.8
Smartgroup Corporation	15.5
Treasury Wine Estates	14.8
ASX	10.4
Infomedia	10.0
Macquarie Group	9.1
BHP Group	8.9
Brickworks	7.3
AMA Group	7.3
Australian Pharmaceutical	7.1
Servcorp	6.9
Cedar Woods Properties	6.9
Magellan Financial Group	6.8
Collins Foods	5.6
Breville Group	5.3
Woolworths Group	5.2
IRESS	4.9
DWS	4.7
Objective Corporation	2.9
SeaLink Travel Group	2.4
Bluescope Steel	1.2
Technology One	0.6
OFX Group	0.6
Harvey Norman Holdings	0.5
Fiducian Group	0.2
APN Property Group	0.2
Pacific Smiles Group	0.2
Bapcor	0.0
REA Group	−0.2
Money3 Corporation	−0.4
ARB Corporation	−0.7
Super Retail Group	−0.8
Orora	−1.7

Rio Tinto	−2.0
Vita Group	−2.4
Service Stream	−2.6
Medibank Private	−2.7
Ansell	−2.8
Cochlear	−2.8
Codan	−2.9
AGL Energy	−3.1
JB Hi-Fi	−3.1
1300SMILES	−3.4
Sonic Healthcare	−3.5
Supply Network	−3.6
GWA Group	−4.5
Adelaide Brighton	−4.7
NIB Holdings	−4.8
Westpac Banking	−5.1
Integrated Research	−5.1
McMillan Shakespeare	−5.2
GUD Holdings	−5.5
Flight Centre Travel	−5.6
ANZ	−5.9
Nick Scali	−6.2
Ruralco Holdings	−6.7
Insurance Australia	−6.9
Corporate Travel Management	−7.6
Commonwealth Bank of Australia	−9.3
Virtus Health	−13.4
MNF Group	−13.5
CSR	−14.5
Platinum Asset Management	−14.9
National Australia Bank	−15.3
Webjet	−15.4
AUB Group	−16.2
Schaffer Corporation	−17.3
Caltex Australia	−17.6
Orica	−17.8
Lifestyle Communities	−18.0
Perpetual	−18.3
Regis Resources	−18.7
SG Fleet Group	−19.3
Monadelphous Group	−21.3
Credit Corp Group	−22.1
TPG Telecom	−22.7
Sandfire Resources	−26.1
Beacon Lighting Group	−27.9
Blackmores	−29.3
Citadel Group	−30.0
Brambles	−30.3
Mineral Resources	−31.8
Mortgage Choice	−34.0
Hansen Technologies	−35.2
Northern Star Resources	−40.9
GR Engineering Services	−42.5

Table J
Debt-to-equity ratio

A company's borrowings as a percentage of its shareholders' equity is one of the most common measures of corporate debt. Many investors will be wary of a company with a ratio that is too high. However, a company with a steady business and a regular income flow—such as an electric power company or a large supermarket chain—is generally considered relatively safe with a high level of debt, whereas a small company in a new business field might be thought at risk with even moderate debt levels. Much depends on surrounding circumstances, including the prevailing interest rates. Of course, it is often from borrowing that a company grows, and some investors are not happy buying shares in a company with little or no debt.

There are various ways to calculate the ratio, but for this book the net debt position is used. That is, a company's cash has been deducted from its borrowings. For inclusion in this book no company was allowed a debt-to-equity ratio of more than 70 per cent. Some of the companies had no net debt—their cash position was greater than the amount of their borrowings—and so have been assigned a zero figure in this table. The ratio has no relevance for banks, and they have been excluded.

Company	%	Company	%	Company	%
Altium	0.0	Service Stream	0.0	Cedar Woods Properties	28.0
APN Property Group	0.0	Technology One	0.0	Bell Financial Group	30.3
ARB Corporation	0.0	Vita Group	0.0	JB Hi-Fi	30.6
ASX	0.0	Webjet	0.0	AGL Energy	32.4
Australian Ethical Investment	0.0	Mortgage Choice	0.7	Pacific Energy	34.1
Beach Energy	0.0	Wellcom Group	1.0	AMA Group	35.6
Bluescope Steel	0.0	Alumina	2.8	GWA Group	37.0
Breville Group	0.0	Clover Corporation	3.1	Lifestyle Communities	37.3
CIMIC Group	0.0	Perpetual	6.0	Beacon Lighting Group	39.2
Citadel Group	0.0	AUB Group	7.1	Money3 Corporation	41.4
Codan	0.0	McPherson's	7.7	Sonic Healthcare	41.9
Corporate Travel Management	0.0	SG Fleet Group	8.9	Blackmores	45.5
CSR	0.0	Ansell	10.5	Adelaide Brighton	45.9
Data#3	0.0	IPH	10.6	Bapcor	46.1
Fiducian Group	0.0	Brickworks	11.3	DWS	46.9
Flight Centre Travel	0.0	Smartgroup Corporation	11.8	IRESS	47.4
GR Engineering Services	0.0	Accent Group	12.3	Super Retail Group	47.4
Infomedia	0.0	Brambles	13.4	MNF Group	47.5
Integrated Research	0.0	Cochlear	14.2	GUD Holdings	47.6
Jumbo Interactive	0.0	NIB Holdings	15.7	McMillan Shakespeare	51.3
Magellan Financial Group	0.0	BHP Group	17.8	Australian Pharmaceutical	51.4
Medibank Private	0.0	Schaffer Corporation	18.0	Virtus Health	52.6
Monadelphous Group	0.0	REA Group	19.0	Ruralco Holdings	52.9
Nick Scali	0.0	Rio Tinto	19.1	SeaLink Travel Group	53.1
Northern Star Resources	0.0	Woolworths Group	19.3	Orora	54.1
Objective Corporation	0.0	Harvey Norman Holdings	19.6	TPG Telecom	55.0
OFX Group	0.0	Fortescue Metals	19.6	ALS	57.3
Pendal Group	0.0	Treasury Wine Estates	20.1	Hansen Technologies	59.6
Platinum Asset Management	0.0	Supply Network	20.4	Collins Foods	60.3
Pro Medicus	0.0	1300SMILES	21.4	Orica	61.6
Regis Resources	0.0	Wesfarmers	22.4	Mineral Resources	63.1
Sandfire Resources	0.0	Insurance Australia	23.0	Southern Cross Media	67.0
Servcorp	0.0	Pacific Smiles Group	24.5	Caltex Australia	69.4
		Credit Corp Group	25.9		

Table K

Current ratio

The current ratio is simply the company's current assets divided by its current liabilities. Current assets are cash or assets that can, in theory, be converted quickly into cash. Current liabilities are normally those payable within a year. The current ratio helps measure the ability of a company to repay in a hurry its short-term debt, should the need arise. Banks are not included.

Platinum Asset Management	13.1	Infomedia	1.5
Money3 Corporation	12.8	Pendal Group	1.5
Credit Corp Group	7.5	Rio Tinto	1.5
Magellan Financial Group	6.2	Citadel Group	1.4
Sandfire Resources	5.0	Australian Pharmaceutical	1.4
Clover Corporation	4.2	JB Hi-Fi	1.4
IPH	3.9	Fortescue Metals	1.4
ARB Corporation	3.8	Servcorp	1.3
Pro Medicus	3.8	DWS	1.3
Jumbo Interactive	3.6	AGL Energy	1.3
Cedar Woods Properties	3.2	Objective Corporation	1.3
Ansell	3.1	Mortgage Choice	1.3
Regis Resources	3.0	Orica	1.3
GUD Holdings	2.9	Flight Centre Travel	1.3
Mineral Resources	2.8	Corporate Travel Management	1.3
GWA Group	2.7	Ruralco Holdings	1.3
Adelaide Brighton	2.6	Super Retail Group	1.3
Supply Network	2.6	Nick Scali	1.3
Breville Group	2.6	Caltex Australia	1.3
APN Property Group	2.5	Service Stream	1.2
McMillan Shakespeare	2.5	Orora	1.2
Treasury Wine Estates	2.5	Accent Group	1.2
Australian Ethical Investment	2.4	Wesfarmers	1.2
Fiducian Group	2.4	Brickworks	1.2
Bapcor	2.3	SeaLink Travel Group	1.1
CSR	2.1	ASX	1.1
Northern Star Resources	2.1	ALS	1.1
GR Engineering Services	2.1	IRESS	1.1
Medibank Private	2.1	AUB Group	1.1
Southern Cross Media	2.1	Lifestyle Communities	1.1
Blackmores	2.0	Data#3	1.1
Monadelphous Group	2.0	Smartgroup Corporation	1.1
McPherson's	1.9	Beach Energy	1.0
NIB Holdings	1.9	1300SMILES	1.0
Perpetual	1.9	Sonic Healthcare	0.9
Schaffer Corporation	1.9	Webjet	0.9
Codan	1.9	CIMIC Group	0.9
BHP Group	1.9	Collins Foods	0.9
Hansen Technologies	1.9	AMA Group	0.8
Wellcom Group	1.9	Vita Group	0.8
Altium	1.8	Technology One	0.8
Integrated Research	1.8	Woolworths Group	0.7
Cochlear	1.8	Pacific Smiles Group	0.7
Bluescope Steel	1.8	REA Group	0.7
Beacon Lighting Group	1.7	Virtus Health	0.7
Harvey Norman Holdings	1.6	Pacific Energy	0.6
MNF Group	1.6	Alumina	0.3
Brambles	1.6	TPG Telecom	0.2

Table L
Price/earnings ratio

The price/earnings ratio (PER)—the current share price divided by the earnings per share figure—is one of the best known of all sharemarket ratios. Essentially it expresses the amount of money investors are ready to pay for each cent or dollar of a company's profits, and it allows you to compare the share prices of different companies of varying sizes and with widely different profits. A high PER suggests the market has a high regard for the company and its growth prospects; a low one may mean that investors are disdainful of the stock. The figures in this table are based on share prices as of 2 September 2019.

Company	PER	Company	PER
Fortescue Metals	5.5	Money3 Corporation	17.0
Bluescope Steel	6.9	Wellcom Group	17.2
Alumina	7.5	McPherson's	17.3
Vita Group	8.1	Ansell	17.7
DWS	8.6	Citadel Group	17.7
Schaffer Corporation	8.9	Flight Centre Travel	18.2
Sandfire Resources	9.0	Codan	18.3
Pendal Group	9.8	1300SMILES	18.6
Beach Energy	10.0	Supply Network	18.7
Mortgage Choice	10.2	Bapcor	20.1
Adelaide Brighton	10.3	Credit Corp Group	20.6
SG Fleet Group	10.3	ALS	20.9
Cedar Woods Properties	10.5	Service Stream	20.9
Brickworks	10.7	NIB Holdings	21.4
Bell Financial Group	10.9	Insurance Australia	21.5
CSR	11.0	Data#3	21.6
APN Property Group	11.1	GR Engineering Services	21.9
Caltex Australia	11.1	Wesfarmers	22.3
Virtus Health	11.5	Medibank Private	22.3
Australian Pharmaceutical	11.8	Corporate Travel Management	22.5
Super Retail Group	11.9	Blackmores	23.0
ANZ	11.9	Integrated Research	23.3
Westpac Banking	12.0	Sonic Healthcare	24.0
AGL Energy	12.0	Magellan Financial Group	24.7
Mineral Resources	12.3	Orica	25.0
Southern Cross Media	12.4	Smartgroup Corporation	25.0
GUD Holdings	12.5	Monadelphous Group	25.7
Harvey Norman Holdings	12.8	Collins Foods	25.8
Rio Tinto	12.8	ARB Corporation	26.1
Nick Scali	12.9	AMA Group	26.4
CIMIC Group	12.9	Webjet	26.4
National Australia Bank	13.0	Woolworths Group	27.4
Macquarie Group	13.4	Hansen Technologies	27.7
Lifestyle Communities	13.9	Brambles	28.5
Beacon Lighting Group	14.0	Pacific Smiles Group	28.6
Platinum Asset Management	14.1	Breville Group	31.4
BHP Group	14.4	Treasury Wine Estates	32.3
Perpetual	14.4	IRESS	32.6
Fiducian Group	14.5	MNF Group	32.7
McMillan Shakespeare	14.7	ASX	33.7
TPG Telecom	14.7	IPH	34.0
JB Hi-Fi	14.8	Australian Ethical Investment	36.4
Orora	15.4	Objective Corporation	40.9
SeaLink Travel Group	15.8	Infomedia	43.5
Ruralco Holdings	16.0	Cochlear	45.1
Servcorp	16.0	Technology One	46.3
Regis Resources	16.1	REA Group	47.0
Accent Group	16.3	Clover Corporation	47.7
OFX Group	16.3	Northern Star Resources	48.2
Commonwealth Bank of Australia	16.4	Jumbo Interactive	51.0
GWA Group	16.9	Altium	65.3
AUB Group	16.9	Pro Medicus	196.7
Pacific Energy	17.0		

Table M
Price-to-NTA-per-share ratio

The NTA-per-share figure expresses the worth of a company's net tangible assets — that is, its assets minus its liabilities and intangible assets — for each share of the company. Intangible assets, such as goodwill or the value of newspaper mastheads, are excluded because it is deemed difficult to place a value on them (though this proposition is debatable), and also because they might not have much worth if separated from the company. The price-to-NTA-per-share ratio relates this figure to the share price.

A ratio of one means that the company is valued exactly according to the value of its assets. A ratio below one suggests that the shares are a bargain, though usually there is a good reason for this. Profits are more important than assets.

In some respects, this is an 'old economy' ratio. For many high-tech companies in the 'new economy' the most important assets are human ones whose worth does not appear on the balance sheet.

Companies with a negative NTA-per-share figure, as a result of having intangible assets valued at more than their remaining net assets, have been omitted from this table.

Brickworks	1.2
Bluescope Steel	1.3
Cedar Woods Properties	1.4
APN Property Group	1.4
ANZ	1.4
Sandfire Resources	1.6
Fortescue Metals	1.6
National Australia Bank	1.7
Harvey Norman Holdings	1.7
CSR	1.8
Mortgage Choice	1.9
Westpac Banking	1.9
Money3 Corporation	1.9
Schaffer Corporation	2.0
Mineral Resources	2.0
Servcorp	2.1
Commonwealth Bank of Australia	2.3
Alumina	2.3
Adelaide Brighton	2.3
Caltex Australia	2.4
Beach Energy	2.4
AGL Energy	2.7
Macquarie Group	2.7
BHP Group	2.8
Rio Tinto	2.8
Pacific Energy	2.8
Australian Pharmaceutical	2.8
Lifestyle Communities	3.0
GR Engineering Services	3.1
Beacon Lighting Group	3.2
Orora	3.2
Credit Corp Group	3.5
SeaLink Travel Group	3.6
Brambles	3.6
Regis Resources	3.7
Monadelphous Group	3.8
Supply Network	4.3
Bell Financial Group	4.6
ARB Corporation	4.7
Perpetual	5.3
Treasury Wine Estates	5.3
Insurance Australia	5.6
OFX Group	5.7
Medibank Private	6.4
Pendal Group	6.6
Nick Scali	6.6
Codan	6.8
Northern Star Resources	6.8
Platinum Asset Management	6.9
Flight Centre Travel	7.0
Orica	7.2
McMillan Shakespeare	7.3
Wesfarmers	7.4
CIMIC Group	7.8
Ansell	8.0
Pacific Smiles Group	8.5
Clover Corporation	9.5
Blackmores	9.7
Ruralco Holdings	10.0
Fiducian Group	10.2
McPherson's	10.6
Integrated Research	10.9
Breville Group	11.3
ASX	11.4
NIB Holdings	12.0
Woolworths Group	12.3
Data#3	12.7
TPG Telecom	13.8
Australian Ethical Investment	14.4
Magellan Financial Group	14.8
Accent Group	17.4
Wellcom Group	17.6
1300SMILES	21.9
Objective Corporation	21.9
Jumbo Interactive	22.2
Altium	25.3
GUD Holdings	26.2
Corporate Travel Management	31.4
Cochlear	41.5
AUB Group	59.2
IPH	60.8
Vita Group	77.7
ALS	79.5
REA Group	114.0
Pro Medicus	120.9
Technology One	149.4
JB Hi-Fi	545.2

Table N
Dividend yield

Many investors buy shares for income, rather than for capital growth. They look for companies that offer a high dividend yield (the dividend expressed as a percentage of the share price). Table N ranks the companies in this book according to their historic dividend yields. Note that the franking credits available from most companies in this book can make the dividend yield substantially higher. The dividend yield changes with the share price. The figures in this table are based on share prices as of 2 September 2019.

	%
Alumina	14.7
Pendal Group	7.8
Bell Financial Group	7.6
Vita Group	7.5
Harvey Norman Holdings	7.4
SG Fleet Group	7.4
DWS	7.3
National Australia Bank	7.2
Platinum Asset Management	7.1
Perpetual	6.9
Nick Scali	6.7
Westpac Banking	6.6
Adelaide Brighton	6.6
CSR	6.5
GR Engineering Services	6.5
GUD Holdings	6.4
Southern Cross Media	6.3
AGL Energy	6.2
ANZ	6.0
BHP Group	5.9
Virtus Health	5.9
Australian Pharmaceutical	5.7
GWA Group	5.6
Fortescue Metals	5.5
Super Retail Group	5.5
Commonwealth Bank of Australia	5.5
Mortgage Choice	5.3
Accent Group	5.1
CIMIC Group	5.0
APN Property Group	5.0
Caltex Australia	4.9
Cedar Woods Properties	4.9
Rio Tinto	4.8
Servcorp	4.8
Schaffer Corporation	4.7
McMillan Shakespeare	4.7
Orora	4.7
Macquarie Group	4.6
Fiducian Group	4.6
Wesfarmers	4.6
McPherson's	4.4
Beacon Lighting Group	4.4
JB Hi-Fi	4.4
Money3 Corporation	4.4
Data#3	4.2
OFX Group	4.2
SeaLink Travel Group	4.1
1300SMILES	4.1
AUB Group	4.1
Insurance Australia	4.0
Sandfire Resources	3.8
IRESS	3.8
Medibank Private	3.7
Supply Network	3.6
Smartgroup Corporation	3.6
Pacific Smiles Group	3.5
Ruralco Holdings	3.4
Brickworks	3.4
Flight Centre Travel	3.3
Service Stream	3.3
Mineral Resources	3.3
NIB Holdings	3.3
Wellcom Group	3.2
Regis Resources	3.1
Blackmores	3.1
Monadelphous Group	3.1
Magellan Financial Group	3.0
ALS	2.9
Sonic Healthcare	2.9
Woolworths Group	2.8
Citadel Group	2.8
IPH	2.7
ASX	2.7
Pacific Energy	2.6
Brambles	2.6
Bapcor	2.5
Credit Corp Group	2.5
Integrated Research	2.4
Orica	2.4
Ansell	2.4
Australian Ethical Investment	2.3
Breville Group	2.3
Collins Foods	2.3
Corporate Travel Management	2.2
ARB Corporation	2.1
Treasury Wine Estates	2.0
AMA Group	2.0
Codan	1.9
Hansen Technologies	1.8
Webjet	1.8
Infomedia	1.7
Jumbo Interactive	1.6
Cochlear	1.5
Objective Corporation	1.3
Technology One	1.2
MNF Group	1.2
Northern Star Resources	1.1
Bluescope Steel	1.1
REA Group	1.1
Altium	0.9
Beach Energy	0.8
Clover Corporation	0.8
Lifestyle Communities	0.8
TPG Telecom	0.6
Pro Medicus	0.2

Table O

Year-on-year dividend growth

Most investors hope for a rising dividend, and this table tells how much each company raised (or lowered) its dividend in its latest financial year.

	%
Pacific Energy	150.0
Jumbo Interactive	97.3
Alumina	87.4
Fortescue Metals	87.0
Clover Corporation	75.0
Schaffer Corporation	55.6
Northern Star Resources	42.1
BHP Group	35.2
Pro Medicus	33.3
ALS	32.4
Data#3	30.5
Magellan Financial Group	26.9
Altium	25.9
Infomedia	25.8
Australian Ethical Investment	25.0
Accent Group	22.2
APN Property Group	22.2
Lifestyle Communities	22.2
Service Stream	20.0
Treasury Wine Estates	18.8
Smartgroup Corporation	18.6
McPherson's	17.6
CIMIC Group	15.6
Pendal Group	15.6
Rio Tinto	15.1
NIB Holdings	15.0
Collins Foods	14.7
Nick Scali	12.5
Breville Group	12.1
Integrated Research	11.5
Fiducian Group	11.5
Corporate Travel Management	11.1
IPH	11.1
Technology One	10.0
AMA Group	10.0
Cochlear	10.0
Harvey Norman Holdings	10.0
Webjet	10.0
Bapcor	9.7
Woolworths Group	9.7
OFX Group	9.6
Macquarie Group	9.5
REA Group	8.3
Ansell	8.2
GUD Holdings	7.7
JB Hi-Fi	7.6
Credit Corp Group	7.5
Supply Network	7.4
Australian Pharmaceutical	7.1
ARB Corporation	6.8
Brickworks	5.9
Codan	5.9
ASX	5.7
Money3 Corporation	5.3
Cedar Woods Properties	5.0
Wellcom Group	4.8
IRESS	4.5
1300SMILES	4.2
Orora	4.0
Sonic Healthcare	3.7
SeaLink Travel Group	3.4
Medibank Private	3.1
GWA Group	2.8
Super Retail Group	2.0
AGL Energy	1.7
McMillan Shakespeare	1.4
AUB Group	1.1
Vita Group	1.1
ANZ	0.0
Beach Energy	0.0
Bluescope Steel	0.0
Brambles	0.0
Commonwealth Bank of Australia	0.0
Hansen Technologies	0.0
National Australia Bank	0.0
Objective Corporation	0.0
Orica	0.0
Regis Resources	0.0
Ruralco Holdings	0.0
Southern Cross Media	0.0
Westpac Banking	0.0
Adelaide Brighton	−2.4
Caltex Australia	−2.5
CSR	−3.7
Pacific Smiles Group	−4.9
Flight Centre Travel	−5.4
SG Fleet Group	−5.6
Insurance Australia	−5.9
Bell Financial Group	−6.7
Virtus Health	−7.7
Beacon Lighting Group	−9.0
Perpetual	−9.1
Servcorp	−11.5
Sandfire Resources	−14.8
Platinum Asset Management	−15.6
DWS	−20.0
Wesfarmers	−20.2
Citadel Group	−21.7
Monadelphous Group	−22.6
MNF Group	−26.9
Blackmores	−27.9
Mineral Resources	−32.3
GR Engineering Services	−45.5
TPG Telecom	−60.0
Mortgage Choice	−66.7

Table P

Five-year share price return

This table ranks the annual average return to investors from a five-year investment in each of the companies in the book, as of September 2019. It is an accumulated return, based on share price appreciation (or depreciation) plus dividend payments.

	% p.a.		
Pro Medicus	108.0	Alumina	13.1
Jumbo Interactive	77.6	MNF Group	13.1
Service Stream	65.6	SG Fleet Group	12.0
Altium	65.2	Vita Group	11.8
Smartgroup Corporation	52.7	AGL Energy	11.5
Accent Group	49.0	Rio Tinto	11.5
Codan	48.8	McMillan Shakespeare	10.6
Northern Star Resources	48.2	CIMIC Group	10.3
Australian Ethical Investment	40.4	Harvey Norman Holdings	10.3
Clover Corporation	39.1	GR Engineering Services	10.1
AMA Group	36.8	ARB Corporation	9.7
Webjet	35.9	Beach Energy	9.6
Magellan Financial Group	33.7	Ansell	9.0
Collins Foods	32.5	Ruralco Holdings	8.5
Lifestyle Communities	32.3	CSR	8.4
Treasury Wine Estates	32.1	Wesfarmers	8.3
Data#3	29.3	Southern Cross Media	8.1
Integrated Research	27.8	Mineral Resources	8.0
Credit Corp Group	26.9	Insurance Australia	7.7
IPH	26.9	GUD Holdings	7.2
Regis Resources	25.9	IRESS	6.6
Cochlear	25.8	Brambles	6.3
Bapcor	25.0	Pendal Group	6.3
Blackmores	23.2	BHP Group	5.2
Fiducian Group	22.8	Brickworks	5.0
Objective Corporation	22.7	DWS	4.7
Schaffer Corporation	22.3	Commonwealth Bank of Australia	4.4
Nick Scali	22.0	AUB Group	4.1
ASX	20.9	GWA Group	4.1
Fortescue Metals	20.6	Super Retail Group	4.0
Corporate Travel Management	20.5	ALS	3.9
Hansen Technologies	20.5	Monadelphous Group	3.7
Macquarie Group	20.3	1300SMILES	3.6
Breville Group	19.7	Flight Centre Travel	3.5
APN Property Group	19.4	Orica	3.3
Wellcom Group	19.1	Woolworths Group	3.0
Technology One	19.0	TPG Telecom	2.6
Bluescope Steel	18.6	Sandfire Resources	2.3
SeaLink Travel Group	18.5	National Australia Bank	2.2
REA Group	18.4	Adelaide Brighton	2.0
Money3 Corporation	18.3	Pacific Smiles Group	2.0
JB Hi-Fi	18.0	Australian Pharmaceutical	1.8
NIB Holdings	17.8	Cedar Woods Properties	1.5
Infomedia	17.5	Westpac Banking	1.5
Bell Financial Group	17.2	Beacon Lighting Group	1.4
Pacific Energy	14.9	Servcorp	1.2
Citadel Group	14.6	ANZ	0.6
Orora	14.2	Caltex Australia	−0.2
Medibank Private	14.0	Perpetual	−0.6
McPherson's	13.5	OFX Group	−1.2
Sonic Healthcare	13.4	Platinum Asset Management	−1.7
Supply Network	13.2	Virtus Health	−7.1
		Mortgage Choice	−8.1

Table Q
Non-interest income to total income

The final three tables rank the banks only. Many of the banks are working to diversify away from their traditional lending and deposit-taking businesses into other operations where they see potential for faster growth and higher profits (although these ventures are not always successful — recently we have been seeing some of the banks divest themselves of money management subsidiaries that did not live up to expectations). This table ranks them according to their success, showing how much of their income derives from non-interest sources.

	%
Macquarie Group	86.2
Commonwealth Bank of Australia	25.8
Westpac Banking	25.6
National Australia Bank	25.1
ANZ	24.5

Table R
Cost-to-income ratio

All the banks are working to reduce their high costs. The cost-to-income ratio — expressing costs as a percentage of operating income — is one of the measures commonly used by analysts to ascertain their success.

	%
Westpac Banking	43.7
National Australia Bank	45.2
Commonwealth Bank of Australia	46.2
ANZ	48.1
Macquarie Group	69.7

Table S
Return on assets

Banks have large assets, and the return on assets ratio — after-tax profit as a percentage of average total assets — is another popular measure of their efficiency.

	%
Macquarie Group	1.5
Westpac Banking	0.9
Commonwealth Bank of Australia	0.9
National Australia Bank	0.7
ANZ	0.7

DISCARD

  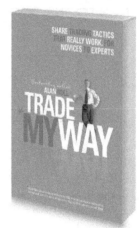

Best-selling author Alan Hull presents the complete
sharemarket solution for novices to experts. Whether
you're managing your portfolio, trading tactically on
the sharemarket or investing in blue chip shares,
Alan Hull explains the ins and outs of investing and
trading in easy-to-understand and engaging language.

Available in print and e-book formats

9 780730 372073